Perspectives on
Teaching Theatre

PETER LANG
New York • Washington, D.C./Baltimore • Bern
Frankfurt am Main • Berlin • Brussels • Vienna • Oxford

Perspectives on Teaching Theatre

Edited by
Raynette Halvorsen Smith,
Bruce A. McConachie,
& Rhonda Blair

PETER LANG
New York • Washington, D.C./Baltimore • Bern
Frankfurt am Main • Berlin • Brussels • Vienna • Oxford

Library of Congress Cataloging-in-Publication Data

Perspectives on teaching theatre / [edited by] Raynette Halvorsen
Smith, Bruce A. McConachie, and Rhonda Blair.
p. cm.
Includes bibliographical references.
1. Theater—Study and teaching. I. Blair, Rhonda.
II. McConachie, Bruce A. III. Smith, Raynette Halvorsen.
PN2075.P45   792'.07—dc21   99-12875
ISBN 0-8204-4033-7

Die Deutsche Bibliothek-CIP-Einheitsaufnahme

Perspectives on teaching theatre / Raynette Halvorsen Smith... (ed.).
–New York; Washington, D.C./Baltimore; Bern;
Frankfurt am Main; Berlin; Brussels; Vienna; Oxford: Lang.
ISBN 0-8204-4033-7

Cover design by Nona Reuter

The paper in this book meets the guidelines for permanence and durability
of the Committee on Production Guidelines for Book Longevity
of the Council of Library Resources.

Printed in the United States of America

Acknowledgments

The Editors would like to thank The Johns Hopkins University Press for permission to publish versions of the following essays:

Sam Abel, "Gay and Lesbian Studies and the Theatre Curriculum" *Theatre Topics,* Volume 4, Number 1 (31–44) March 1994. Baltimore: The Johns Hopkins University Press."

Paul C. Castagno, "Informing the New Dramaturgy: Critical Theory to Creative Process," *Theatre Topics,* Volume 3 Number 1, (29–42) March 1993. Baltimore: The Johns Hopkins University Press.

Jerry Dickey and JudyLee Oliva, "Multiplicity and Freedom in Theatre History Pedagogy: A reassessment of the Undergraduate Survey Course." *Theatre Topics,* Volume 4, Number 1 (45–58) March 1994. Baltimore: The Johns Hopkins University Press.

Robin Murray and Margaret Millen Swanson, "Towards a Multicultural Theatre Course" *Theatre Topics,* Volume 2, Number 2 (105–11) September 1992. Baltimore: The Johns Hopkins University Press.

Patricia VandenBerg, "Integrating Production and Curriculum in a Liberal Arts Setting" *Theatre Topics*, Volume 1, Number 2, (149–53) September 1991. Baltimore: The Johns Hopkins University Press.

Contents

Introduction

Bruce A. McConachie

A primary catalyst for this anthology was an Association for Theatre in Higher Education Annual Conference, focused on curricular and pedagogical issues in college theatre education. While planning the anthology, we expected to be able to divide the essays from the proceedings and elsewhere into three roughly equal parts, matching the general teaching orientations of each of us: acting and directing for Rhonda, design and technology for Raynette, and dramatic literature, history for me. It soon became apparent, however, that there were many important issues facing all theatre educators, regardless of their specializations within the field. We were also discovering that some of the most provocative articles we might decide to publish would bridge these specializations in significant ways.

At the same time, we were becoming more confident about the importance of our project. Theatre educators for the past several years had been responding to the crisis in our profession with radically new ideas for teaching their courses, but there was very little in print about any of this work. This crisis, in turn, was directly related to major problems in the culture and politics of American society—the continuing attacks on artistic freedom and higher education, the increasing victimization and oppression of ethnic, class, and sexual minorities, and the trivialization of socially responsible advocacy in mainstream culture, among many others. We began to hope that our anthology might encourage educational revisions and reforms that would assist theatre educators in exploring structural and pedagogical ways of grappling with these problems.

The ATHE Conference itself, entitled "Imagining the Future," focused our concerns and clarified our strategies for the book. Conference presenters detailed many of the challenges facing theatre educators, explored teaching methods aimed at diversifying core readings and empowering minority students, and charted new ways for theory, pedagogy, and production practices to inform each other. Anna Deavere Smith's Keynote Address on the need for committed theatre, as well as the example of her ongoing performance of *Twilight: Los Angeles, 1992*, energized our resolve to locate the educational reforms many ATHE members were advocating in the context of a progressive politics for our culture and society. Several themes emerged that became focal points for us in selecting and organizing articles for the anthology: institutional constraints and opportunities for reform, the challenges and possibilities of teaching theatre in our postmodern culture, methods of empowering students in classroom and production work, and strategies for dealing with racial, sexual, and class differences in theatre education.

As co-editors, we realize that the approaches advocated in the following pages would take theatre education in several diverse directions, some running parallel but others potentially at cross-purposes. Empowering theatre students, for instance, does not guarantee that their education will honor and enhance multicultural diversity. We may want our theatre programs to undermine modernist ideals of foundations and totalities, but the postmodern embrace of contingency and historical specificity can also confuse and disempower students, despite (and partially because of) their immersion in postmodern crosscurrents. Ironically, institutional dynamics, in addition to smothering efforts at reform, can make it more difficult to teach diversity through practices that encourage the sexual and racial resegregation of the curriculum. In short, this anthology is not a package deal for a single model of progressive theatre education.

Nonetheless, the following essayists are asking the right kinds of questions to challenge many of our present structures and processes. Further, contributors to this volume sidestep assumptions and concepts that implicitly run counter to progressive possibilities for change. None are assuming that certain texts or modes of teaching contain or unlock timeless, essential truths that must not be omitted from theatre classrooms. Nor does anyone dispute the need for shared intellectual standards among theatre scholars and students, regardless of their cultural backgrounds—an argument that sometimes masquerades as multicultural, but finally corrodes the values of diversity.

Perspectives on Teaching Theatre is the first book of its kind; no other anthology attempts to encompass the major concerns that confront college teachers of theatre and to suggest new strategies for teaching in the classroom, on the stage, in the Dean's office, and in other arenas of public life. Even so, there are many omissions. We were hoping for more articles from departmental chairs and other administrators of theatre programs. We sought essays from a wider ethnic range of contributors than we finally received. Our coverage of some significant areas of the typical theatre curriculum is light or nonexistent. And we've included very little about how many of the reforms suggested by our essayist might eventually challenge and change the professional theatre. So this anthology, in many ways, is only a first step. However, we are confident it is a step in the right direction.

Not So Special Vehicles

Anna Deavere Smith

Introduction

When planning an Association for Theatre in Higher Education annual conference, "Imagining the Future: Theatre Education in the 90s," I felt it was important to set a tone for the overall proceedings with a focused, substantial keynote address. The issues before us had to do with teaching and making theatre, the role of theatre in the culture at large, and the challenges of functioning in a culture in which issues of difference, power, social and economic equity, and simple community form the ground for struggle and negotiation.

It was important that the keynote speaker be a person who lived in both the professional and academic theatre worlds, and who had a powerful sense of the ways that theatre illuminates our personal and communal conditions and can actually be an element in building community.

Anna Deavere Smith came immediately to mind. Actor, writer, interviewer, social critic, and master teacher, she—possibly more than any other person I can think of—rigorously and concretely holds up our world for examination by using theatre's tools.

In her keynote for ATHE, printed here with some minor editing, Smith lays out a range of problems confronting us as theatre-makers, teachers, and citizens. I am always moved by her call for us to get in our small "rowboats" and move between the fortresses of difference—exploring, being ambassadors, carrying the word that, inevitably, we are all in this together. This is a call which we all must heed if we are to move successfully into the new millennium.

I am grateful to Smith for her contribution to ATHE, to this volume, and to the face and force of theatre in the United States today.

—Rhonda Blair

As we begin to imagine the future, there are ethnic, generational, class, and gender gaps to transcend. Today I will be talking about new ways to work in those gaps and about how we might try to re-evaluate the way we integrate ourselves into academia, into popular culture, into communities, and into society at large. I will be talking about new ways to look at being "*in*" our differences, and I will be talking about the development of skills.

First of all, I believe that skills for theater cannot be developed inside of theater or in academia alone. Most of my work is with actors and playwrights. However, I am also beginning to see how crucial it is for non-commercial theaters in particular to find new kinds of skills in the audience development departments. Let me address that first.

I have attended two of the Theater Communications Group's workshop/retreats on diversity. We seem to go round and round about how to diversify audiences. In this organization as well, people like Rhonda Blair have worked to try to change the composition of the organization, and it has been a hard battle. All you have to do to see that we are in for some tough work is to look at the graduate student population at the conference. When I was here two years ago, I attended the Women in Theatre pre-conference, which is a group that has spoken about diversifying ever since it began in the 1970s. The last time I was here, 40% of those who attended were graduate students. They were all white. I was standing just outside the meeting room one evening, and Kate Carney and Beverly Byers Pevitts walked past, peeped into the room, and said to me, "What happened? It didn't use to be this bad." Kate and Beverly are among those who began the Women in Theatre pre-conference and to their eyes, by 1991, it had gone backwards in terms of diversity. Common sense stepped into my idealism and told me that if all the graduate students were white, the future of the organization was clear. Although my colleagues talked about diversity at the conference, particularly in terms of curriculum, something inhibited the most obvious action when they were on their own campuses. Curriculum, or the addition of multicultural or feminist texts, was not going to yield raw results in the long run. The place to put creativity if one is going to diversify a membership like this one, and ultimately if we are going to diversify theater, is in the recruitment and mentoring of graduate students. Likewise, in the recruitment and mentoring of all students of theater if one begins to look for directors, designers, managers, who are other than white, the list is short. The list gets shorter if you want to collaborate with people who do other than ethnocentric work. There are reasons why people in the last twenty years have been doing ethnocentric work, and I will get to that later. The future, I think, will call for some artists who can move, on occasion, beyond the boundaries of ethnic, gender, and political beliefs.

I think that the issue of audience development, which to me is akin to the issue of diversifying the pool of theater workers, cannot be addressed solely within the world of theater. I think we need to look at how other people who interact with the public do this. I know that it is not going to warm your hearts for me to suggest to you that we talk to politicians, but I think we could begin there. I know this avenue is limited. However, overall, I am advocating beginning relationships that can work like two-way streets. For example, during the run of my show *Twilight: Los Angeles 1992*, the District Attorney of Los Angeles sent a note inviting me to lunch. He promised good food and information, which was the case. I was, however, surprised at the end of the lunch, actually quite moved, that he said to me, with an astounding sincerity: "Is there anybody that you talked to during the time of working on your show, that I should meet?" I referred him to Twilight, a gang member, who in fact inspired the name of the show. There are people in public service who do want to find ways of learning more about this mysterious "they" out there. There are people in the media, in politics, in community work, who know and understand the limitations of their own ability to get to the public. We in theater are in the same position, and we need more skills. We normally exchange information among ourselves in atmospheres like this very conference. We need a broader arena.

When I came to Crown Heights, I became indebted to a man named Robert Sherman who was then with the Human Rights Commission of the Mayor's Office of the City of New York. He is now the head of an organization called the "Increase the Peace Corps" which was developed literally out of the Crown Heights riot. When I met Sherman, I became fascinated with how his office went out into the middle of the riot, and found, while rocks and bottles were being thrown, the people in the community who were going to help maintain peace in the future. The mayor's office, for all its shortcomings, did have a seed for organizing, and they have called on that seed many more times throughout the last two years. As the scene created itself in my mind, it looked something like this: The mayor's human rights people in orange jackets and in a yellow van with a megaphone on the roof cruised around the streets. They already had a few community activists with whom they had relationships. Even community activists have a limited amount of contact with the anonymous "they." One of them, a man named Richard Green, spotted a black man in his twenties standing in the middle of a riot with a group of little kids, talking to them about the power of the vote. This man, Henry Rice, is also someone I met while I was in Crown Heights. Against his better judgment, he did join up with the folks from the mayor's office and has been an important force in building bridges between Blacks and Jews in Crown Heights. I do not want to paint a rosy picture, because there are limits to the building of that bridge, but at least they were able to put down a few planks of wood, wet and muddy planks maybe, but planks nevertheless. What I am trying to tell you is, we cannot sit in our offices, in our theaters, or our classrooms and effect change. If audience development doesn't become an activist activity, many regional theaters will become dinosaurs. Here the need for activism is not only about ethnicity, it is about age. How will we begin to bring younger people into theater? How do we let them know that theater is here for them, and it can be about *them*? We have to make our presence obvious. We need orange jackets and megaphones. Presence is after all the gift of the actor. It is the heart and the voice of theater. People didn't create a circle and wait for the show to begin. Actors and writers drew a circle around the crowd and put a show in the middle.

In theater we have not fully realized what the drama of race is. This is because we have been creating it as a series of monologues. One race speaks, the other listens. In mainstream theater, it often happens that artists of color go onto the stage and perform for largely white audiences. They talk, white people watch. How often does it happen that white people create plays about themselves in *race* for audiences of color? Not often. One might say that for years the white drama has been played before the world through media for audiences of color. However, as one Korean woman, Mrs. Han, in Los Angeles told me:

> I used to think America was the best
> I still do
> I don't deny that now
> Just because I am victim
> When I was a little girl
> I used to think all Americans were rich
> I used to see many luxuries
> Hollywood lifestyle movies
> And I also thought all Americans were white
> I never saw any Black
> maybe one housemaid?

That comes as no surprise. There is a reticence in white mainstream drama about race. Who can talk about race? Who owns the discussion of race? Who wants to talk about race? Who needs to?

The Training of Artists

I think that the training of artists does not need to be so sterile as we have thought in the past. My own way of working has been to introduce social concerns, largely because I like to construct courses that allow me to cross list and to make a class body which is mixed with actors and non-actors, or people who want to act, but also people who have been thinking about social issues and would like to try acting them out, as a way of knowing the issues differently.

I know very well, maybe a little too well, that there are some among you who feel that this will inhibit the development of talent. I am not here to convince anybody about what theater should be. We know that theater can be many things.

I would hate to see my remarks reduced to such questions as "What about art?" "Doesn't political theater hurt art?" Or as one man said to me at a panel that my colleague Rush Rehm at Stanford organized on Democracy and Theater: "As for Miss Smith, I think she should just worry about herself, I saw a wonderful play in San Diego called *For Colored Girls*, I would suggest she write something like that." First of all, we only have to look at the press around *For Colored Girls*' arrival in New York in the mid-seventies to see how boldly it crossed boundaries. Yes, my entry into theater is political. Largely because of my race and gender. I am political without opening my mouth. My presence is political. The way I negotiate my presence becomes political. If I tried to deny my politicalness, I would be even more political. Personally, I do believe that all art is political. Even Noel Coward. The movies that Mrs. Han saw in Korea as a little girl were political.

On the other hand, as an acting teacher, as a playwriting teacher, I am also very concerned about the level of skills in American theater, and I hope our tendency to categorize art as art and politics as politics will not inhibit a discussion of skills. I am saying, let's move around, let's look for the answers by collaborating with others on our campuses and in society who are like minded, and who also have an interest in learning more about who and what society is and how to speak for it, and about it. I am talking about a collaborative, public advocacy which will make our voices stronger, and our will to communicate large enough to carry over the noise. My prediction is society is going to get noisier.

Four years, three years, two years, is a short time for developing that illusive thing we call "major talent." However, no major talent really becomes major talent without finding some way to speak *for* and with his or her own times. Is it possible that the lack of work is because we have spent too much time training our students to mirror themselves, to show the world what's *inside* of the artist rather than the world *around* the artist?

Theater training in our universities provides Hollywood with an incredible group of people. Many start out as actors, but go on to other less visible careers. Some repertory theater directors complain that Hollywood steals all of the major talent, and that it is difficult to develop relationships with actors and playwrights, directors, too, I would imagine, although the major concern seems to be playwrights, because they want to go where the money is. Here I think is another collaboration that we have not worked out very well.

There are real contradictions in the way that we think about television and movies, and how our training intersects with it. I, for one, find teaching "How to Audition" courses one of the least gratifying experiences in the world. I do it, because I, like everybody else, think it is important to teach our students about the so-called "real world." I frequently find my own tone changing from teaching to warning.

On the one hand, we depend on the visibility of our successful students; on the other hand, we talk about Hollywood and television as though they were shallow and beneath our great artistry. And I have seen how my students look, after they meet with the "people from the industry." Some look shocked, dazed, confused. The ones who have been praised or recognized in these one-day, or sometimes one-hour, sessions come out glowing. The ones who are praised or recognized are usually different from the ones whom we have been praising and recognizing. We cannot control that, and I think we should find another way to have influence. I believe, as I have been told, that the television industry is run by very smart people who have to work very fast. Some of the smartest students I have had and some of my smartest friends have gone that route. Motion pictures also can boast fine artists. I think that one reason we kind of write off those industries is because we know we cannot teach our students about the power dynamics there, and that they have to learn that themselves. How can you teach that in a term? Getting yourself ready for the big audition is what the whole long haul is about.

The first thing I suggest is get your students ready for the "*real* real world," not the real world of how to get a job. We actually have something quite wonderful to offer these industries. In twenty years, let's try to create a new actor, an actor who is less self-conscious, less concerned about the pose of acting, and more concerned about details. As much as I critique our reliance on Stanislavski, I certainly sound like him now.

I am also concerned about the kinds of people we send into theater and into the "industry." Are they humanitarians? Are they self-absorbed? Do they have humility? We use the word vulnerability over and over again, but are they vulnerable? Vulnerable to whom and to what? What in the way we train them creates humility and vulnerability? Who are these human beings? What kinds of values do they have? I know from visits to some of your universities that some of you are very concerned about that. These last four years have shown me a student who is more anxious, more frightened, more close-minded, more intolerant than I have ever seen. I know that some of you have tried to intervene. I think it is crucial that we find more ways of actively intervening. What kinds of people are we recruiting? What kinds of people do we send into the world in the name of theater. Actors used to be, in the days of commedia, humanitarians, gymnasts, actors, singers, psychiatrists rolled into one. Provocateurs. The clowns and fools were willing to say what others would be shot for saying. *Whom do our actors speak for? Whom can they speak for? They should speak for whom?*

We must take our responsibility for helping to provide leadership in the arts and for society more seriously. These are the role models that many will look to. I am saying that the buck doesn't stop in the right place.

I was on an audition tour for the University/Resident Theatre Association (U/RTA) one year. I do not know if this particular chair was serious, but I took it seriously, as a metaphor, when he said to me: "In the last year we bring in the dentists." Okay. I understand that. I understand that. The dentist is important, but when the dentist comes, the students should not stop talking. In fact, they should then be working harder to communicate what is in their hearts because presumably the dentist will have done something in the interest of cosmetics that will interfere with speech. Speaking from the heart is what must be encouraged against all obstacles. Furthermore, speaking from the heart does not mean confessions, as talk show television would lead us to believe, and it does not mean being unkind. It simply implies that as artists we have more resources from which to draw than the mind. We *need* those. Society needs those resources tapped *through* our evocation.

I went to UC Irvine to hear Helene Cixous a few years ago. At the time I had been doing experiments with gender crossing in acting training. Afterwards, I asked her what she thought about crossing gender in theater. She said she thought it was transvestism, and implied that it was silly. Then she said, "First of all, an actor has to have a soul." What about that? She said that when an actor walks in the room, she can tell right away if there is a soul there. Can we? Or have our eyes become cloudy? We cannot let the industries dictate to us what major talent is. We cannot tell them. They do not know. And we do not know. However, we can participate in the definition. The best way for us to participate is to send them something different, something more expressive in terms of real visible range of expression, and someone who is larger, more wide-eyed, more interested in life. For the years that I spent in agent offices, and in auditions, I can tell you that I saw a masquerade of poses called actors. Let's urge our students to give up that masquerade.

The Japanese mime, Mamako, said when I studied with her at the American Conservatory Theater (ACT): "Have a rich life and Haiku will come." That's just about all she said, but it was quite enough for me. And yet, I would call that mentorship. Most of my students want to hear a lot more than that. As teachers, I think we should watch more, and say less.

More on Skills and Technique

I have found in what is now nearly twenty years of teaching actors that they have a much broader expressive range than they use, or are encouraged to use. They are seldom pushed to find and to commit to gestural specifics that create a picture of behavior that is as complex as actual human behavior. When I have tried to urge my students to do this, their response is resistance, largely because of the way they have previously been indoctrinated to believe in psychological realism. I believe in it, too, but I think that it is only part of the picture. If we want the general public to pay attention to us, we are going to have to dazzle it with something that is more specific. If we could create on stage twenty minutes of an interaction of almost any life interaction, that is first of all a complex interaction, it would be dazzling. On the one level, we would find greater variety in external behavior.

Now, for fun, let's make that a political interaction. For those of you who subscribe to *The New Yorker*, you know that there was a big controversy on Valentine's week, because of Art Spiegelman's drawing of a Hasidic man in an embrace with a Black woman with dreadlocks. To give this a context, last year in New York, there was a high level of tension between Blacks and Hasidic Jews because of the riots and the events that led up to the riots, the killing of a seven-year-old Black boy by a party of the head Rabbi's motorcade, and the retaliatory killing of a Hasidic scholar by a group of young Blacks. Hasidic men don't even *shake* the hand of any woman that they are not married to (they don't touch what "does not belong to them"), let alone embrace one, and the Hasidim do not intermarry. The Hasidim were outraged, and so were Blacks. Some remarked that if this were reversed, and a Black man were embracing a Hasidic woman, the outrage would have been even greater. Now, what if we did that in theater? If we did, we could give the time to explore this image. It would be controversial, but I am not so sure it would actually be as controversial as that cover was. First of all, depending on the way it was cast, there is a likelihood that the personality of the actors would actually intervene and dampen the controversy. However, if we did carefully create such a moment, and carefully observe and re-enact the physical behavior, it could be some of the most loaded theater one could imagine. As far as a public controversy, of course, the problem is that it's likely that more people saw the cover of *The New Yorker* than would see the play.

I am not actually talking about non-traditional casting here, because we have used the term "non-traditional casting" so much that we have tamed the idea into something that does not sound very exciting, kind of like what the term "politically" has done to a multitude of issues. What I am proposing is creating theater that juxtaposes worlds that are far apart in order to create an aesthetic contract out of politically explosive interactions. We could then capture a raw, natural, and genuine modern drama which could ultimately influence how societies negotiate difference.

It is difficult within the university structure to supply actors with adequate physical, vocal, and social training. If we want to create an actor who is really transformative, we are going to have to be more clever about how to use the resources of the university to do it. As we all know well, it is nearly genius when a group of artists get a university to support conservatory training or something like it. We have to find new collaborators within the university that will allow us to look at acting as a study of human behavior and as a tool for researching communication skills and for expanding our knowledge of what expression is. The resources are there, and through performance studies departments, there are the beginnings of this. However, you know performance studies departments are actually not interested in training performers the way that we are. The word performance is used so much in the university and in culture that soon we should start a movement to reclaim it.

In terms of the interactions we have had with others in the university, I am not sure we have found situations that benefit us the best. I am sure some of you, as I have, for example, taught acting to lawyers and business students. I frankly, after having been at the federal trial for the Rodney King case, have an ethical problem with that. I saw a lot of bad acting. I saw acting reduced to manipulation. I do not think the lawyers went to acting school, or took acting classes, but I'm sure some of what I saw was based on watching actors "do" lawyers, in movies. In fact, one lawyer reminded me very much of a portrayal I had recently seen by a major movie star in a very popular movie. The problem is most actors are not lawyers. They don't know the language of the law. The language of the law could have a drama of its own, if lawyers would let that language create their plays. When they let the histrionics of acting tell them how to speak their own language, the result is something which is bad acting, and which frequently speaks down to the public, rather than up towards the ideals of the law. In this way, our work is about life and death. Because people in life base their performance of themselves, whether that is how they act in the courtroom, how they act on a date, how they act Asian, how they act like a man, a woman, on the performances they see in the media. We have to give them more to work with. We can only do that if we are working, from the undergraduate level, with very mature students, who come to the work already with an unusual/not cosmetic/expressive range. We need chameleons, transformers. Mercurial people. The times are hot, but there's not enough mercury in the thermometer. That's why we do not have an accurate display of the climate. We need mercurials. We do not need mimics.

Skills and the Peformance of Ethnicity

Our performance of ethnicity depends on the movies, television, advertising, and especially on the fashion industry. If we took away all of our clothing, how could we perform ethnicity and gender as current? I interviewed Elaine Brown, former Chairwoman of the Black Panther Party, for the show *Twilight: Los Angeles 1992*. Her advice to young Black males or, as she calls them, "Seventeen-year old-young brothers with a gun in your hand" is this:

> Seventeen-year-old young brother with a gun in your hand
> Tough and strong and beautiful as you are. . . . .
> Don't be getting all hung up on your ego
> Or pumping up your muscles
> And putting on some black beret or some kind of Malcolm X hat
> Or other kind of regalia or symbolic vestment that you
> Can put on your body
> Think in terms of what you gonna do for
> Black people
> I'm saying these are the long haul.

Now let me put the opposite picture out here. When I taught at the University of Southern California, the women students would not take off their jewelry when they did scene work. It did not matter what the role was, they wore whatever earrings they had on, usually large gold bangles, and their rings. Even when asked to play men in *American Buffalo*. It was like pulling teeth to ask them to costume themselves fully and to take off their jewelry. This resistance oddly reminded me of a similar resistance I met when I taught in Harlem—the kids would not take off their jackets when they acted. What is that resistance to taking off some piece of your identity?

Technique versus Art

I think we have a road to go on to develop more technique. I know, however, that technique is only part of art. I am collaborating with Judith Jamison on a dance piece for the Alvin Ailey American Dance Theater for the celebration of the thirty-fifth anniversary of the company. I met up with the dancers twice while they were on tour this year, and interviewed all of them. I'll speak their words and Ms. Jamison is choreographing a dance around their words. One of the themes that kept recurring among the twenty or so dancers was "The dance is not the steps." "The technique is the dance; the dance comes from within you."

What is inside ethnicity? Most of us know the steps. We learn them very quickly, and we are willing to change them each year. We keep some each year. But we change. This is not to trivialize the origins of these hair cuts, colors, adornments. This is not to trivialize them, but what is inside? If we could dance the steps of ethnicity, across the boundaries of ethnicity, we could give American culture something it needs: a beautiful revelation of what lives inside our respective ethnic houses. Now we are living in a society that daily moves further and further behind its fortresses. We cannot afford to be fortressed. If the university is gated, if it is keeping you inside—move out. If institutional theater is a fortress, move out. We are supposed to be on the outside, as theater people. One way to ensure our "outsideness" is to dare to learn the steps of all the dances and to do them until we find the dance. We need the proper dancemasters. We should not and cannot trust every teacher with all the dances. We know that, and the last twenty years of theater in their respective homes—theater in ghettos: Black, Native American, gay, Asian, and others—has been a result of that awareness.

Advocating Theatre and Theatre Practitioners That Are Other Than Ethnocentric

This is, I think, the only radical thing I have to say. I am aware that I am talking to a predominately white audience. Possibly that will change in twenty years. In a way, this part of my talk is written for what I imagine this audience might look like in twenty years from now. If I wait till then, this will not be of use.

Theater in the last twenty years has been ethnocentric. I would really have to look at funding requirements twenty years ago to see the reason for this. If I were to sit down at a table with some of my favorite theater artists, I would find myself with an Asian playwright who was educated at Stanford, a Black director educated at Brown, an Asian American critic who went to Harvard, a white woman playwright who went to Bryn Mawr, et cetera, et cetera, et cetera. I am not going to continue the list, because I would leave people out, and I don't want to do that! The point is, it is not just education that led to this. Some very well-educated theater people hit the streets and did not go immediately to mainstream theater. They tried to start theaters of their own that were about them. I am not sure if that was their organic idea, or if that was supported by grants, etc.—and yes, it was supported by education and by how ethnic studies was conceived *at that time*. Now, I think, is the time to create ways of moving between the fortresses, and in so doing to encourage a new generation of artists, who live in work, for lack of a better image, in *boats*.

This will not be easy and this will be inhibited, because among people of color, and among whites, we have not yet decided who can speak for whom. When I began working on *Twilight: Los Angeles 1992*, I asked Gordon Davidson to hire a team of dramaturgs, rather than one, because I was afraid that my own ethnicity would tell this story about L.A. in a way that reduced it to Black and White—that is what I knew about race in America, Black and White. L.A. is a multilingual, multiethnic city, and the explosion was by some accounts a poverty riot in which Latinos participated in great numbers and in which Asians, and Koreans in particular, were the most visible victims. Or so the media told us. The media, interestingly enough, told us very little about how whites reacted to the city burning down.

I asked Dorinne Kondo, a Japanese American anthropologist, feminist, and MacArthur Chair at Pomona College, to join me. I also asked Hector Tobar, a reporter for the *Los Angeles Times*, who covered the riots, and of Guatemalan descent, to join me. Eventually I worried that I was too vulnerable and thought I'd better not rely on my own judgment to watch out for the Black voice, and asked the African-American poet Elizabeth Alexander, from the University of Chicago, to join me. Emily Mann, who was the director, felt that Oskar Eustis would be a good addition to the team, because of his theatrical experience. What a battleship of dramaturgs. We met every night of previews. Our meetings were a scene to behold. There I learned a lot about "who can speak for whom." Dorinne and Hector in particular became more and more passionate as the work went on and felt a great sense of responsibility finally for "their communities." I understand this.

Dorinne, now, also thinks that this issue of who can speak for whom is a very interesting dynamic in work that tries to be multicultural. She has gathered and given me notes from her associates, mostly academics, and mostly but not all Asian American. First of all, it was interesting to her that they said things to her that they would not say to me. Second, there is a way in which she senses from them that they feel she has let them and the race down to the extent that she was not able to get me, or the work, to represent them adequately or with enough complexity. Of the notes that Dorinne has shared with me I am most interested, for the purpose of this discussion, in the critique from some that the Korean and the Spanish I spoke in the show was not perfect: "If she is going to speak the languages, then her accent should be right." Apparently, a colleague of Dorinne's, Marcyliena Morgan, a linguist and anthropologist at UCLA, said in my behalf (again none of this came to me directly), "Why should she speak Korean perfectly—you don't speak English perfectly."

Obviously, I will work harder on my Korean and El Salvadoran accents. I like this critique because it really says to me in a graphic way that, as I advocate cross-ethnic work, work that tries to cross the boundaries of ethnicity will be met with caution. And it should be.

A question I was frequently asked about my work in L.A. was "Did you meet anybody who unified the voices?" Didn't you meet anyone who could speak for everyone? I interviewed 175 to 180 people. The answer is no. One, I am not looking for such a voice, because I think there is a lot that needs to be heard in difference. Number two, there is nothing in our educational system in the last twenty years that has encouraged the development of a voice that can speak for more than itself. The tragedy of both Crown Heights and Los Angeles was that there was not one who could speak across lines. The future will demand that we have people who can.

Vehicles

We need to educate people who can move from place to place. We cannot just tear down the walls of ethnicity. Those walls are there for good reason. There is a fine history of Asian American Theater, Black Theater, Gay Theater, Latino Theater, Women's Theater, White Mainstream Theater and so on. Some have been around longer than others. Time is not the issue. We must capture this moment, wherever we are now, whatever ground, behind whatever fortress, and we must encourage fabulous, passionate, goodhumored, bright-eyed people to get in boats, small boats, row boats, boats that carry only one person in some cases, two or three in others, and help them push off, help them move out of the sand so that they can move from fortress to fortress—ambassadors, explorers. Exploration is not colonization. The good part of the story is that it is unlikely that any of the fortresses will allow a colonizer in. The past twenty years have taught us how to identify colonialism. And that's good.

Not So Special

A real danger in theater and in theater education is the idea of "specialness." A "special talent," a "special gift." We tell our students that they are special, that theater is special, and we hold up models of specialness. Something is shortsighted about that. We should be teaching them to identify the specialness in the world around them, and teaching them how to perceive a special moment in time, and how to capture it.

To encourage our students to be not so special, we have to give up the idea that we are special. That is the only way we will be the "Not So Special Vehicles" we need to be. The theater is disenfranchised at this moment. It is on the outside. The moment to capture is the moment of our not so specialness.

Limbo

I will close with my favorite quote. Twilight is a gang member in South Central and an architect of the gang truce in L.A. The title of my show was inspired by his *nom de guerre*, "Twilight." When I asked him how he got his name he spoke about limbo, and of being in limbo. I want to close with him because I think that thought, after reading the ATHE brochure, that the group is in a kind of limbo. And my speech has been a reaction to that idea of limbo.

Twilight said to me:

Twilight
is that time
between day and night
limbo
I call it limbo. . .
So a lot of times when I've brought up ideas to my homeboys
they say
Twilight
That's before your time
that's something you can't do now
When I talked about the truce back in 1988
That was something they considered before its time
Yet in 1992 we made it realistic
So to me it's like I'm stuck in limbo
Like the sun is stuck between night and day
in the twilight hours
You know I'm in an area not many people exist
Night time to me
is like a lack of sun
And I don't affiliate darkness with anything negative
I affiliate darkness of what was first
because it was first
and then relative to my complexion
I am a dark individual
and with me stuck in limbo
I see darkness as myself
I see the light as the knowledge and the wisdom of the world
And in order for me to be a true human being
I can't forever dwell in darkness
I can't forever dwell in the idea
of just identifying with people like me
and understanding me and mine.

Twilight is a prophet, and he is a person who can do what we try to teach people to do for four years. He can speak as he thinks. He can render a poetic idea as though it were normal because it is normal. He met with me twice. He spoke quickly, softly, and patiently. Each time, he ended abruptly. When I said good-bye, he simply nodded and said all right, quite unimpressed with himself or with the occasion of the interview. We asked him to meet once to have his picture taken for *Vogue* magazine. He came with three homeboys and an old car. He never came to the show that bears his name and carries his words as a major theme. We invited him several times. *I should have taken the show to him.*

PART I: Institutional Dynamics

Raynette Halvorsen Smith

We live in a time in which continuous change is the only constant. Teachers of theatre must confront radical change within two institutions: the professional theatre and theatre in higher education. The authors of essays in this section challenge standing traditions ranging from the content and process of specific courses to how theatre fits into higher education and larger cultural concerns.

Robert Wills' essay invites us to a future where we "will be asked routinely to think about and do things which now seem unthinkable." He sums up current challenges of teaching theatre by quoting the Pew Higher Education Roundtable Program, "Relying on what worked in the past has become an uncertain means of knowing what will succeed in the future." Our attention is focused on how, as part of this changing environment, teachers of theatre are forced to negotiate seemingly contradictory demands. For example, the desire to become more inclusive, admit new ideas, cultures, forms, and practice versus the need to satisfy the ever increasing demand for accountability which implies a more stable, measurable progress against established norms. How do we embrace a movement towards interdisciplinary teaching strategies that rely on collegiality and community, while recognizing the many ways of knowing and individual learning styles of the students?

The remaining essays in this section demonstrate concrete examples of these struggles. Stratos Constantinidis lays out the challenges of teaching theory in an ever-changing landscape. This includes problems such as, where does the teacher position him- or herself as a teacher of criticism and theory in relationship to the material and the student now that he or she can no longer make claims of neutrality? He further questions the position of the teacher of theatre criticism in the institution. Constantinidis states that "… [if] the school is *the* dominant Ideological State Apparatus in modern society, then we need to look more closely at how academic theatre 'hails' some students and faculty and 'ousts' others from its various programs."

Dickey and Oliva, who reviewed the syllabi for thirty-seven undergraduate theatre history sequences, complain that "no other discipline in the visual or performing arts lacks such an awareness of global developments." They reassess existing teaching strategies and their merits and suggest alternative approaches to content, projects, and the overall philosophical perspective on undergraduate history courses: "The rapidly-changing nature of our world will no longer allow us to rely on what we once understood to be the geographical boundaries of nations nor can we rely on pedagogical practices that are now as outdated as our maps in geography."

Patricia VandenBerg chronicles her experience with breaking out of the institutional theatre production mold to combine class work with production work. Along this theme, Rhonda Blair outlines strategies employed at Hampshire College. Blair points out that as a good "child of the sixties," Hampshire actively challenges and restructures institutional authority. Through its emphasis on interdisciplinary course structure and individually tailored classes, it becomes one model of dynamic institutional restructuring. Blair concludes that, although this constant aggressive rethinking about what theatre-making and theatre-teaching is all about can be exhausting and frustrating, "As the system demands that my students and I be much more individually and specifically present to each other, we learn to be more present to ourselves."

The Future of Theatre Education:
Thinking the Unthinkable

J. Robert Wills

Philosopher Peter Caws once drew attention to a certain ancient encyclopedia where it is written that animals are divided into the following classifications:

1. belonging to the emperor
2. embalmed
3. tame
4. suckling pigs
5. mermaids
6. fabulous
7. dogs running free
8. included in the present classification
9. which behave like madmen
10. innumerable
11. drawn on camel skin with a very fine brush
12. et cetera
13. which have just broken their leg
14. which from a distance look like flies

Those of us in the United States today, Caws would suggest, are probably astonished at this taxonomy. We see it as imaginative, fanciful, unconnected to reality—and certainly not an accurate way of accounting for animals. However, what should strike us, instead, as we consider the different logic of another system of thought, is the very real limitation of our own: we should be amazed that we could never think *that*.

The future will bring theatre educators to this same point with increasing regularity: how, we will ask, could we possibly think *that*? Or, harder yet, how could we possibly *do* that? For in the future we will be asked routinely to think about and do things that now seem unthinkable.

That is the primary premise of this particular invitation to discussion and debate, and why the title of this essay—"The Future of Theatre Education"—has a subtitle—"Thinking the Unthinkable."

There is a secondary premise at work here, as well: namely, that to begin any discussion about the future of theatre in higher education means first exploring, however briefly, the twin futures of higher education and of theatre. No amount of theorizing or philosophizing about future theatre education will have any impact unless it acknowledges the changed educational and theatrical realities of our time.

Let me begin with higher education.

Clark Kerr once wrote for the Carnegie Council that some 66 institutions that existed in 1530 "still exist today in the Western world in recognizable forms: the Catholic church, the Lutheran Church, the parliaments of Iceland and the Isle of Man, and 62 universities," (qtd. in Pew 1). Higher education has, indeed, survived for centuries, and for many of those years it remained essentially unchanged. In our time, however, change has relinquished its glacial speed and now rages through our campuses as never before. Worse yet, the changes we face on campus have been, and will continue to be, neither planned nor anticipated nor regular in any way. Instead, as the Pew Higher Education Roundtable Program has asserted, "ours is an age of discontinuous change—of unexpected turns, sudden shifts, and unexplained connections. Relying on what worked in the past has become an uncertain means of knowing what will succeed in the future" (2). Such discontinuous change, as most of us know too well, is driven largely by financial constraints, public opinion, a new necessity for accountability, and the general infusion into higher education of all of society's joys and problems.

If the very idea of ongoing change were not discomforting enough, even more unsettling is the notion, again put forth by the Pew Higher Education Roundtable Program, that "the changes most important to the university are those that are external to it." In other words, whatever pressures and constraints we face inside academe are now surpassed by the new "use of societal demand ... to reshape" our institutions, by the external forces and regulations and manipulations which abound.[1] The isolation and autonomy higher education has traditionally enjoyed is vanishing, replaced by a vastly different social contract.

Then, too, higher education is also rapidly (and I think, wisely) joining the mass of corporate life in a rush toward dismantling our traditionally hierarchical systems of organization. The disappearing tradition in this regard is based on held information, a strong sense of turf, a known chain of command, and rules devised to be followed. In such hierarchical systems, power is limited to a few, and groups advise while leaders decide. In higher education, however, as elsewhere in the world, hierarchies are breaking down, pyramid organizations are disappearing, and there is a clear shattering of traditional authority.

Luckily, there is a new tradition emerging, opposite in almost every way. This new tradition has to do with organizing ambiguous networks rather than hierarchies; it works horizontally, not vertically; it proceeds, not to the top of the ladder or the peak of the pyramid, but in seemingly random meandering—sometimes fast, sometimes slow, sometimes overlapping and contradictory. Some would say that our traditional way of doing things is like hiking, the planning of fixed routes to known destinations. The emerging way of doing things, by way of contrast, is more like surfing, positioning oneself to catch waves without a destination fixed beforehand.

In any case, higher education in the 1990s is changing, changing in ways more profound than at any time since the early 1900s.

By way of contrast, in theatre at the moment, perhaps just the opposite is true. After a burst of rather significant change in the 1960s and 1970s, theatre—at least mainstream theatre—now finds itself at the end of a decade or more of relative stagnation. As Daniel Yankelovich has said, the "period of the 1980s was a prolonged mental holiday, a national suspension of reality" (qtd. in Edgerton 5), and most of theatre, like most of society, joined the inactivity. There are isolated differences to this broad generalization, to be sure, but overall the premise holds true. Will this change in the time ahead, as new world leaders try to shape a new world order, and as the nation further responds to the wake-up call it first heard in the early 1990s? Perhaps. However, in the meantime, those of us in theatre in higher education must be aware, not of rapid change in the theatre, but of two slow-moving, long-term trends that continue to develop.

First, theatre is painfully, slowly, sometimes inharmoniously, but relentlessly and purposefully becoming a more inclusive art because of three fairly straightforward changes: (1) theatre artists and producers are increasingly recognizing, using, and trying to appeal to a broader and more representative array of people, people earlier either marginalized or excluded from theatre and from most of our national life—women, people of color, gays and lesbians, older adults, persons with disabilities, and others heretofore underused and undervalued by both society and the arts; (2) theatre people in the West are increasingly utilizing non-Western theatre traditions, ideas, and practices drawn from many cultures around the world; and (3) theatre artists are increasingly incorporating emerging artistic practices, especially those practices that expand the cutting edge of our discipline.

This first trend holds the real possibility for enriching and enlarging our efforts. The second trend, however, should bring real fear, for it relates to the current health of theatre, and really all the arts. That health is fragile right now, measured by almost any means. In fact, it's downright precarious. The American Council for the Arts (1993), for example, points out that twenty-five professional theatres have closed in the last five years, that the accumulated financial deficits for 182 other theatres have more than doubled recently, and that theatre touring has been reduced by 40% in the last two years. At the same time, in just a decade symphony orchestra deficits have grown from $2.8 million to $23.2 million. Obviously, public support for theatre and the arts has diminished. So also has governmental support. Federal support in "real" dollars has dropped 25% in the last decade, during which time state support dropped by an even larger 29%. And on July 15 of 1993, 240 members of the House of Representatives voted to reduce funding for the National Endowment for the Arts after 105 members of the House—not enough in the end—actually voted to eliminate all NEA funding.

Closer to home, the arts on many campuses have been battered by recent decisions brought about by financial stresses. In fact, Carl Shoenfeld has suggested that among the best ways for "school and college deans to protect their divisions from the downsizing and restructuring abroad in academe today" is to "get out of [theatre and the] fine arts."[2]

Consequently, any future vision for theatre programs in higher education must, first of all, acknowledge the rapid and continuing change, the external pressure, and the organizational transformation which is occurring in higher education. That vision must also recognize the current debilitating environment for theatre in society and on many of our campuses.

Given these prospects, what can be said about the future of theatre education in colleges and universities? How can the conversation begin? Where should we be looking for whatever will come next?

There are several simple questions we can begin to ask, even though the answers to such questions may not be so simple. They range across concerns evident on campus and in contemporary society. Let me suggest a dozen and a half of them for your consideration, just as a beginning:

1. Our theatre programs are frequently closed shops. How can we best create more inclusive campus theatre programs, knowing that inclusiveness must embrace, as a minimum, access—for new people, new ideas, new cultures, new forms and practices.

2. The professional theatre world is far from perfect. How can we educate and prepare students to change the theatre they will confront, rather than merely fit into it? Or, as Jonathan Warman has recently written, in our current programs students "are not being taught that they have the power to formulate their own performance paradigms, manipulate the paradigms already extant, create their own niche" (1–2).

3. How can we educate students so they can both enjoy a full, rich, meaningful life, and be adequately prepared for multiple and flexible career paths?

4. How can we incorporate into our curricula new teaching and learning strategies, especially those strategies that rely heavily on collegiality and community. At the same time, how can we recognize more fully the many ways of knowing and the individual learning styles and capabilities we now know exist?

5. How can we assess (measure) the quality of what we actually accomplish? The demand for accountability has arrived, and it is no longer adequate for theatre programs merely to assert their excellence. The world wants proof, and the proof must relate to our classrooms, laboratories, studios, and stages.

6. How can theatre programs both enhance and influence institutional mission? Said another way, how can theatre programs become more campus-specific?

7. How can theatre programs develop greater campus political strength?

8. How, at both the undergraduate and graduate levels, can we achieve the appropriate balance between education and training, between teaching and research, between production and non-production, between old and new, and between all the other seeming opposites that provide appropriate and healthy tension for our work?

9. How can we continue to serve well the dwindling number of traditional students while also serving more effectively the new majority of non-traditional students? Look who's coming to college these days. It's a different population from the one we have served in the past.

10. How can theatre programs in higher education actually begin to have an influence on what happens in the theatre at large? Of all the disciplines taught on campus, theatre is perhaps the least important to the industry it strives, in part, to serve.

11. How can theatre programs best face the realities of continued budget restraint?

12. How can academic theatre programs best intersect with and influence the national discourse on major issues of our day: the crisis in ethics and human values, the shifting of economic and social goals, the resolution of racial, gender, and class conflict, the changing realities of American families, and all the others.

13. How can theatre programs best relate on campus to the new interdisciplinary endeavors, to the growing connectedness of human knowledge and creativity—to women's studies, for example, or global studies, ethnic studies, environmental studies, and the like?

14. How can theatre programs best prepare students for a global world, a global economy, a global workforce?

15. How can campus theatre programs (and this relates in part to the question about mission) develop more distinctiveness, so that each emphasizes individual strengths and strives for different purposes?

16. How do we as faculty and students decide what to teach, what to learn—or more importantly, what not to teach, what not to learn—in an age where learning everything has become impossible?

17. How should theatre education relate to dance, music, video, TV, film, the visual arts, the electronic and interactive media, and to all of the other arts and sciences that now touch its activity?

18. How do we deal with issues of faculty morale and productivity, tenure, a dwindling job market, below-average academic salaries, campus marginalization, and the like?

19. A bonus question: What are the other questions we should be asking of ourselves as we face the 21st century?

Well, there you have it, and there's lots more, of course. Even so, perhaps these few questions can serve as a beginning. As I wrote earlier this year in a related context, "there will be no 'business as usual' for higher education for the next several years. Nevertheless, all of the changes which lie ahead can be met successfully if we are willing to adapt, to change, to admit freely a new reality, and to design our own future with purpose and care" (Wills "What Lies Ahead?" 6). Let me conclude with an allusion drawn from medieval cartography. Those very early maps placed known geography at the center of large scrolls. Around the edges of the scrolls, near where the oceans dropped off into the unknown, were written the words, "Here Be Dragons" (Wills "Here Be Dragons" 6). Everyone knew that where the dragons lived, there also lived great challenge, even terrifying fear. Everyone also knew that facing the dragons meant challenging the unknown, daring to discover whatever lay hidden beyond the current horizon. For most, crossing into the unknown was unthinkable. Those who thought the unthinkable, however, found themselves transforming nothing less than a "new world."

I hope in the years ahead that we in theatre in higher education can face our dragons triumphantly, so that we can increasingly think the unthinkable as we face the challenges that lie ahead.

Notes

1. The Pew Roundtable is talking specifically about doctoral-granting research institutions, but its premise actually applies to all colleges and universities in the United States and, indeed, around the world.

2. Schoenfeld, for the record, also recommends that deans distance themselves from the humanities, social sciences, and education. In other words, support for what we do, both on campus and off, is not exactly at its highest levels.

Works Cited

American Council on the Arts. *Update.* July, 1993.

Edgerton, Russ. "The New Public Mood and What It Means for Higher Education: A Conversation with Daniel Yankelovich." *AAHE Bulletin* (June 1993): 3–7.

Pew Higher Education Roundtable Program. "A Transatlantic Dialog." *Policy Perspectives* (June 1993): 2–4.

Schoenfeld, Carl. "Scholars Study Budget Cuts." *Academic Leader* (July 1993): 2–4.

Warman, Jonathan. "ATHE Does Need a Performance Studies Focus Group." *TASC Newsletter* (July 1993): 1–2.

Wills, J. Robert. "Here Be Dragons." *Theatre News* (October 1981): 6–8.

————. "What Lies Ahead? Higher Education in the Twenty-First Century." *VASTA Newsletter* (Winter 1993): 3–5.

A Teacher of Theatre Criticism:
Why Did Kamikaze Pilots Wear Helmets?

Stratos E. Constantinidis

Hitherto men have constantly made up for themselves false conceptions
about themselves, about what they are and what they ought to be.
    —Karl Marx and Friedrich Engels, *The German Ideology*

The radical self-doubt of criticism is such that it is not even able to say
whether it is an "amateur" or "professional" pursuit. It cannot, surely,
be *professional*, for nothing is more natural than reading. It is simply a
matter of turning the pages until you get to the end—turning them,
naturally, with a peculiar attentiveness, but an attentiveness which,
though it can be nurtured and informed, cannot ultimately be taught.
Yet it can not be *amateur* either, for it is unthinkable that the labor-
intensive industry of literary inquiry—schools, university faculties,
publishing houses, literary bodies—turns on a mode of cognition more
akin to wine tasting than chemical experiment. When English literary
studies were first academically institutionalized in Britain, this dilemma
was "resolved" by a judicious blending of the two modes.
    —Terry Eagleton, *Criticism and Ideology*

In criticizing the theories of Ludwig Feuerbach, Bruno Bauer, and Max Stirner
in *The German Ideology*, Karl Marx and Friedrich Engels envisioned assertive,
versatile individuals who would be capable of building on their own a new and
different social role for themselves by abolishing the inhibiting conditions of
their existence (92–95). If these versatile individuals were teachers of theatre
criticism, then, presumably, Marx and Engels would have been pleased to see
them do the following: assume an independent viewpoint, move from one theory
to another, question the long-winded positions of any theory, and encourage their
students to erase the life-long imprint of any theory from their syllabi. After all,
Marx and Engels believed that current "reality is only a product of the preceding
intercourse of individuals themselves" (87).

Attitudes have changed since 1845. Nowadays, a teacher of criticism, who
wishes to introduce theatre students to more than one conception of theory, faces
a problem: the dominant mind-set ordains that there is no impartial way of
teaching a theory or a cluster of theories. Terry Eagleton reiterated this position
in his book, *Literary Theory*: "Since there is in my opinion no 'neutral', value-
free way of presenting it, I have argued throughout a particular *case*"—that is the

case of Marxist theory (vii). But Eagleton's position, his theory, is only one among many, and it has been resisted by other critics. "Hostility to theory," Eagleton remarked, "usually means an opposition to other people's theories and an oblivion to one's own" (viii). His sarcastic remark cuts both ways.

To mitigate possible student resistance to a theory, an instructor may explain to them that the term "theory" is a narrow term with an expansionist agenda. Theory (as a collective noun) is often defined as "the criticism of criticism" or as "metacriticism." It has been fashionable to distinguish among critics, theorists, and metacritics—the theorists supposedly affording a greater degree of detachment, clarity, or abstraction than the critics; and the metacritics, likewise, from the theorists (Raval 239). This questionable labor division among critics, theorists, and metacritics implies that a theory and its (meta-) theorists can presumably stand on higher, safer ground (not necessarily outside the vortex of theatre criticism), and can achieve a better (over)view or clearer viewpoint than other theatre critics. However, a theorist's "academic" distancing from his object of study can also make him appear, in his ivory tower, to be a step further removed from the mundane concerns of theatre professionals.

Terry Eagleton's book *Literary Theory* offers a prime example of theory as the "criticism of criticism" by introducing the student to several formalist, structuralist, semiotic, and deconstructive theories as he passes them through the eye of the Marxist needle. What Eagleton did in his book, other instructors may do in their syllabi—savoring their pet theory and influencing the viewpoint of their students. In such cases, theory stands for ideology, and student hostility to a theory may be a symptom of resistance to a particular ideology. Eagleton briefly explored the relationship between "criticism" and "ideology" as two separate entities when he raised the question about the role of the teacher as a mediator between a text and a student in his earlier book, *Criticism and Ideology* (11). If the task of a criticism teacher is to explain a difficult [portion of a] text to a student so that it may be more easily understood or accepted, how can a teacher avoid interposing his/her own "shadow" between the text and the student? This "shadow" casts a spell on many epistemological and ideological issues regarding interpretation. Unlike Louis Althusser, however, Eagleton was cautious in raising Marxist theory to the level of a science, which presumably stood above [bourgeois] criticism and ideology. "Historical materialism," Eagleton wrote in a wisely ambivalent statement, "stands or falls by the claim that it is not an ideology, but that it contains a scientific theory of the genesis, structure, and decline of ideologies" (16).

It would seem then that the challenge for some teachers of theory in the 1970s and the 1980s was how to deal with the subject at hand so that criticism would become more than a narrow analytical tool for any particular viewpoint. On the one hand, for Marxist critics and other sociologically oriented critics, criticism becomes futile if its theories fail to discover their footing outside the text within the social reality. On the other hand, the old claim of the historical materialists to have been able to theorize the conditions that make "long perspectives" possible by situating their critique outside the field of competing viewpoints no longer seems efficable—let alone credible. As Eagleton correctly observed, "this, doubtless, seems a somewhat unfair, deftly convenient advantage to claim over the adherents of such alternative methods. Nor is Marxist criticism rendered any more popular by its simple incompatibility with empiricist and intuitionist techniques" (17).

In order to establish a more useful distinction (or rather, relationship) between criticism and theory, I will adopt the plural number (theories), and I will provisionally define theatre criticism as an ever expanding body of clusters of complementary and rival theories. As Marvin Carlson put it, "the term 'theory' then, I have taken to mean statements of [general] principles regarding the methods, aims, functions, and characteristics" of the art of theatre (9). In this sense, I will try to sketch my observations about some problems that affect the teaching of criticism—i.e., the teaching of various theories of the theatre. The term "teaching," of course, is a broad term about an activity that can take place in formal institutional settings (e.g., university classrooms) as well as in informal settings (e.g., dining rooms). My focus here will be on academic instruction, even though I value non-academic lessons highly and I know of no theatre scholar who has taught theory without some recourse to evidence outside of educational theatre.

I will concentrate on the problems of teaching criticism—not on the problems of any particular theory whose validity is either sanctioned or debated in academic circles—even though these two kinds of problems are interrelated. Furthermore, I will limit my observations to my experience in teaching two courses entitled THEATRE CRITICISM I and THEATRE CRITICISM II at the Ohio State University from 1989 to 1993. Due to the anecdotal nature of my essay, I will present my own observations primarily, but will also occasionally include the views of others. Experience has taught me that problems generally arise from the way an instructor responds to four basic perceptions: (1) his or her role as a professional teacher, (2) the role of criticism in the discipline of Theatre Studies, (3) the role of the art of theatre in his or her society, and (4) the role of the students as future academics or theatre professionals.

One of my tasks as teacher of criticism is to help students read, understand, discuss, and evaluate texts about the art of theatre as theorized and practiced since the days of Aristotle. I teach a total of nineteen texts in translation in these two ten-week courses, namely: Aristotle's *Peri poiãtikẽs*, Horace's *Ars poetica*, St. Augustine's *De civitate Dei* (I:1–2), Bharata's *Nãtyasãstra*, Castelvetro's *Poetica d' Aristotele vulgarizzata e sposta*, Cervantes' *Don Quixote* (I:47–48), Rapin's *Reflections sur la poetique d' Aristote*, Heinsius' *De tragodiae constitutione*, Sidney's *Defense of Poesy*, Dryden's *Essay of Dramatic Poesy*, Goldsmith's *Essay on the Theatre*, Diderot's *Paradoxe sur le comedien*, Lessing's *Hamburgische Dramaturgy*, Hegel's *Aesthetik* (III:III:3), Coquelin's

L'art du comedien, Shaw's *The Quintessence of Ibsenism*, Tolstoy's *Chto takoye iskusstvo?*, Nietzsche's *Die Geburt der Tragödie*, and Bergson's *Le rire*. I selected these texts because some of the other texts I had in mind were out of print, or were not available in translation, or were truncated translations squeezed between the covers of some anthology.

Some of these texts I have studied privately and have had long, repeated discussions over many years with friends (most of them certified philologists). However, as soon as I turned my personal reading list into a course syllabus, I had to defend it from those students who in the beginning of the course thought that I was teaching a section of the Eurocentric canon, as well as from those students who at the end of the course thought that I was teaching against the grain of the Eurocentric canon. One of them gave me a piece of his or her mind (with a vengeance) by mailing me an anonymous evaluation of my teaching during my fourth-year review for tenure and promotion. According to my critic, (who wrote that he or she wanted to see me shipped back to Greece) my thoughts in class should have served the ideas of the authors of the assigned texts, and I should have saved my critique of their ideas for private conversations with friends. However, my critic did not tell me (nor can I tell) where exactly my thoughts as a private person end and my thoughts as a teacher of criticism begin.

Although student comments rarely infringe on a teacher's academic freedom, the pressures placed on a professional teacher of criticism are not confined to syllabus preparation and classroom performance. His or her syllabi and classes are not isolated phenomena. They are part of a department's required or elective curriculum, and they share in the history of curriculum development or "curriculum erosion"—as my predecessor humorously preferred to call curriculum revisions. My predecessor, who taught these two criticism courses before he passed them on to me, was an avowed neo-Aristotelian (Kenneth Burke's term). However, unlike the Chicago critics (such as Crane, Keast, Maclean, and Olsen), my predecessor totalized Aristotle's text by leaving no room for alternative interpretations and theories. He mainly assigned Aristotle's *On Poetics* to his students, and he gave this text a very close reading for two academic terms. He believed that classroom teaching was like playing a dramatic role on the stage, and he would often play the devil's advocate in class for educational purposes. However, during the era of anti-Aristotelian theories, he found himself siding with the devil. His own beliefs and skills were being tested. As he phased into retirement, he had to cope with changing that seemed to undermine the very skills and beliefs in that he had a life-long investment.

If indeed the attitudes of students, faculty, even administrators about the role of teachers of criticism and the significance of certain theories (Aristotelian, Marxist, feminist, you name it) are slowly shifting, then an instructor with a pet theory (even in an updated "neo-something" form), which was popular for some time, may be trapped in the quicksand of criticism—or worse, may find himself labeled as "deadwood." Familiar classroom routines (lectures, discussions, student reports, term papers, final exams, grade rosters) may be giving some criticism teachers a false sense of security, especially if they encounter few unexpected demands from students. Since some teachers do not have the motivational reserves to endorse a new viewpoint or the resources to retrain themselves in new theories, they may resort to criticizing the rhetoric of change and its agents—an equally useful activity in my opinion. They may do so in the manner of my predecessor who noted two paradoxical situations: first, he experienced several curriculum changes in his long career, but no tangible improvements. Second, the more the university managers demanded quality education and higher professional standards from faculty, the less they increased financial support to most faculty members in comparison to their own salaries. One of my tenured colleagues wrote a letter of protest to the Governor of the State of Ohio. In this letter, my colleague emphasized the fact that his salary at the rank of Associate Professor of Theatre at The Ohio State University was lower than the salary of the average high school teacher with comparable years of teaching in the Columbus metropolitan area.

The teaching of criticism and its theories in a classroom is not insulated from social and academic politics. The budget cuts and hiring freezes in the early 1990s, which were launched under the slogan "let's save the core curriculum," have in fact arrested the development of curricula and have silenced non-core teachers. They have also raised the question whether or not the teaching of criticism should be part of the "core" in Theatre Studies. To date, theatre criticism has not been part of the core curriculum in the undergraduate theatre program and the graduate programs in acting, directing, design, and technology at the Ohio State University. M.F.A. students, who are required to accumulate 99 graduate credit hours for their degree, are obligated to take up to six credit hours of literature, history, *or* criticism. Students always opt for two courses in dramatic literature, sometimes in history, but rarely in criticism. If acting, directing, design, and technology students and their advising faculty think that criticism and its theories are marginal to their professional interests in this and other universities, then criticism courses and their teachers may be expendable in the minds of those in authority who regard criticism either as a secondary, parasitic imposition on the art of theatre, or as an annoying commentary on their art of managing departments of theatre and colleges of the arts.

During a period of declining enrollments and shrinking fiscal resources, a criticism teacher who is perceived as "deadwood" may be induced to resign or to request an early retirement—if tenure places layoff constraints. In implementing such face-saving layoffs some administrators take a crusading posture. For example, they claim that they infuse new blood in their departments because layoffs based on seniority rather than competence are unfair. In addition, they would claim that they are protecting students from being shortchanged by unmotivated teachers, protecting the reputation of a history-criticism-literature program from being tarnished by poor teachers, or even generously protecting those competent teachers who are overworked, underpaid, and underappreciated for their efforts.

As an underappreciated criticism teacher, my predecessor solved his salary problem by investing his free time, not in academic research and class preparation, but in real estate. During the 1989–90 academic year, according to *The Ohio State University Personnel Budget 1989–90* (1989, vol. 1. p. 24E), his salary as associate professor on a full-time nine-month appointment was $45,120 after twenty-six years of teaching; whereas the Theatre Department chairperson's salary as full professor on a full-time twelve-month appointment was $76,080 after thirty-six years of teaching; and my salary as assistant professor on a full-time nine-month appointment was $30,720 after five years of teaching. My predecessor retired in 1990, and died in 1992. In his Last Will and Testament, he left half-a-million dollars to the WOSU radio and television station, but not a penny to the OSU Department of Theatre. Given the emphasis placed by some administrators on a teacher's value in the academic market-place, which has affected salary structure and promotion opportunities, some associate professors in doctoral programs of theatre perceive themselves to have gone backward in their careers. The incentives for quality teaching are not there, and without incentive there can be no significant change. Holding back salary increases depends on the hope that the so-called "conscientious" teachers of criticism will not become disillusioned and will not eventually invest their research skills and time in real estate.

It would seem that the challenge is no longer how to turn criticism into something more than a narrow analytical tool for any particular viewpoint; rather, the challenge becomes how to turn criticism teachers from expendable commodities (expressed in dehumanizing metaphors such as "deadwood" and "dinosaurs") into stimulating workers who mine rather than undermine new theories about the art of theatre. The two challenges are interrelated. Thomas Kent has suggested that we should worry less when we construct totalizing theories or reduce analytical discourse to a body of knowledge that can be taught; instead, we should worry more when we fail to find a way to collaborate with others and to restructure work relationships in our academic institutions (265). Feminist scholar Mary Belenky has recently reminded us that the structure of academic life fosters competitive and comparative individualism, which becomes especially evident in the race for tenure, promotions, teaching loads, travel grants, research grants, salary increases, and research leaves (Ashton-Jones and Thomas 33–34). In this environment, some instructors are afraid to admit that they have problems teaching criticism because they assume that their colleagues will regard them as incompetent. Fear may lead to stress; stress may lead to ineffective class performance; and ineffective class performance may lead to a loss of confidence. This syndrome may claim as its victims novice and veteran criticism teachers who have been competent and confident for a number of years.

A criticism teacher who questions the epistemological assumptions that govern the views of his colleagues about acting, directing, designing, reading, or seeing plays may soon discover that hardly anyone shares his excitement about criticism or his kind of criticism. Some faculty members (including criticism teachers) find a theory (e.g., Stanislavsky's "empathic" acting theory, Charlotte Bunch's "nonaligned" feminist theory, etc.), stick to it, get comfortable with it, and consider germane only those views that reinforce that theory and practice. Often they and their students add an interdisciplinary or philosophical dimension to their explorations. The added dimensions definitely expand their professional and theoretical domain, but they do not necessarily lead teachers and students out of the comfortable cage of tradition—their tradition. Since my Aristotelian predecessor was teaching THEATRE CRITICISM I and THEATRE CRITICISM II during my first three years at the Ohio State University, I was assigned to teach THEATRE CRITICISM III—a course that focused on deconstruction by request of the students. Ironically, my training (if not my teaching) was rooted deeper in the classical tradition than my predecessor's. How can a "Greek" teach deconstruction? After all, it is unavoidable that a teacher of criticism will take his or her own training and background as a guide.

According to Jacques Derrida, one can be steeped in the classical tradition and still be able to teach deconstruction. Derrida admits that, as a teacher, he always starts with the texts and rules of the Western tradition, which demand discipline and demonstration, before he transgresses established norms. "If you're not trained in the tradition," Derrida said, "then deconstruction means nothing" (Olson 131). This stipulation by Derrida offered me a comfortable justification for teaching that course, but I always get suspicious when I get comfortable. While Derrida's philosophical project opposed "essentialism" by attacking the notion that signs have "inherent" meanings, still Derrida's teaching project made training in classical norms an "essential" precondition to deconstruction. For Derrida, a student cannot ignore some "minimal requirements" of knowledge of the great texts in the European tradition, even if the student is schooled in an open-ended, flexible, multicultural canon. But these minimal requirements are not shared by all students or academic institutions in Europe, let alone the United States of America. Europe has never existed as a unified linguistic, cultural, or national entity despite the ambitious (often ambivalent) results of expansionist military or economic plans—the North Atlantic Treaty Organization and the European Economic Community are the most noteworthy since the Second World War. Then, the question becomes "minimal requirements for which students in whose tradition?"

I have taught these three criticism courses to a total of fifty-four graduate students. The ratio of male to female students was 2:1. The ratio of American to foreign students was 5:1. The ratio of white to black students was 6:1. Two of my students were older than me. The mean age of male students was thirty-four and the mean age of female students was thirty-one. The foreign students were from China, France, Ghana, Greece, England, India, Korea, Poland, South Africa, and Saudi Arabia. The American students were also worlds apart in subcultural and personal values. Suffice it to say, one student had abandoned the order of the Schoenstatt Sisters of Mary before she was admitted to the M.A. program of Theatre, another student became a nun after she graduated, and yet another student was a lesbian feminist who had a child by *in vitro* fertilization. My reading list from Aristotle to Bergson could not anticipate the active social forces and histories that these students carried with them into the classroom and expressed in the form of questions, discussions, reports, papers, and exams. However, as a teacher, I could not slight them; nor would some of my students have let me, if I had tried.

Progressively, we had an influence on one another although it was not always intended. On the one hand, my students became my teachers, in the sense that some of their questions and answers began to influence my selection and interpretation of the assigned texts. On the other hand, a tradition of texts (which was abridged by my reading list) was transformed by some Ph.D. students, who were taking their doctoral candidacy examination, into a practical reading list. This list, in a sense, certified them as "educated" in matters of theatre criticism. However, I had not wished my syllabi to reaffirm a canon or invent one. I simply had used a sample from a tradition of texts to show to my students how some theories, which had a provisional status in the form of lecture notes (e.g., Aristotle's *On Poetics*, Hegel's *Aesthetics*) or admonitory letters (e.g., Horace's *Poetic Art*), have established themselves as a developing body of analytical practices and framing concepts for the production of knowledge about the theatre.

The efficacy of the analytical practices and framing concepts from Aristotle to the present has been determined by acceptable procedures of validation. The acceptability of these procedures (and subsequent practices and concepts) has been a matter of consensus among theatre critics and other theatre professionals who have established circles, movements, schools, academies, and even national (artistic/scholarly) traditions with minimal requirements or criteria of supposedly objective knowledge. Of course, all institutionalized knowledge is not necessarily objective, and many logical paradoxes occur when the criteria that are enforced by academic and non-academic theatre groups are internal—in the sense that they are indoctrinating, defying common sense and empirical evidence. If, for example, a theory (say, Aristotle's theory of tragedy or Georg Hegel's theory of tragedy) can be defined only in terms of internal coherence, then anyone can set his or her own criteria of validation of what kind of play is (or, is not) a tragedy or even what kind of experience is (or is not) of the theatre. Likewise, if a group of theatre professionals (such as the presidents of the national theatre associations who met at the Miami University Summit Conference in Theatre in Oxford, Ohio, in 1992) could set any number of programmatic requirements of what is (or, is not) a proper, coherent, or redundant education in theatre, then any group of, say, religious fanatics would have as much claim to being practitioners of theatre criticism regardless of their anti-theatrical prejudice.

Inevitably, my teaching was controlled to a certain degree by the internal requirements (courses, exams, papers, grades) of the academic unit that employed me, by the expectations of the senior faculty members who evaluated my teaching annually, and by the expectations of my theatre students whom I was hired to educate in matters of criticism. In order to give myself elbow room, I explained to my students, who came from so many different theatrical traditions, that theatre criticism, and its object of study, cannot be defined in terms of some universal logic for progress or in terms of some singular conception of what critical or theatrical knowledge should be. In saying so, I inadvertently undermined the credibility of criticism, because some of the students thought that criticism was a futile enterprise if the activities of the critics did not follow a singular, universal logic, or universally applicable criteria. Why should students waste their time and money to train themselves in criticism if its various theories are the result of subjective activities that belong to the domain of values rather than to the domain of facts? I was subsequently reminded that the thirst for validity and accuracy dominates the investigations of all critics, and that the neutral criterion of "truth" surfaces in all rival theories. Therefore, according to some students, only those theories can be reliable that are proven to be immune to any limiting personal, social, cultural, and historical circumstances.

It has been difficult to make this kind of student realize that the critical theories are only provisional answers that make explanations about the theatre possible, not reliable. My task became easier when he or she would agree to let me break down the vague criterion of "truth" into a set of seemingly neutral criteria (such as "accuracy," "consistency," "clarity," or "practicality"). Then, I could show how the application of "neutral" criteria, such as the above, historically allowed judgment to be passed on some theories as being inaccurate but practical, and on some other theories as being accurate but useless. Although I failed to persuade some of my students on this and other points, I succeeded, through the length of a course, to instill in most of them the notion that no theory that is handed down to us can substitute for a fresh, concrete analysis of a [re]current problem in the field of theatre—no matter how accurate or practical this theory may seem to be. Eventually, my students accepted a notion of pluralism that facilitated polite class discussions, but some of them abandoned it in their term papers.

Of course, none of my students has ever introduced himself or herself to me as a capitalist, sexist, or racist. In fact, some of them introduced themselves as Marxists, feminists, or postmodernists. In saying so, they were no different from many eager medical students who define themselves as doctors, assuming that a successful academic life will prepare them to become what they are not yet.

However, some of my students sounded phony on paper, not because they were insincere, but because they wrote their papers in an obscure postmodern jargon. They put more effort into imitating an elitist discourse and less effort into describing or solving a down-to-earth problem for theatre professionals. Jargon can be useful. Medical jargon, for instance, assists a doctor to record his diagnosis of an illness in more precise and concise terms than ordinary language. The same jargon, however, can help a quack disguise his lack of understanding of the symptoms that he observes and temporarily fool his patient. These theatre students were not quacks, but in their effort to speak the fashionable language of postmodernism, they failed to describe and solve specific theatre problems—however small. Their papers remained a classroom exercise, a "language game" (Wittgenstein's term).

Moreover, elitist language inhibits a democratic dialogue between scholars and the other theatre professionals inside and outside the academic world because it does not encourage the non-specialist to understand or respond. For this reason, my answer was simple when one of my postmodern students asked why I bother to teach premodern critics. I said that some "postmodern" critics are less democratic, flexible, or even dialectical than some "premodern" critics. Like numerous present-day academics, many modern and not-so-postmodern theatre theorists (from Gordon Craig to Peter Brook) endorse "vanguardism," i.e., the notion that theatre will change only where small groups of leaders (*didaskaloi, gurus, shamans*, experts, department chairpersons, directors of theatre, etc.) discipline and enlighten the theatre professionals. As a remedy to this managerial notion, I assigned my students to read and compare Aristotle to Plato, Castelvetro, and Lope de Vega because I think Aristotle understood how precarious the life of theatre and democracy becomes when critics (such as his teacher Plato) entrust judgment only to the philosophizing rulers, who exploit the communicative incompetence of the public which is described in *The Republic* as short-sighted, hard of hearing, ignorant, and pleasure-seeking (VI, 488 B–E).

In his *Politics*, Aristotle objected to leaving matters only to the reasoning of experts or specialists. He did not subscribe to the notion that the best men to judge a physician are other physicians, that the best men to judge a critic are other critics, that the best men to judge a playwright are other playwrights, and that the best men to judge a teacher are other teachers (III, VI, 1282a, 1–21). Instead, Aristotle preferred the collective judgment of a more or less educated public at a time when the trend was to prevent the people from gaining control. For example, in the case of the medical profession, Aristotle points out that "physician" means the practicing medical doctor as well as the teacher of medicine and the student of medicine.

(εἰσὶ γὰρ τινες τοιοῦτοι καὶ περὶ πάσας ὡς εἰπεῖν τὰς τέχνας, ἀποδίδομεν δὲ τὸ κρίνειν οὐδὲν ἧττον τοῖς πεπαιδευμένοις ἢ τοῖς εἰδόσιν). (III, VI, 1282a 3–8)

In all arts, there are such men, so to speak, but we assign the right of judgment just as much to the students as to the experts.

Aristotle was confident that the collective judgment of a group of men who enjoyed basic freedoms was "better or at least as good" as the judgment of an expert. He also thought that the professionals who offered goods and services to the public were neither better judges of their products and services than the consuming public, nor should they be the only ones to exercise this judgment.

οἷον οἰκίαν οὐ μόνον ἐστὶ γνῶναι τοῦ ποιήσαντος, ἀλλὰ καὶ βέλτιον ὁ χρώμενος αὐτῇ κρενεῖ (χρῆται δ' ὁ οἰκονόμος), καὶ πηδάλιον κυβερνήτης τέκτονος, καὶ θοίνην ὁ δαιτυμῶν ἀλλ' οὐχ ὁ μάγειρος. (III, vi, 1282a 15–24)

For instance, the ability to judge a house belongs not only to its builder, but even more so to its user (that is, the householder). Likewise, a steersman judges a rudder better than its carpenter, and the gourmet judges a meal better than its cook.

Evidently, Aristotle saw the teacher as a member of his community, not the opinion leader of a mindless crowd. Aristotle's advice remains useful in educating the educators of today who hold doctoral degrees, have impressive curricula vitae, and possess the skill of professional gab:

οὐδέν γὰρ κωλύει τὸν παιδοτρίβην ἕνα τῶν γυμναζομένων ἐνίοτ' εἶναι καὶ αὐτὸν ὥσπερ ὁ κυβερνήτης εἰς ἐστὶν ἀεὶ τ ὧν πλωτήρων· ὁ μὲν οὖν παιδοτρίβης ἢ κυβερνήτης σκοπεῖ τὸ τῶν ἀρχομένων ἀγαθόνε ὅταν δὲ τούτων εἰς γένηται κ αἰ αὐτὸςε κατὰ συμβεβηκὸς μετέχε·ι τῆς ὠφελείαςε ὁ μὲν γ ὰρ πλωτήρε ὁ δὲ τῶν γυμναζομένων εἰς γένεται παιδοτρίβ ης ὢνζ (III, iv, 1279a 3–8)

Nothing therefore prevents the teacher from becoming a trainee himself occasionally, just as the captain is always a member of a crew; the teacher or the captain looks after the benefit of those under his authority, but he also, incidentally, shares the benefits when he becomes one among them, because the one is still a sailor, and the other becomes one of the trainees even though he is a teacher.

Critical theory has become an academic specialty and requires years of study to master its jargon. This jargon, however, empowers only a privileged few who speak it and write it, and entombs theoretical conversation outside the classroom, disempowering the non-specialist and discouraging M.F.A. theatre students from taking a course in criticism as an elective. How many academic experts address the daily concerns of theatre professionals who could care less about Jacques Derrida, but care desperately that live theatre is losing its grip on the people? By professionalizing and specializing the discourse about theatre even further, we are responsible for marginalizing critical theories. I therefore advise my doctoral students to remain non-specialists at heart and to rethink their public role even if this may require some degree of de-academization.

Like so many other teachers of criticism, my goal then was to democratize theatre criticism by helping my students realize five things: that criticism is not only an academic project that is made inaccessible to the average theatre folks; that theatre folks can rearticulate critical theories in the vernacular without diminishing their diagnostic power; that students become critics when they override the dicta of the so-called experts—such as their teachers; that any dictum should always be studied in the context of past and present social and economic conditions; and that no methodological jargon and theories can save the day by reinventing what is possible if they are not applied to the solution of the practical problems of theatre professionals.

Of course, a goal such as the above is easier set than accomplished. In my search for a lineage of texts and scholarship, for instance, I had hardly any classroom time to bridge the issues of the past with the problems of the present. When I attempted to stop my exhaustive and exhausting exegetical work of the classics and the neoclassics, I ventured to turn the attention of my students to critiques of the entertainment industry and the academic industry. I justified my attempt by claiming that the theoretical lineage from Aristotle to Bergson matters less than the deconstructive practice of exposing the artifice of canonical texts, and exploring the distinction between "high" and "low" entertainment. If deconstruction were to be liberated from being just another interpretive approach to appreciating dramatic literature, I had to demonstrate to my students in my lectures how the hidden contradictions in the texts of famous drama theorists were smoothly integrated as truths into the world of professional theatre. My book, *Theatre Under Deconstruction?* which, in part, grew out of my lecture-notes, provides a record of this endeavor.

Nonetheless, during these three ten-week courses (I, II, III of 3 credit hours each), I could not shake off the thought that for three hours a week I was turning the classroom into a fast-food restaurant where I was serving my students foreign dishes selected from Greek, Italian, Indian, French, Spanish, Dutch, and German menus in an Americanized (i.e., translated) context. I was force-feeding them with the "pastiches" of texts drawn from diverse cultural sources and historical periods. If what criticism teachers and theatre students read, discuss, and write about the art of theatre in the classroom helps them create a "prefiguration" (Marcuse's term), i.e., an image of its future in their minds, then I wonder what kind of prefiguration the academic cosmopolitanism of my classes has created in the minds of my students, and how long it will take before this image fades away in their memories.

Perhaps, I need to repeat two things here in the form of a conclusion: first, the conceptual and empirical sophistication that is needed for understanding what is going wrong with the complex art of live theatre as an economic and cultural institution can be communicated in an accessible language. Otherwise, as my predecessor bemoaned, things may not change much as the educational and professional crisis is protracted for one more decade, albeit under different privileged groups. The working relationship between learned academics and theatre professionals, which Lope de Vega satirized in his amusing speech, *The New Art of Writing Plays in This Age*, presented to a Madrid literary society in 1609, may still be relevant. There is no point in doing what we should not be doing at all.

When, for instance, I was invited to visit a criticism class of my Aristotelian colleague in the late 1980s, I observed that he and his students gave Ingram Bywater's English translation of Aristotle's *On Poetics* a close reading—explaining and discussing major terms and concepts from page to page. When I was assigned to visit a criticism class of a feminist colleague of mine in the early 1990s, I observed that she and her students gave Ben Brewster's English translation of Louis Althusser's *Ideology and Ideological State Apparatuses* a close reading—explaining and discussing major terms and concepts from page to page. I was surprised to see these two instructors use the same teaching method because the departmental grapevine had prepared me to think of them as having diametrically opposed personal and professional orientations. He was, reportedly, an old-fashioned, single elderly man with an anti-feminist attitude and a fixation on Aristotle. She, on the other hand, was, reportedly, a progressive, single, middle-aged woman who defined herself as a materialist feminist. Regardless of their alleged personal and professional differences, they engaged themselves and their students in the same teaching method, which is known as *"explication du texte."* I did not speak out against this method of teaching criticism, which is considered to be outdated by my fashion-driven colleagues, nor did I raise an eyebrow as would my philologically minded colleagues who question the scholarly validity of explaining, not the original text, but its translation, because I am, reportedly, obsessed with deconstruction. In fact, I found some merit in this "old" method of teaching. However, I will mention one of my major reservations here: if we continue to do what we always did when we teach criticism, we will get what we always got—that is, critics who spend their time and the time of the next generation of critics in reading and explaining texts from Aristotle to Althusser. Unfortunately, neither Aristotle nor Althusser could anticipate (let alone describe or solve) the problems that plague the theatre profession at the beginning of the twenty-first century. However, we can, and so can our students if we teach them (and ourselves) how to practice alternative teaching and research methods.

Second, I remain concerned about the institutional ways in which teaching and research are organized (read, "compartmentalized") in large departments of theatre, contributing to the decline in communication between the students or faculty who are entrenched in two lines of programs: the B.A./M.A./Ph.D. programs in literature, history, and criticism, and the B.F.A./M.F.A./D.F.A. programs in playwriting, acting, directing, design, and technology. As teachers of theatre criticism, we are in the business of (re)producing and disseminating new knowledge about the art of theatre. If, as Louis Althusser and his disciple Pierre Macherey believed, the school is *the* dominant Ideological State Apparatus in modern society, then we need to look more closely at how academic theatre "hails" some students and faculty and "ousts" some others from its various programs. As teachers of theatre criticism, our silence or eloquence (whichever applies in one's case) may contribute to the reproduction of the existing relationships of production in theatre departments. When criticism teachers and students get together to reflect on the nature and function of theatre, they make this incursion into theory with a view of making progress in understanding not only criticism and the art of theatre, but also the conditions that make their investigations possible.

Note

Unless otherwise indicated, all translations in this essay are the author's. A version of this essay was delivered at the annual conference of the Association of Theatre in Higher Education in Philadelphia in August of 1993 under the provisional title "After the Fact: Teaching Criticism to Theatre Students."

Works Cited

Agger, Ben. *A Critical Theory of Public Life: Knowledge, Discourse, and Politics in an Age of Decline*. London: The Falmer Press, 1991.

Althusser, Louis. Introduction. *Proletarian Science? The Case of Lysenko*. By Dominique Lecourt. Trans. Ben Brewster. Norfolk: NLB, 1977.

Aristotle. *Politics*. Trans. Harris Rackham. London: William Heinemann, 1932.

Ashton-Jones, Evelyn, and Dene Thomas. "Composition, Collaboration, and Women's Ways of Knowing: A Conversation with Mary Belenky." *(Inter)views: Cross-Disciplinary Perspectives on Rhetoric and Literacy*. Ed. Gary Olson and Irene Gale. Carbondale: Southern Illinois UP, 1991. 27–44.

Carlson, Marvin. *Theories of the Theatre: A Historical and Critical Survey from the Greeks to the Present*. Ithaca: Cornell UP, 1984.

Constantinidis, Stratos E. *Theatre Under Deconstruction? A Question of Approach*. New York: Barland Publishers, 1993.

de Man, Paul. *The Resistance to Theory*. Minneapolis: U of Minnesota P, 1986.

Eagleton, Terry. *Criticism and Ideology: A Study in Marxist Literary Theory*. London: Verso Edition, 1976.

———. *Literary Theory: An Introduction*. Minneapolis: U of Minnesota P, 1983.

Horkheimer, Max. *Critical Theory: Selected Essays*. Trans. Matthew O'Connell et al. New York: Herder and Herder, 1972.

Horkheimer, Max, and Theodor Adorno. *Dialectic of Enlightenment*. Trans. John Cumming. New York: Herder and Herder, 1972.

Jacoby, Russell. *The Last Intellectuals: American Culture in the Age of Academe.* New York: Basic Books, 1987.

Jameson, Fredric. "Postmodernism or the Cultural Logic of Late Capitalism." *New Left Review* 146 (1984): 53–93.

Kent, Thomas. "Talking Differently: A Response to Gayatri Chakravorty Spivak." *(Inter)views: Cross-Disciplinary Perspectives on Rhetoric and Literacy.* Ed. Gary Olson and Irene Gale. Carbondale: Southern Illinois UP, 1991. 261–66.

Marcuse, Herbert. *Eros and Civilization.* New York: Vintage, 1955.

———. *An Essay on Liberation.* Boston: Beacon Press, 1969.

Marx, Karl, and Frederich Engels. *The German Ideology.* Ed. S. Ryazanskaya. Moscow: Progress Publishers, 1964.

Olson, Gary. "Jacques Derrida on Rhetoric and Composition: A Conversation." *(Inter)views: Cross-Disciplinary Perspectives on Rhetoric and Literacy.* Ed. Gary Olson and Irene Gale. Carbondale: Southern Illinois UP, 1991. 121–41.

Raval, Suresh. *Metacriticism.* Athens: The U Georgia P, 1981.

Wittgenstein, Ludwig. *Philosophical Investigations.* Oxford: Basil Blackwell, 1953.

Multiplicity and Freedom in Theatre History Pedagogy:
A Reassessment of the Undergraduate Survey Course

Jerry Dickey and JudyLee Oliva

> The task of today's historian, then, would seem to be to recognize the new multiplicity of the discipline created by the challenge of modern theory and to utilize this freedom for the positive expansion of the discipline.
> —Marvin Carlson

The much-acclaimed documentary filmmaker Ken Burns recently described the reasons for his ongoing fervor with events and individuals from the past. "History," Burns said,

> is always about the present. Only superficially is it past in terms of the events examined happening before our time. But what we choose to remember is always related to who we are today ... How can you possibly know where you want to go if you don't know where you've been? (Interview)

In an age when the relevancy of the study of history receives popular challenges, those of us who teach history to others might do well to keep Ken Burns' attitude in mind.[1] According to Burns, the study of history forms part of a rigorous process of self-examination and discovery. Far from adhering to Henry Ford's belief that "History is more or less bunk" (qtd. in *Macmillan* 252), Burns believes that a study of history aids in the shaping of one's identity and sense of purpose.

None of us who teach theatre history questions the validity and usefulness of its study for any individual wishing a career or further education in the performing arts. Surprisingly, however, undergraduate theatre students typically approach their required courses in the history of their art with apprehension at best—and downright dread at worst. With practically every theatre program in colleges and universities around the country requiring an undergraduate survey course or courses in theatre history, one marvels at the relative paucity of published material pertaining to the pedagogy of this subject. Now, with exciting new methodologies in theatre history being introduced into the field, an opportune moment arises to inspect the place of the survey course in the theatre curriculum and to review the particular demands placed upon the teacher of theatre history.[2] Specifically, we need to examine what we are doing in the classroom to determine if the activities and projects we employ are the most appropriate forms for exploring historical material. Perhaps most importantly, we need to question whether or not we are resisting the adoption of new pedagogical approaches.

We begin by recognizing that an implicit model exists for undergraduate theatre history surveys, although this model contains numerous variables. As part of a syllabus exchange project and pedagogy panel for Theatre History Focus Group constituents of the Association for Theatre in Higher Education, we appraised thirty-seven undergraduate survey sequences including sixty-six separate courses.[3] The most frequent design of these survey courses contains a chronological discussion of major theatrical developments through a combined study of production innovations and dramatic literature, frequently augmented by a required research paper and two or three exams. The focus typically rests largely on Western Europe and America, sometimes with an all too brief look at theatre of the Orient. The overall length of the survey provides one variable within this dominant model, with courses ranging from one quarter to four semesters. Additionally, some surveys exist within a liberal arts curriculum, while others form part of a professional training program. Some serve majors only; others combine the theatre student and the non-major within the same setting. Finally, a few surveys connect to their respective institution's general education program, either as part of a history of western civilization sequence, as an option for an arts or humanities requirement, or occasionally as an interdisciplinary unit of the curriculum.

For the teacher of any of these various history surveys, at least one general characteristic typically holds true: students enrolled in such a course have had little to no exposure to the field of theatre history in their previous education. Faculty consider themselves lucky if their students possess a working knowledge of the history of America and Western culture. In many cases, students' conditioning leads them to believe that the study of history equates with a tedious memorization of names, dates, and battles. Very possibly, students have encountered previous courses in history that provide the information in a lecture format so predictable and methodical that they lose interest. Understandably, then, students approach the theatre history course with that feeling of apprehension or dread. The syllabus of one colleague in theatre history acknowledged students' hesitations with the disclaimer, "Cheerful silence and non-participation are not worth much but are preferable to sullen ugliness" (Dickey 81). Furthermore, as Oscar Brockett points out, the primary goals for most students in the undergraduate theatre history course include "first of all, to pass the course and, only secondarily, to learn something about the subject" (43). As the course progresses and students feel relatively assured of their desired grade (or have given up hope of ever achieving this grade), attendance usually wanes.

As teachers, we counter these attitudes and habits with an arsenal of weapons. Many syllabi examined for this study reveal similar strategies, such as strict attendance policies or rewards for participation, stringent warnings against plagiarism, and handouts that extol the merits of studying theatre history (the type of sincere advocacy Brockett fears might "create more doubt than any other one could devise" (43). The hope of inspiring the student toward self-analysis and discovery usually dissipates before midterm.

The tone of many of these syllabi sadly reflects our frustrations as historians/teachers at having to teach not only theatre history, but also writing, research, behavior, group dynamics and textual analysis. Curiously, though we charge ourselves and our students with the above responsibilities, little evidence exists to suggest that we teach students how to achieve them. We ask students to write a research paper but do not teach them about basic theatre history research. In fact, we ask students to be creative, spontaneous, and participatory in class, but then rarely give them an opportunity beyond responding to lecture notes.

The principal difficulty for the teacher/historian in organizing a survey course is that of making excruciatingly difficult decisions about what material to omit, or of determining the minimal amount of time to cover adequately, for example, the drama of the Middle Ages. Additionally, the theatre historian must possess familiarity with a vast array of subject areas. Theatre historians commonly explicate their field by drawing upon social history, philosophy, religion, and other performing and fine arts, as well as various aspects of stage performance and production. In many programs, the historian must impart this knowledge single-handedly for a chronological period covering some 2,500 years relating to countries all over the globe.

The prevalence of a host of new methodologies within the last couple of decades place increasing demands on the historian/teacher. The new emphases on theatre historiography, feminist, interdisciplinary and intercultural studies, semiotics, and the new historicism reveal numerous areas of historical omission that, for a variety of reasons, are not included in the traditional body of material that comprises the history book or the survey course. These omissions include the achievements of women, ethnic and racial theatre traditions, the complexity of social forces that define the theatrical event, techniques for analyzing and reconstructing performance activity, and aspects of theatre in popular culture.[4] Additionally, the field of performance studies identifies theatrical elements in a wide array of human activities that traditionally escape the purview of the theatre historian. As R. W. Vince notes:

> The list [of potential subjects] appears endless. But there remains a suspicion that any attempt to limit the list, to restrict the area of investigation by defining "theatre" in any particular way as a precondition of study, will prove both arbitrary and self-defeating. (14)

The influx of new approaches and subjects creates a daunting dilemma for the teacher/historian: to add even more material to a survey of the prehistoric origins of theatre to postmodernism and beyond without overwhelming the introductory theatre history student.

Vince further concludes theatre historians/teachers struggle with a problem of professional identity. Methodologies lie somewhere between literary and performance. Often academic institutions view the survey as a "service" course that must meet a variety of needs depending on the academic association of the course. Vince raises the equivocal question when he asks, "Will theatre history be able to take advantage of new historiographical theories and methods and establish itself as an independent discipline devoted to the historical and theoretical study of the performance event?" (16). As an independent discipline, perhaps the historian would spend less energy on confining and selecting the content of courses and more on enlarging and expanding the perspective in which the discipline is viewed.

In practice, the advent of the new methodologies clearly influences the teaching of the undergraduate survey. An examination of the submitted course material reveals that instructors attempt to expand the traditional subject matter of the history survey. Typically, teachers devote a lecture (perhaps two) to the role of women in theatre. Most courses include a section on African-American theatre. Sometimes performance reconstruction projects ask the student to use imaginatively some aspects of the new historicism, semiotics, or reception theory. Unfortunately, these efforts constitute a tiny fragment of the design of these respective courses.

Even as previously neglected material augments the history survey, new problems surface. As with most textbooks, previous omissions from history now enter into the canon only by marginalizing the added subjects. Discussions of women and blacks need not be treated as though they are separate units. As James V. Hatch laments in his essay, "Here Comes Everybody: Scholarship and Black Theatre History":

> A student who reads "American" in the title of a theatre text should expect more than European ethnics.... This continuing apartheid in an era when our scholars show increasing sophistication in national and multiethnic theatre history is unfair to students—and dishonest.... The study of American theatre should become an integrated history, not a book with a chapter on Black performers. (148–60)

In addition, significant geographical omissions emerge. Although almost all theatre history survey courses include the teaching of dramatic literature, none of the surveys examined include a single play from Mexico, Latin or South America, Canada or Australia. Similarly, contemporary dramas in Asia rarely appear in either textbooks or course outlines.[5] The continent of Africa fares a little better, although only three of the thirty-seven surveys examined include a play by Nobel Prize-winning Nigerian playwright Wole Soyinka, or any other black African. No other discipline in the visual or performing arts lacks such an awareness of global developments. In short, the undergraduate theatre history survey needs urgent re-examination in light of the changing face of the discipline.

The descriptions above accurately reflect the current state of theatre history survey courses. However, many of us teaching the survey course recognize the discrepancies between process and product. No pedagogical revolution looms on the horizon, but with awareness and sometimes frustration comes reform, perhaps renaissance.

So, where does one begin in the classroom? The following section outlines several organizational options currently in practice, and includes a few guiding principles to consider in the formation of the undergraduate survey. The goal is not to offer a prescribed recipe for the politically correct course, but to suggest some possible approaches to address historical omissions and to reverse students' attitudes. This section also offers a discussion regarding existing teaching strategies, the merit of such strategies, and proposes some alternative ways to address not only content, projects, and presentations, but also the overall philosophical approach to the undergraduate history course.

Provide Greater Attention to Expanding the Traditional Boundaries of Historical Inquiry in an Integrated Fashion

An examination of the syllabi submitted reveals that the design of the overwhelming majority of survey courses mirrors the organization and subject matter of the required textbook, with Oscar Brockett's *History of the Theatre* serving as the required or recommended text in twenty-three of the thirty-seven survey sequences.[6] Exceptions exist, however, to this organizational structure that focuses primarily on Europe and America. At the University of Hawaii at Manoa, the undergraduate survey in "World Drama and Theatre" unfolds in a four-semester sequence, team taught by an Asian and Western theatre specialist. The final course in the sequence, titled "The Pluralism of Twentieth-Century Drama and Theatre," not only covers the stylistic and philosophical developments of theatre in Europe and America, but includes units on leftist theatre in Japan, the rise of modern drama in India, theatre and modernization in China, feminism and theatre, twentieth-century African theatre, and Japanese anti-realism and nativism: Suzuki Tadashi, and much more. Students read plays by Apollinaire, Pirandello, Brecht, Odets, Artaud, Miller, Beckett, Baraka, Churchill, and Shepard alongside numerous lesser-known Asian and African counterparts. Admittedly, Hawaii's rather unique geographical setting provides an ideal situation for an east-west binary analysis of theatre, and the vast majority of theatre programs do not even have a full-time voice coach much less a specialist in Asian theatre.

We outline the Hawaii model for two reasons. First, we cite this sequence because of the importance Hawaii gives to the study of history in terms of faculty resources and overall space in the curriculum. In an age when the glut of professional training programs seems wildly out of proportion with the number of available jobs in theatre, we would all do well to remind our faculties and administrators of the merits of teaching our students critical judgment through historical analysis. Second, we detail the Hawaii approach not to point out how poorly prepared most of us are to teach an expanded survey of Asian and African theatre, but to show that whatever our teaching conditions—one semester/four semesters, majors/non-majors—no reason exists why course content needs to mimic the organization of the required textbook.[7] We may use the textbook as an invaluable resource for our teaching, but supplement it with omitted material as we are able (and we need to keep trying to make ourselves more able).[8]

In addition to global expansion, similar historical omissions need redressing in regard to issues of gender, race, and class. In a recent article, Tracy Davis poses a series of questions to use as guides toward a feminist methodology in theatre history. The questions appear deceptively simple:

1. How does the ideology of the dominant culture affect women's status?
2. How do social, class, and economic factors affect privilege?
3. How is the status quo maintained or challenged in artistic media? (68–71)

As Davis asserts, these questions help make "the invisible visible in female and male experiences" (68). With only slight semantic changes, all three questions may also pertain to issues of race, ethnicity, and interdisciplinary studies. Using these types of questions as part of an ongoing discourse with students on the nature of theatre history easily expands the traditional boundaries of study without marginalization. The questions also provide students with a set of filters through which they may examine their own culture, thus imbuing their historical inquiry with a rush of immediacy.

Explore Methods of Organization Other Than That of Linear Chronology

Although following a linear construct contains obvious advantages, the chronological approach need not be the only means to explore theatre history. Sam Abel formerly of Dartmouth College has spoken on several occasions about his efforts in developing a topic-oriented history survey. He insightfully identifies how the linear approach gives the student the false illusion of comprehensiveness by apparently chronicling in order all of theatre history's most significant developments. In an effort to provide as much thoroughness as possible, the chronological format all too easily can become, as Abel puts it, "a marathon road race, with the only goal being to get to the end, somehow, before collapsing into an exhausted stupor" ("Alternate" 7).[9] Since the survey course by its very title cannot provide comprehensiveness, we need not attempt to make it do so while continually berating ourselves with guilt for failing to accomplish what we should not attempt in the first place. Thomas Postlewait reminds us that "No single system of designation—political, normative, aesthetic—can fully comprehend and subsume all other modes of designation" ("Criteria" 318).

Abel's survey at Dartmouth replaces chronological phases with units investigating various approaches throughout history to the development of the physical theatre space, performance organization and reception, and theatre's relationship to social constructs. Discussion topics range from such areas as "How to Represent Space: Theatrical Scenery, Static and Moving," to "Theatre Which Exercises Power/Theatre Which Criticizes Power." A more radical approach might include teaching the survey course in relation to social trends, specific innovators or the development of religion. Another approach might consider viewing theatre history beginning in the present and tracing conventions of today back to their roots. Approaching the survey course with a broader perspective allows for a "multiplicity" of teaching strategies, without the burden of comprehensiveness.

Draw on the Knowledge of What We Know to Understand and Explain What We Do Not Know

Some of the more creative teaching strategies in regard to specific projects and presentations possess the same philosophical bent. The value of using what we know to understand what we do not know constitutes a unifying factor in many of the activities presented in the submitted syllabi. Several examples serve to make the point. Geraldine Maschio, University of Kentucky, asks her students to write letters to their parents trying to convince them of the value of the acting profession. The students must cite both historical and contemporary references to justify their case. Kenneth Stilson, from Stetson University in Florida, asks his students to write "think" papers in which they identify human needs potentially satisfied by theatre. At Milliken University in Illinois, Denise Myers helps her students understand the components of comedy and tragedy by asking them to rewrite the story of the three bears, first as a comedy and then as a tragedy. Ralf Remshardt, who teaches at Denison University in Ohio, offers an even more challenging task. His students must rewrite a scene from *Othello* in the style of *The Cherry Orchard*. They must decide how to transfer Shakespeare's world into Chekhov's. They quickly learn that much of what is said outright in Shakespeare recedes into subtext in Chekhov.

This notion of teaching by drawing on areas of familiarity to illuminate the unfamiliar does not represent a formalized teaching approach, but it certainly could. The benefits are inviting. For example, students are more likely to understand significant relationships between two cultures if they can place themselves in a historical and foreign culture by using contemporary conventions. If by reading Shaffer's *Equus* they can better understand the use of a chorus, then perhaps we should begin with *Equus*, followed by *Oedipus*, instead of waiting until we get to contemporary theatre in another semester. Although not necessarily a novel idea, this notion appears not readily practiced as a formalized teaching strategy.[10]

Explore Opportunities for Students to Conduct Historical Inquiry Through Applied Research

With the increased acceptance of the role of the dramaturg in America since the 1970s, we might logically extend such practical application of historical research to undergraduate students' clear interests in production. A number of the survey courses examined tailor research projects to fit production activity that engages the individual student. Many of the courses require students to attend live performance. Brockett speaks of the usefulness of inviting the director of the viewed production to discuss with the class:

> what historical information, if any, he or she found useful in planning the production, or how he or she sought to make a play from the past meaningful to present-day spectators. In many production courses, students are told that they should do research, often involving the historical background, but usually they are given no help in determining what they should be looking for or what they should do with what they find. Seldom are they taken through the process in a systematic way. (51)

New curricular developments in dramaturgy advocate such an approach, but most of these courses exist solely on the graduate level.

Provide Greater Attention to Historiography

Numerous courses examined begin with a brief unit on the many factors that influence historical interpretation of theatre. In his essay, "Historiography and the Theatrical Event: A Primer with Twelve Cruxes," Thomas Postlewait concisely articulates these various factors. We may easily apply one or more of them in detail to topics encountered throughout the survey. This approach has clear value: students learn theatre history not as a set body of facts, but as a process of interpreting sometimes elusive, fragmentary, and all too often contradictory data. Students increase their self-analysis as they become aware how their own values, biases, and beliefs might impact their organization and interpretation of these data.

Re-Examine Pedagogical Presentation Style in an Effort to Encourage Active Learning

Thus far, we have broached the areas of content and form in theatre history pedagogy—but not that of style, the way in which anything is made or done. This aspect of pedagogy remains slippery to discern and rarely if ever discussed, even among ourselves. How do we lecture? Do we have a particular style that suits the content and form of the course work? This last question is perhaps the pivotal one. Tradition dictates the components of style, especially in history courses, in the form of lecture and discussion. The professor gives the notes, the students take the notes, and sometimes both sides engage in interesting if not predictable discussions. Sometimes roles reverse so that students give reports both individually and within groups.

We will not attempt to evaluate the advantages or disadvantages of this traditional style, because as we all know and have experienced, there are professors who are brilliant lecturers. More seminal to our concerns is the realization that our style of teaching influences our students' learning. Logically, presentation style should be compatible with the content and form of the course. The challenge is then twofold. First, we need to investigate our own individual style, and in some way evaluate its success. Next, we might experiment with style as it relates to content and form. Just as a director must have a particular approach and method to realize a production, so must an instructor find the most appropriate means to teach the material and reach the student.

No models exist in our discipline regarding style, except in generalized versions on classroom management and in even more generic epistles on college teaching. We must therefore experiment and be willing to fail in some instances until we find some alternative stylistic choices. To begin, it may be as simple as changing the physical arrangement of the classroom—a circle perhaps, or even an alternative space altogether. Creative choices are sometimes more obvious than we may realize. For example, we might have class in the university chapel or in historically significant architectural structures that can simulate or suggest an atmosphere not unlike some of those in periods being studied. The origins of liturgical drama for instance take on greater resonance once we remove students from secular surroundings.

Other issues in style appear less concrete. Perhaps tone or physical manner inhibit receptivity. Perhaps the lecture format, whether formal or informal, does not provide the best choice for the content of a particular unit in theatre history. Perhaps we employ a passive rather than active style. Active learning might take on a different meaning if we experiment with such a notion in a theatre history course. Active learning implies a physical component at best and at least learning that requires some kind of ongoing participation by the student. Passive learning implies that students take no part in the action of the course. They remain submissive and acted upon. Active learning requires active teaching. The question, again, is one of style.

Active teaching and active learning require more energy. Both teacher and student must assume more creativity and diligence in their pursuits. However, the old adage that one "gets out of life what one puts in" applies here. The more a teacher expects of a student (not necessarily in terms of just quantity; but also in terms of quality) the more the teacher gets from that student. The examples that follow may serve to explicate the notion of active learning as well as to reify the philosophical nature of the idea.

1. Create activities in which the students learn from each other. The

professor serves as mediator and guide. In-class group activities can be productive, such as assigning teams to discuss different aspects of Greek tragedy followed by a creative presentation to demonstrate what they have discovered. This creative presentation could involve drawings, a brief dialogue with choric exchange, or even a chart to delineate comparisons and/or contrasts.

2. Offer choices that meet the needs of the students while recognizing students' abilities and backgrounds. Mary Alice Mark, who teaches at a Dade Community College campus in Dade County, Florida, offers one interesting example of active learning. Mark teaches nontraditional students whose interest in theatre specifically—and education generally—lacks commitment and focus. She interests her students in theatre history by asking them to improvise their versions of particular developments. For example, one exercise requires them to create an improvisation on how and why Thespis became the first actor. Why did he or whoever step away from the chorus? What might have been the circumstances on that particular day?

3. Establish an atmosphere that allows for flexibility and spontaneity. Rather than locking into a rigid syllabus, establish potential time slots to use for continuing a valuable discussion, exploring an idea, a play, a problem in greater depth, or to follow through on a particular project that has merit. As in any university or college community, specific issues come up that politicize the student in some way: the firing of a football coach, the arrest of a classmate for drunk driving, or maybe a larger, more global issue, such as the United States presidential campaign. By having some time to address issues of importance to the students and to help them relate their own cultural context to the period of history about which they are learning, the teacher also encourages analogous thinking while reaffirming the students' value as active, thinking participants in their culture.

4. Offer alternatives and choices in the evaluation of students. Of the individual theatre history survey courses reviewed, 70% relied upon examinations for at least half of the student's overall grade. However imaginative the test format, exams typically compel students to emphasize facts rather than concepts to prove their grasp of the subject.[11] Rather than using examinations primarily to test whether or not the student has read and processed the material, required reading may be useful as part of in-class discussions and reconstruction projects, or as the basis for more detailed reading journals, annotated bibliographies or written analyses. It may be useful to experiment with letting students make up their own exams, if an exam proves necessary. Allow them to offer suggestions for what should be included in a theatre history text. Let them have some input in the method by which they will be evaluated. Every class is different, with different dynamics. The use of the same type of test, same type of evaluative tools for every class every year seems illogical. We

must continue to examine what is important, what it is we really want our students to know and understand, and what is the larger context in which we educate our students.

At Rutgers University in Newark, Donald Borchardt offers an alternative by having his students complete assigned readings before participating in group decision-making panels pertaining to a variety of historical and contemporary theatre issues. For example, students explore fundamental aspects of ancient Greek theatre architecture, dramatic festivals, and performance style while working within their campus environment to secure an appropriate space for the staging of *Prometheus Bound*, a performance offered by a hypothetical professional touring theatre devoted to historical "authenticity."[12]

Clearly, the idealistic nature of this discussion of alternative teaching strategies is meant to raise eyebrows, to call into question traditional pedagogical practices, and to stimulate further dialogue amongst those of us who teach theatre history. The rapidly-changing nature of our world will no longer allow us to rely on what we once understood to be the geographical boundaries of nations; nor can we rely on pedagogical practices that are now as outdated as our maps in geography.

As teachers we may feel less bound to follow the guidelines and parameters of existing textbooks. We must teach our students to find comfort in the ambiguity of open-ended questions, and to distrust their ingrained beliefs that the study of history remains tantamount to the study of names, dates and "facts." We should use our textbooks only as the initial resource for the chronological development of various aspects of theatrical performance. Suddenly a lot of time opens in the course outline. Attention may shift to specific individuals, events and trends in greater detail, not as examples of universal truths, but as contributors to and products of the many disparate forces that shape a theatrical event. We can then *show* our students how to conduct historical inquiry on their own. As Marvin Carlson suggests in the quote that began this discussion, we must use a "multiplicity" of means to address the multicultural nature of our discipline and our world. Furthermore, we must do so with the "freedom" of idealism grounded in an ongoing pedagogical exploration of the content, form and style of the theatre history survey course.

Notes

1. See, for example, Paul Gagnon, "Why Study History?" *Atlantic Monthly* Nov. 1988, 43–66, for a summary of these challenges as well as a defense of the role in history in civic education.

2. Joseph R. Roach's "Theatre History and the Ideology of the Aesthetic," *Theatre Journal* 41 (1989): 155–68, provides but one recent example of new analytical methodologies in theatre history.

3. We gathered no formal statistical information from the collected syllabi. The observations in this paper summarize trends observed in the material received. Although both large and small programs submitted a diverse collection of syllabi, we recognize that the collection represents only a random sampling rather than a comprehensive compilation. This study omitted syllabi for courses with a focus primarily upon dramatic literature, play analysis, graduate studies, or special topics. In the latter regard, excluded courses involved those of a very limited time span, geographic, ethnic or gender focus (such as "Medieval Theatre" or "Women in Twentieth Century American Theatre").

4. A surprising discovery involves the number of history texts and survey courses that make slight mention, if any, of American musical theatre, to use but one very large example. For instance, the 6th edition of Oscar Brockett's *History of the Theatre* reserves less than a handful of paragraphs for a discussion of popular musical theatre.

5. One noteworthy exception is Felicia Hardison Londré's recent publication, *The History of the World Theater From the Restoration to the Present* (New York: Continuum, 1991). Grant McKernie and Jack Watson's *A Cultural History of Theatre* (White Plains, NY: Longman, 1993) also provides expanded discussions of world theatre, typically in the form of boxed inserts labeled "A Global Perspective." For a critique of six frequently used history texts, see Sam Abel's "Globalizing the Theatre History Textbook," a paper presented at the 1991 Annual Conference of the Association for Theatre in Higher Education.

6. Edwin Wilson and Alvin Goldfarb's *Theater: The Lively Art* is a distant second, being required in six surveys. Only one survey did not require or recommend a history text.

7. The course mentioned at the University of Hawaii at Manoa requires the Wilson/Goldfarb text, which does not share a similar organizational structure with the course content.

8. For example, we have barely begun to witness the possibilities in the field of theatre history for alternative learning techniques involving interactive computer technology.

9. Thomas Postlewait has also suggested that a topically organized study allows for greater connections of trends from one age to another. Speaking of Richard Southern's topically-oriented text, *Seven Ages of Theatre*, Postlewait concludes that "uninhibited by chronology, political orders, or national lines, [Southern] is able to connect medieval Christian performances to Tibetan festival theatre, the Elizabethan stage to the Japanese Noh, the continental opera theatre to the Kabuki. The principle of resemblance, not diversity, organizes history...." Postlewait cautions, however, that replacing chronology with topics may de-emphasize "the political, social, and economic forces that shape the theatre" ("Criteria" 313). Such a warning does not take into account the fact that topics need not be paired only in terms of shared performance style, but also by similar political, social, and economic factors as they influence theatre.

10. Francis Fergusson, among others, speaks about this approach in *The Idea of a Theater* (New York: Princeton UP, 1949), 23.

11. Only 8% of the survey courses reviewed used examinations to constitute 25% or less of the student's final grade.

12. Borchardt explicates in detail this approach, labeled "Guided Design," in a now out-of-print teaching manual, *Think Tank Theatre*, published by University Press of America in 1984.

Works Cited

Abel, Sam. "An Alternate Model for Teaching Theatre History in the LiberalArts Curriculum." ATHE annual conference. San Diego, Aug. 1988.

———. "Globalizing the Theatre History Textbook." ATHE annual conference. Seattle, 9 Aug. 1991.

Borchardt, Donald A. *Think Tank Theatre: Decision Making Applied*. Lanham, MD: University Press of America, 1984.

Brockett, Oscar. "Historical Study in the Theatre Curriculum." *Master Teachers of Theatre*. Ed. Burnet M. Hobgood. Carbondale: Southern Illinois UP, 1988. 37–57.

Burns, Ken. Interview. CNN Headline News. CNN, 29 Jan. 1992.

Carlson, Marvin. "The Theory of History." *The Performance of Power*. Eds. Sue Ellen Case and Janelle Reinelt. Iowa City: U of Iowa P, 1991. 272–79.

Davis, Tracy C. "Questions for a Feminist Methodology in Theatre History." *Interpreting the Theatrical Past: Essays in the Historiography of Performance*. Postlewait and McConachie 59–81.

Dickey, Jerry, comp. "Syllabus Exchange 1992." Unpublished collection. University of Arizona, Tucson.

Fergusson, Francis. *The Idea of a Theatre*. New York: Princeton UP, 1949.

Gagnon, Paul. "Why Study History?" *Atlantic Monthly*, Nov. 1988: 43–66.

Hatch, James V. "Here Comes Everybody: Scholarship and Black Theatre History." Postlewait and McConachie 148–65.

The Macmillan Dictionary of Quotations, New York: Macmillan, 1989. 252.

Postlewait, Thomas. "The Criteria for Periodization Theatre History." *Theatre Journal* 40 (1988): 299–318.

———. "Historiography and the Theatrical Event: a Primer with Twelve Cruxes." Theatre Journal 43 (1991): 157–78.

Postlewait, Thomas, and Bruce McConachie, eds. *Interpreting the Theatrical Past: Essays in the Historiography of Performance*. Iowa City: U of Iowa P, 1989.

Roach, Joseph R. "Theatre History and the Ideology of the Aesthetic." *Theatre Journal* 41 (1989): 155–68.

Vince, R. W. "Theatre History as an Academic Discipline." Postlewait and McConachie 1–18.

Toward Democratic Education Through Theatre Production

Patricia VandenBerg

We had problems at Calvin College. The theatre faculty was overworked; the students were restless. More immediately, who was going to supervise the student-directed lab bills? For years this responsibility had been assumed on a non-credit (read "volunteer") basis by the Director of Theatre. As the new hire in that position, I knew that I could not do a good job of supervising the lab bills in addition to all of my other responsibilities. I refused to do so and asserted that none of my colleagues should be expected to volunteer for the job either.

Confronted with the likelihood of student outrage if their directing opportunities were eliminated, but having no faculty volunteers to allocate to the cause, my department was compelled to hunker down and get creative. One of the benefits of directing a theatre program under the auspices of a Department of Communication Arts and Sciences is that some of my non-theatre department colleagues came to the problem of theatre production/curriculum with few, if any, preconceived notions. Their innocence gave us fresh insights, and the solutions proved more far-reaching than the issue of the lab bill alone. Our departmental deliberations convinced us that in order to alleviate student and faculty burnout we had to more effectively integrate production and curriculum.

We have now created a system by which all of our productions grow out of classes. Students receive at least partial academic credit for work on any of the four productions that we do annually. Faculty workloads are now more reasonable. In addition to relieving the burnout problem, our solutions have resulted in some pedagogical benefits, among which are more possibilities for exploring multicultural and democratic education. While our plan is very specifically geared to our program and institution, I believe that it could, with modifications, be used in numerous contexts.

In this essay, I will first describe the curricular/production program we have implemented at Calvin and its benefits. I will then give an example of the way in which our approach engages the students in a manner that broadens their worldview.

Calvin College is a private, liberal arts college. The Theatre program employs three theatre faculty as well as a staff technical director, costume designer, and costumer. We produce four theatrical productions per year: three are faculty or guest-directed; the fourth is the previously mentioned student-directed lab bill. Like most theatre programs, we serve our own majors as well as many students from other fields.

Fortunately, we did not have to start from scratch in integrating productions and curriculum at Calvin. Our major fall and spring productions had long come out of a class called Theatre Production. It is a curious hybrid whose precursor was a drama club. During the 1960s the former Director of Theatre cleverly plotted a strategy whereby the students in the class received 1/4 credit hour per term for participation. (This was intended to parallel the credit policy of the choirs and band at Calvin.) To this day, students audition/interview for the class. If accepted they may participate in it throughout their four years at Calvin and can accumulate up to two full course credits toward graduation. The group normally numbers around seventy and includes students from many majors. The class becomes a company of sorts that produces the major play each term. Only those in the class are allowed to audition for, or to crew the two mainstage plays. Competition to get into the class is stiff, drawing around 115 applicants for 20 positions that become vacant each fall. In addition to producing the plays, the class meets once a week for one hour, and the instructor receives one course teaching credit per term for producing the plays and leading the class.

There are some drawbacks to this plan, but we have found that the benefits outweigh the problems. One obvious drawback is that there are students on campus who would like to participate in mainstage productions but who either are not accepted into the class or do not audition because they don't have the time or the inclination to make the commitment to the course. (There are numerous other production outlets for these students, however, both within the department and sponsored by the student-run Drama Guild.) Another problem with the system is that directors are limited in casting to those who have been accepted into the class.

The benefits, however, are many. The class sessions provide an opportunity for all students involved to be part of a systematic approach to play production. The class explores various aspects of the play in production, such as the genre, the playwright, the social context in which the play was written, the world view from which the play emerged, and the matter of production style. Students are privy to why the play was selected, the production concept, and the design process. The entire class participates in workshops relating to specific needs of the production, like mask making and period movement. Over four years the students are exposed to a wide range of plays and playwrights. Each student has the opportunity for hands-on experience in numerous areas of production. We have found that the class fosters a lifelong appreciation of theatre even in the students who pursue non-theatre-related careers. For those who pursue theatre professionally, it serves as a solid base for further study or training.

After considerable rumination on the problem of lab bills, one observant member of our department pointed out that the catalog featured a departmental seminar that had not been offered in years. We agreed to use that course as a theatre seminar culminating in the production of student-directed one-act plays. The course is now offered annually, taught by department faculty on a rotating basis. The instructor chooses a theme or topic for the class: a playwright, a genre, a style; the subject changes annually and the class may be taken more than once.

The first half of the term is dedicated to studying the topic; the second half, to production meetings and rehearsals. Class members who wish to direct submit proposals including play choice and production concept to the class. The class votes to determine which one-act plays will be included in the bill. After the directors are determined, the class assigns itself other production responsibilities. Usually, all positions, including design positions, can be filled by class members. Acting auditions are open to the entire campus. Our production staff is available to give guidance, but the student members of the class essentially own the production. The results over the past five years have been very exciting.

As a professor, one has the flexibility to explore areas of interest or research. One also has the joy of watching as students grow empowered both intellectually and practically. The discussion of the play selection is in itself momentous. For the first time the students begin to understand the challenges of selecting plays which will be appropriate for the audience, include an acceptable number of women's roles, be technically feasible, etc. The students respond with great enthusiasm to the learning experience because they are discovering things for themselves and from one another. They understand the process of theatre production—selecting the bill, creating publicity, arranging for house management, and dealing with the myriad details necessary to making the production happen. Because the students participate in grading themselves and their classmates, their sense of responsibility to the group and to the importance of collaboration in the theatrical endeavor is heightened.

And finally, the product is better. The production is conceived in a context of exploration and understanding. The playbill has a cohesiveness that contributes to the audience's potential learning experience. The evening of theatre has flair and polish (via such attention to detail as entr'actes and lobby entertainment). In addition, the audiences love it. We play three nights on a weekend toward the end of the spring term to full and lively houses. These productions are eagerly awaited and heavily attended by students.

Having integrated three of our four productions into courses with happy results, the department looked to integrate our interim term production into a course as well. Calvin's interim term, which takes place in the month of January, is a time when the college faculty is encouraged to offer innovative courses. In the past, when we offered a theatrical production during the interim, a faculty member had to teach a class in addition to directing the production. Now we offer the production as a class and usually do the kinds of things we would not do during the regular season, such as readers' theatre or children's theatre or a smaller play that would not be chosen for the mainstage. Recent offerings have included a readers' theatre production of Michael Quigley's *April Is the Cruelest Month*, a children's theatre presentation of our faculty member, Debra Freeberg's *And the Book Ran Away with the Spoon*, and productions of Davis's *Mass Appeal* and Glaspell's *Trifles*. Students who wish to work on the production enroll in the class. Auditions are open to the entire campus. Students are supervised by the theatre staff and receive a full course credit for their work.

In the four years we've been using this approach, there have always been more students interested in taking the class than we've been able to accommodate. The hands-on nature of this course fits in well with the experiential nature of many interim-term courses offered.

Thus, by working creatively within the given structure, we have made a good start at effectively integrating curriculum and production at Calvin College. It feels right in terms of pedagogy, workload, and the respect it engenders for theatre as a discipline. It also greatly facilitates the goals of moving beyond a Eurocentric curriculum and production program to a broader worldview. Calvin College is a generally conservative institution which, like so many others, has only recently begun to value and actively pursue a more multicultural and democratic approach to education. Our theatre structure (particularly the theatre seminar and interim-term course/productions) offers infinite possibilities for exploring various worldviews. Let me illustrate:

Most all of my students come from highly patriarchal homes and communities. I was becoming increasingly irritated at the fact that almost none of them seemed to have a clue as to why there might be so few plays by women compared to those by men. I decided to offer a theatre seminar on women playwrights. (You will recall that our theatre seminar is the course out of which the student-directed lab bills are produced.) For reasons unrelated to the seminar topic (scheduling, prerequisites, etc.) I ended up with a class consisting of nine males and four females.

We began by reading Virginia Woolf's *A Room of One's Own*, as well as numerous articles addressing the question, "Where Are All the Women Playwrights?" We then proceeded to study the works of such playwrights as Kennedy, Churchill, Wasserstein, Shange, Norman, and Daniels. Meanwhile, students who wished to direct looked for short pieces to propose to the class as possibilities for inclusion in our evening of theatre.

Discussions were always lively and covered student-initiated inquiries ranging from the naive, "Why would a woman's perspective of reality be any different from a man's?" to the more sophisticated, "What are the implications of a man directing a play by a woman—or a woman directing one by a man?" and even further, "a white person directing a play by a non-white or vice versa!"

My favorite class session was also the most confrontational. One of the students had brought in for production consideration a short play, *Reservations for Two*, by Lori Goodman. The play is an encounter between two young professionals, Ann and Jim, who meet at a nice restaurant for dinner. It is their first date. At one point Ann notices Jim's briefcase and inquires whether he has just come from work. He confesses that he has not but has brought his briefcase in the hope of going home with her that evening. Ann becomes irate and the evening rapidly deteriorates.

The class's response to this piece was explosive. There was hot disagreement over the appropriateness of the characters' behavior, and the divisions in the class were clearly along gender lines. The discussion began something like this:

"Isn't that just like a guy. What a tacky jerk."
"He was just being considerate."
"Considerate!!!?"

At which point the women in the class lambasted the male who had defended Jim's behavior. The males then loudly defended their maligned brother.

Heated discussion led to the suggestion that it would be interesting to see the piece performed twice; once under the direction of a male, and once under the direction of a female. We proceeded with the plan acknowledging that, in fact, the gender perspectives of the directors should not necessarily be made the central issue of the performance, and that eventually the audience might not be able to differentiate gender perspectives in the two pieces. We agreed, however, based on the observation that seeing the same scene done differently in acting and directing classes was always instructive, that in any case the audience could benefit from seeing the same piece twice.

Excitement ran high as the class selected other pieces to complete the evening and began auditions and rehearsals. They named the evening of theatre "Women Aloud" and word of the curious work being done spread rapidly across campus.

The results were very interesting. The major difference in the two versions of *Reservations for Two* was in production style. Anton, the male director, saw the play as hilarious. Both the design and acting styles were heightened, creating an almost slapstick scene about a guy who means well and is surprised and mortified by his date's response. Judi, the female director, created a piece which pointed up the frustration of trying to create a relationship. She wrote in her program notes, "I read this piece and my initial reaction was more sympathetic towards one character. I now find myself sympathetic toward the situation itself. Jim and Ann both have expectations of each other, and these expectations contribute to their misunderstanding of one another. In our own lives we often have preconceptions and defenses which hinder and sometimes prevent effective communication." Anton's play was very funny; Judi's, melancholy.

By combining production and curriculum, we were able to explore some of the complexities of allowing numerous voices to be heard in a society and in the theatre. The students experienced first-hand that gender, among many other variables, does make a difference in one's perception of reality, in one's experience of our society, in the message one wants to convey to the world, in the battles one chooses to fight. Furthermore, the students conjectured, if we have begun to get a glimpse of the different ways that males and females experience middle-class America, what about the array of experiences that would be engendered by differences in race, class, age, and religious background? The implications were mind boggling. The seed was sown.

Our "Women Aloud" played to full houses. The audiences started their evening with program notes written by one of the students in the class:

"Each play we have chosen to produce tonight is written by a woman. Why highlight plays by and about women? We have heard women raising their voices, one after another, each calling out, 'I am here: acknowledge me! I am human: listen to me!' Representing perspectives as diverse and valid as those of men, they seek to be acknowledged as significant voices in the chorus of life. Tonight we will listen to these new voices telling our common story. By listening, we participate more fully in the human experience."

In a community in which the issue of whether women should be allowed to hold high church office still rages, this is progress.

Calvin College, like most institutions of higher learning, has a long way to go to achieve true multicultural and democratic education. However, sincere steps are being made, and the theatre program in its current structure is prepared to lead the way.

"I Do—I Understand":
Hampshire College Theatre's Alternative Teaching Model

Rhonda Blair

I hear, I forget;
I see, I remember;
I do, I understand

—East Indian saying

From 1984 to 1995 I taught theatre in a private, experimenting, liberal arts undergraduate institution. From its early years, it has engaged issues that have since moved to the forefront for many of us teaching theatre across the country: interdisciplinarity; portfolio, rather that grade-based, assessment; redistribution of authority among administration, faculty, and students; critique of capitalism, imperialism, patriarchy, gender, and race; and ongoing reassessment of curricular standards and requirements. This environment has given rise to a Theatre Program that is a case study of the application of many alternatives strategies and methods. Working at the college was rewarding, tedious, frustrating, invigorating, exhilarating, and underpaid. I am hopeful a discussion of this program will be useful, especially in terms of thinking about curricula tailored to the individual student and the place of student production within curricula and production seasons.

The Theatre Program is a microcosm of and is utterly embedded in and supported by the larger institution. Founded in the late 1960s specifically to offer an alternative to traditional higher education, Hampshire College[1] requires its roughly 1,100 students to work independently with the 95+ faculty members to construct their own courses of study. These courses of study may follow traditional disciplinary lines, but more often they don't, entailing a high degree of individualized definition and often a good amount of interdisciplinarity.

A student moves through three levels of study. In Division I, a student completes independent projects or a two-course sequence in each of Hampshire's four schools (Humanities and Arts, Social Science, Natural Science, and Communication and Cognitive Science). This variation on a general education distribution requirement is geared toward acquainting the student not with particular "content," but with strategies of inquiry, approaches to research, analysis and creativity across various fields. Division II is typically a two-year program comprising the student's primary area or areas of study, and includes a multicultural component and a community service project. It corresponds to a "major," but is tailored to the student's particular educational goals. The core of Division III, typically the student's fourth year, is a substantial, usually multifaceted independent project (which, of course, is not always at "honors" level). At each level, students negotiate with the faculty of their choice in order to pursue a given course of study. Once an agreement is reached, faculty and students sign a contract that provides guidelines for the work.[2] The completed work is typically gathered and presented in a portfolio, followed by a culminating meeting (rather like an oral exam). Rather than being graded, students receive written evaluations for courses and projects. This kind of review and assessment occurs at all three levels. For example, in the Division II, a committee reviews a student's portfolio a number of times in the course of the two years; this portfolio contains evaluations and items such as course papers, documentation of productions, internships, videos, slides, journals, and, importantly, the student's own written assessment of synthesizing the work— strengths, weaknesses, and future direction. This assessment—or retrospective paper, as we call it—is key, for it requires students to reflect on their educational choices, and gets them to think about their education as a body of work informed by articulated values and personal goals, rather than as a mere accumulation of skills, facts or credit-hours.

A progressive social and political agenda has been part of Hampshire's ethos from the beginning. It was the first institution of higher education in the U.S. to divest its financial holdings in South Africa in the 1970s, has programs in Feminist Studies (started in the 1970s), Third-World Studies, and Public Service and Social Change. These programs, which are centers of intellectual energy (and sometimes conflict) on campus and which often jointly sponsor campus-wide events, include faculty across the four schools. The blurring of boundaries and dissolution of traditional disciplinary lines are also reflected in courses, many of which are team-taught, often by faculty from different schools (e.g., an extremely popular introductory course called "Women's Bodies/Women's Lives" is taught by one faculty member from each of the schools).

As a good "child of the sixties," Hampshire has as one of its missions the responsibility not only to question, but also to redistribute authority. Each faculty member decides which two courses she or he will teach in a given semester; while the dean or other faculty can bring informal pressures to bear in order to try to cover a certain area, these pressures are non-legislated. There is no course-review committee. Faculty are not tenured, but receive multiple-year contracts (after the first seven years, renewal becomes slightly more automatic, though review continues). All faculty within a school, including junior faculty, vote on reappointment and promotion of their school colleagues. Students elected to be voting members of the four schools also vote on reappointment and promotion. A faculty member's whole file is open to all voting school members, as well as to the faculty member her- or himself. The College Committee for Reappointments and Promotion has seven voting members—five faculty and two students; two of the seven votes determining your professional future belong to undergraduate students. In most cases, this committee works well, though it is generally acknowledged that the overall reappointment process is too psychologically grueling and labor-intensive. The college is exploring options for revising it.

The president eats breakfast in the dining commons every Monday morning at 7 a.m. so that any student who wants to—and who gets up early enough—can speak directly with him in an informal setting.

The impression, and often the reality, at Hampshire is that everything and everyone is open to question and negotiation, and that power is fluid.

In the Theatre Program there are three full-time faculty, a staff technical director (shared with the Dance Program), and a part-time costume coordinator. The faculty are a "program" by virtue of the fact that we agree to be. Technically, any of us could operate independently within the school of Humanities and Arts, if we wanted to; our contracts are with the school, not the Program. We have full discretion with our own capital and operating budget. While it is possible to view the Program's curricular and production components separately, they are inextricably intertwined.

In Division I we engage the student with the rudiments of production and performance, lay the groundwork for fundamental skills acquisition, and get students to begin to think critically about theatre's social and cultural function. Using a two-course option, a student completes two courses, typically involving the student in some performance/production skill acquisition and in producing a critical and/or research paper (e.g., completing Beginning Acting and The Design Response). Or a student will complete one course and develop a project and/or paper out of that course (e.g., completing Beginning Acting, then doing an extended scene or scenes for a public workshop, applying readings from Stanislavski, then writing a critical and experimental assessment of the work). Not only writing, but the revision of writing—the back and forth between faculty and student, often through three or four drafts—is crucial. At this level students begin to nose out connections between the things in theatre that interest them and aspects of other disciplines, articulate their interests, and define questions or areas to be explored. We begin acclimatizing students to the faculty's roles as facilitators, experts, guides, resources, and evaluators. We are generally not teachers who require them to "take these particular courses in this particular sequence" or to "do these particular productions"; rather, we lay out what they need to cover for the area in question and help them develop plans for accomplishing that. Finally, they see from the beginning that almost our entire production program is run largely by their peers.

In Division II we have a set of guidelines that all students concentrating in theatre are urged to follow (my avoidance of the word "requirement" is deliberate). We expect a breadth of engagement with various areas of theatre, even though a student may have a single personal focus (e.g., playwriting or design). We don't want students narrowing their vision too soon, before they have sufficient knowledge and experience to make informed decisions. A main goal at this level is to make sure students have a grasp of the interrelationships among the various aspects of theatre, and that they develop ways of thinking about theatre's connection to other disciplines and to the world at large. Under the general guidelines a student completes at least one course each in acting, directing, design (usually a survey of all design areas); completes four courses in theatre literature, history or criticism; completes three courses in a liberal arts distribution; stage manages or assistant directs a production; crews four productions in at least three different areas; serves as house manager for a production; engages in an exploration of multiculturalism/Third-World issues; completes a community service project; and writes ten short analytical papers on canonical plays from a perspective that is related to the focus of the individual student's concentration (e.g., as an actor, director, playwright). We also encourage an annotated bibliography of short papers on other texts that have influenced the student's work. Most students keep a journal (often throughout their time at Hampshire) that is a place both for logging events and for recording thoughts, impressions, research, and struggle around events and projects. If a student is doing a split or dual concentration (e.g., in theatre and psychology, theatre and dance, or theatre and anthropology), we may adjust this curriculum to facilitate the student's interdisciplinary focus. This foundational outline is deliberately minimal in terms of traditional "content," since its goal is to open doors to possible futures and uses of theatre, rather than the acquisition of a predetermined body of knowledge or "professional theatre" skills. Initiative, questioning, and self-reflection are key to the process. We leave room for the student to go after whatever else is necessary for her or his education,[3] e.g., six more courses in performance and acting in a show a semester; courses in European history or art history or physiology; two more courses in lighting and designing dance concerts for theatre productions; spending a year or a semester studying in London, or interning in a regional theatre's administrative offices; two more directing classes and directing two projects; or some combination of the above. At the end of the Division II, a student should be prepared to define, develop, and execute a major independent project. Most Division IIs are well-shaped courses of study. Some Division IIs are thin; if we graded them, they would be a C or C minus. Sometimes they are developed gracefully, and sometimes there is considerable tussle between student and committee in arriving at an agreement regarding the appropriate kind and amount of work.

The easiest way to explain Division III independent projects is to give examples. I supervised a student who wrote and performed the lead in a play about schizophrenia. At the Division II level this student took courses in playwriting, psychology, and performance, among others, spent a summer in the American Conservatory Theatre program, and took a semester leave to research and write, working in a treatment center with people with psychoses. Her interest comes from a personal place; she is a healthy young woman who has a number of immediate relatives who have serious mental illness. This provides great passion and impetus to her work. The same is true of a young woman who developed and performed a one-woman performance on the situation in Bosnia. She has a solid background in performance courses and productions, has done substantial work in European history, dramaturgy, and general theatre studies, speaks Serbo-Croatian and has lived in Bosnia for a couple of extended periods. In the past, Division III students have staged plays by Sartre, Beckett, Franca Rame, Cherie Moraga, Chekhov, Molierè, Euripides, Sharon Pollack, Martin Sherman, Peter Weiss, Howard Barker, Tennessee Williams, Susan Centlivre; they have written original full-length plays (on subjects such as AIDS, interfaith marriage, homosexuality, violence and criminality, and sadomasochism), sometimes workshopping them, sometimes seeing them fully produced; they have produced musicals and cabarets; they have designed sets, lights, costumes for a whole range of performances (at and outside of Hampshire); they have written critical papers on feminism and performance, on European history and *The Golem*. Every production-based project has a written component—at the very least a paper in which the student examines the nature of the process and the work in which she or he has been engaged, contextualizing it within a larger social and theatrical context. My favorite projects are often the multifaceted ones. One student did a performance piece about Gertrude Stein, Picasso and Matisse in the fall and produced and directed *No Exit* (her "capstone") in the spring, writing substantial critical papers to go with each; the Stein project grew out of a modern drama course and a semester-long independent study on Stein, while *No Exit* was founded on an advanced contemporary drama course and three courses in philosophy, focusing on existentialism. Her paper on the way Sartre's philosophy is manifested in his play in theatrical terms revealed the student's insight into how *No Exit* works as psychologically taut, surprising theatre. This student was not academically oriented and we struggled over her writing at the Division II and early Division III stages, but she loved what she was doing and was committed to grappling with the problem, as she put it, of staging philosophy. Her production of *No Exit* was the most alive, funny, and scary I have seen.

Most of the production projects I have described occurred within our Program, which has two black box spaces, one larger and one smaller. Our in-house season typically consists of two Mainstage and four Studio productions with 21 to 24 workshop slots available (typically scheduled three a night, one night a month). Mainstage productions, which happen in the larger theatre, are typically connected to the Division III level; they have larger budgets, full access to the Program's shops and stock, and are expected to meet a higher level of production than Studio shows. Studio productions, in the smaller theatre, may be connected to Division II or III work, and may be overseen by students in their second, third, or fourth year of study; while these shows are fully mounted and have full access to the shops and to scenic and costume stock, they have smaller budgets, are more limited in terms of access to lighting stock, and are expected to have a more modest level of production. Both Mainstage and Studio productions have a seven- or eight-night two-weekend run. Any student enrolled at Hampshire, including one in his or her first semester, can apply for a workshop slot; we usually accommodate most who apply. Workshops can be no more than fifty minutes in length, are given only one performance (often on a bill with one or two other projects), have no budget, and may use only modular furniture, a very simple repertory light plot, and whatever else they can bring from their own dorms or apartments. In order to apply for a Studio slot, a student must have produced (i.e., been responsible for) a workshop. In order to apply for a Mainstage, a student must have produced a Studio. Once a year or every other year the faculty produce, direct, and sometimes design a show in the Mainstage, but all other work is student produced, directed, and designed. Also, each year some four to eight Divisional projects occur "off-site," i.e., in an alternative space on our campus or one of the other campuses, or in a community space. We are also called upon to see students' work in productions at the other consortium institutions.

The Theatre Board, comprising seven student members, two alternates, our technical director, and faculty (who collectively have one vote per issue), selects the season and oversees production use of the theatre spaces. The Board is allotted a budget to distribute, according to policy, among the six funded productions. A program handbook has detailed information and guidelines regarding the production season and procedures, and it is more or less consistently followed.

In mid-spring, students submit formal proposals for production slots, providing information on text, royalties, tentative production staff, and so forth, requesting particular slots and describing how the work is related to their own and other students' Division II and III plans. Usually students who are contractually obligated at the Division III level and have contributed over the years to the production program and are given priority, other priorities being the number of contractually-obligated students signed on to a production proposal and the prior experience of those involved. In some years, the season falls easily into place. In others, there is tough competition for a given slot, or for a slot at all, and people are turned away to find alternative venues. (A good number of students also use alternative venues by choice.) Thus, those on the Theatre Board have a high level of responsibility; they are assessing their peers' qualifications and applications and, are determining what will be produced the next year. Students have the lion's share of the accountability, for, within the guidelines and with faculty counsel, they are the ones setting the agenda.

Our seasons are rarely "balanced" in a conventional sense (e.g., one classic, one contemporary, one small, one large, etc.), because they grow out of particular students' desires and strengths and—more importantly—because the focus is on students taking responsibility for the process of generating and producing theatre, rather than working on a particular range of plays before they graduate. Our students can encounter a traditional "range"—they just tend to do so most often through participating in productions on the other campuses and through field trips to regional theatres in our area (such as Hartford Stage and A.R.T. in Cambridge).

The theatre faculty influences the selection of material through what we produce in the season in alternate years, discussions with students in shaping their Divisional contracts, our participation in Theatre Board discussions, and in introducing students to material they might not otherwise encounter. While the material chosen (or created, since there are always original scripts and performance pieces in the season) does indeed matter, we tend to engage the students in a dialogue clarifying her or his reasons for selecting a given project, rather than offering approval or disapproval. We challenge the student to articulate the merit of the project, its function within the Theatre Program, and her or his personal goals in executing the project.

Typically, once a proposal is accepted for the season, the student producer (who may or may not be the show's director) begins raising funds to supplement those provided by the programs. There are a number of offices and programs on campus to which a student can go, as well as Five Colleges sources and local businesses or "angels." Tapping into an entrepreneurial spirit and resourcefulness, students acquire business and professional interpersonal skills that stand them in good stead when they graduate, since all graduates entering the profession have to present their projects and themselves effectively to strangers in order to succeed.

At this same time, the producer and director finish developing their production team. This is sometimes difficult, since it is done through personal negotiation in an environment in which skilled students in design/technical areas are often in high demand, i.e., there are more positions than there are experienced students to fill them. While each producer/director wants the most skilled production team, the design and technical students—like the producers and directors—tend to approach a sophisticated level of understanding and craft only in their last few semesters. The result is that each production is a "hothouse" tutorial, with the faculty and staff providing intensive guidance to those students in charge, e.g., playwright, director, design, staff and technical director.

At least one of us holds preliminary meetings with students generating the project and, once the process begins, a student director can expect his or her committee chair to attend three or four rehearsals and to hold weekly or bi-weekly meetings. The design faculty member holds regular meetings with the student designers and oversees the progress of their work, attending at least two rehearsals. Each production also is given a "post-mortem," an open session in which strengths and weaknesses of the technical production process are discussed and suggestions for improvement—in regard to students' work and the Program's procedures—are made. Public critiques of the aesthetics and values of productions are also sometimes held, though this kind of response happens most regularly in class discussions (e.g., acting classes are required to attend the productions, write brief response papers focusing on performance, and participate in talking about the shows) and in one-on-one and small-group discussions among faculty and students involved in the production.

There is a tension inherent in being a theatre program here. Theatre is quintessentially a collaborative form, involving an impact on an entire community from beginning to end to aftermath, while Hampshire is built on a premise of individual choice and autonomy. As a faculty member, I sometimes question the value of a project the Theatre Board includes in our seasons (whether due to the material itself, my sense that a student is not prepared to execute the work well, or my belief that the project is simply too big to mount sanely, given our resources). However, I only am part of a single vote among the nine and, barring issues of safety (where faculty indeed have veto), it is often a better pedagogical choice to raise issues during the season-setting meeting, let the students decide, and play out the process. While we sometimes have an unmitigated disaster (as does any program, whether with student- or faculty-produced shows), what a student learns from the flaws in a production process can be invaluable, especially if the student assesses that process thoughtfully with his or her committee and then applies what she or he has learned in a subsequent project.

Inter-student negotiations, relationships, and simple peer pressure on productions can be intense, since students—director, designer, actor, or writer—can have different agendas that are linked to curricular contracts as well as personal goals and personality. In terms of work load, students are constantly balancing doing their own projects with participating in and supporting those of their peers, knowing that they are dependent on those peers to get their own work done. In terms of creative autonomy, for example, a Division II second-year director with one concept of a character may have to negotiate with a Division III costume designer who has another, while the Division II third-year student playing the role has a third vision. In these situations no faculty person coerces a student to work on a particular project or steps in to decide which vision prevails; what we do is bring the parties together and make it possible for them to work out the matter among themselves. Throughout this process, the contractually obligated student is aware that her or his faculty committee must find whatever work is done of sufficient scope and quality to meet the terms of the contract and thereby receive an evaluation (our equivalent of getting credit).

Many undergraduate programs allow students to direct and design. At Hampshire, it is expected—required—that students produce, direct, design, perform, crew, and help determine the course of the production program itself. Apart from one production every year or every other year, only students make the art that goes in our theatre spaces. It is crucial to their education. During a production process the student must be able to talk about the work, and once the show closes the student must write about it.

We do not send a great number of students to graduate school, but when they go, it is to places such as Yale and N.Y.U. (M.F.A., acting), Juilliard (M.F.A. in Directing), and Brandeis (M.F.A., design). Speaking about my own field, I am cautious in encouraging actors to pursue M.F.A.s since there are not many excellent programs and the chances of finding consistent, satisfying work by this route are slim. Not incidentally, the talented young women who have completed M.F.As consistently refer to the misogyny and sexism they have encountered in graduate programs and teachers. We try our best to be realistic with students about what is happening professionally, economically, and politically with theatre in this country, and where the meaningful, thoughtful work is. (It should be a wake-up call to us all that even Neil Simon has given up on his Broadway theatre.)

As a result, and in line with our focus on autonomy and personal responsibility, we encourage students to make independent decisions, developing personal self-knowledge and a range of entrepreneurial skills that will allow them to go more directly after what they want. On graduation, our students often go into internships or regular jobs, sometimes with alternative groups such as Mabou Mines, sometimes with more mainstream theatres such as the Goodman; sometimes they go to L.A. and work in the film and TV industry. Some found their own theatre companies, some of which quickly fold and some of which last for years. Some produce their own work on a show-by-show basis. Some leave theatre and enter another profession.

Whatever it is that students choose to do when they graduate, we do our best to make sure that they have basic skills in theatre production. Equally important, we try to instill in them a sense of theatre as a mode of production within a particular set of social, economic, and political conditions, and a sense of theatre as a very personal and specific art. I am constantly impressed by the level of artistic and social engagement, insight, and individuality that many of our students develop over their four years here.

It is challenging to say how certain elements of our program, housed as it is in an experimenting institution within a rich, diverse consortium, might translate into institutions with different structures and regulations. My guess is that, in any institutional structure, there are potential ways to grant more autonomy, decision-making, and responsibility to students—constantly treating them more like the young fellow artists/scholars they can be, challenging them to go farther, faster, and deeper in their development than might otherwise be the case. For this to happen, faculty have to give up some of the (often illusory) control we think we need and to become almost aggressively interdisciplinary in thinking about what theatre-making and -teaching are all about. My experience of participating in this kind of program, which can be exhausting and frustrating (often because material resources are limited), is that it has been ultimately intellectually and artistically liberating, not only for the students, but also for fostering my own development as an artist and a teacher. As the system demands that my students and I be much more individually and specifically present to each other, we learn to be much more present to ourselves.

Notes

1. Hampshire was developed and founded by faculty and administrators of the University of Massachusetts at Amherst, and Amherst, Mount Holyoke, and Smith Colleges as a direct outgrowth of the progressive social and educational movements of the late 1950s and 1960s. These institutions now form the Five Colleges Consortium.

2. A student works with a two-person faculty committee at the Division II and III level, and a one faculty-one student committee for independent projects in Division I. Hampshire's four-school structure was revised in 1998.

3. Students enrolled at any of the Five Colleges may take courses for free at any of them. We strongly encourage students to work with the many excellent faculty on the other campuses. Because of our small size and the tutorial nature of much of our work, our course offerings in theatre are limited. The consortium is clearly a major factor in making Hampshire's system and the particular approach of our Theatre Program possible.

PART II: Postmodern Challenges and Possibilities

Rhonda Blair

We live in a postmodern world that has radically shifted traditional views of power, authority, art, identity, and culture. When students arrive at college, they tend to know more about television and the shopping mall than they do about history, geography, or theatre. Young people typically enter undergraduate theatre programs with limited perspectives that lead them to define theatre in conventional terms, in regard to both issues of production process and representation. This is complicated by the fact that we educators too often assume we actually know who it is we are teaching without actually taking time to find out. Appropriately, the essays in the section begin by examining our assumptions about who our students are. They then move to consider how we might more effectively dislodge students' assumptions about what the theatrical event is artistically and socio-politically—assumptions about form, character and identity, psychological realism, narrativity, in short, to consider ways of dislodging students' resistance to theorizing, innovation, and a view that encompasses the complexity of the late twentieth-century moment in which we find ourselves.

In "Local Negotiations: Educating Student Spectators and *Etta Jenks*," Stacy Wolf describes what happened when University of Wisconsin-Madison Introduction to Theatre students encountered a deconstructed production of Marian Meyer's *Etta Jenks*, a play about a naive young woman who succeeds in the pornographic film business. Wolf examines how the presentation of an open theatrical text in an open pedagogical context, embracing postmodern strategies, instead of leading to "pleasurable, radical readings of the production" for the students, caused frustration because their expectations regarding narrativity, theatricality, and psychological realism were disappointed. The students wanted—and did not receive—"right" answers to questions raised by the production. Wolf's descriptions of the gap between contemporary theories of emancipated spectatorship and the reality of her students' "unskilled" readings, based on conventional spectating strategies, lead her to ask questions about how to engage students who are "resisting," but not progressive readers. Asserting that her students typically come from communities with different values than those of her department's (postmodern, progressive) theatre producers, Wolf calls for a recognition of these differences, a rite with which many of us are surely familiar. She leaves us with a challenge to see our work as theatre practitioners-educators in ways that acknowledge the realities of students' perspectives and values, and thereby better educate them to become active, progressive spectators.

Patricia Flanigan Behrendt's "Romancing the Stones: Teaching Introduction to Theatre in the Age of the Sound Byte" defines strategies for getting to know our students in just these ways. Invoking the maxim that we teach students, not theatre, Behrendt considers introduction to theatre courses in relation to broader issues in the undergraduate curriculum and describes how she obtains profiles of her students in order to know and teach them more effectively. Like many of us, she generally finds that introduction to theatre students are insufficiently skilled in listening, reading, speaking, and writing, that they lack sufficient general knowledge, and they tend to resist fact-based and culturally diverse materials. In coming to terms with what students don't know and why they resist knowing, with the objective of making students want to know and understand more, Behrendt designs and administers questionnaires to assess specifically how students (mis)understand issues and terms being considered in class and to gather information on work, reading, and leisure habits. She makes a solid argument that the knowledge gained through these surveys about student values and comprehension provides hard information on just who is being taught, and allows more effective interventions for progressive education.

Also addressing the challenge of "non-progressive resistance," Sarah Bryant-Bertail discusses students' initial discomforts in encountering theory in "Teaching Theory to Undergraduates: From Methodology to Ideology." Describing a course in play analysis that involves students in applying a range of theoretical perspectives to playtexts and culminates in students actually performing theory, Brayant-Bertail shows the value of teaching theory to undergraduates when it is approached as a means of making students conscious of their own theoretical and social assumptions (in this regard, she echoes Gary Jay Williams' essay). She describes students' initial resistance to grappling with theory and how she helps them negotiate the transition from learning passively (i.e., being "receptacles" for received information) to using theory as a tool to engage theatre texts actively. The essay includes concrete examples of course structure and assignments, as well as a discussion of problems that can arise in such a project.

Raynette Halvorsen Smith's "Deconstructing the Design Process: Teaching Scene Design Process Through Feminist Performance Art" outlines resistances to contemporaneity and innovation in traditional approaches to teaching scene design, and then proposes the investigation of postmodern strategies and methods derived from deconstruction and feminism. Beginning with a critique of how design teachers, and therefore students as well, are often unconscious of the values underlying conventional production/design processes, Smith reads the design process "against the grain" by looking at it through the lens of feminist performance art. The result is a discussion of dichotomies such as: the text as authority versus the body as text; the theatre of the dominant idea versus the theatre of undecidability; the military versus the ensemble model; and aesthetic "harmony" versus collage. This essay offers practical ways of shifting conventional hierarchies and perspectives in design, illuminating the ground on which they are built, and teaching design in order to accommodate instability and even incompletion, thereby making room for alternative perspectives, values, and materials in the design process.

In "East Decodes West: Russian Formalism and the New American Dramaturgy—Critical Theory to Creative Process," Paul Castagno provides specific tools and exercises for taking playwriting students beyond the limitations of playwriting based on conventional Aristotelian narrative modes, "opening the doors to new kinds of writing." Examining the dramaturgy of contemporary "language playwrights" Len Jenkin, Mac Wellman, Constance Congdon, and Eric Overmeyer in light of selected principles of Russian formalism, Castagno defines commonalities between the new dramaturgy and formalist theory. Out of this, he develops exercises that guide students to engage, among other things, transrational language, impeded form, autonomous properties of language, non-motivational plot devices, and non-psychological character treatments—all strategies and traits planted firmly in the postmodern. The resulting approach can liberate young playwrights from the stranglehold of traditional narrative and psychological realism, significantly expanding their artistic vision.

Local Negotiations:
Educating Student Spectators and Etta Jenks

In her frequently cited article, "Why Doesn't This Feel Empowering?" pedagogical theorist Liz Ellsworth self-reflexively describes and analyzes her own classroom, critiquing the assumptions of critical pedagogy. In her class, she found that using concepts fundamental to critical pedagogy—"empowerment," "dialogue," and "voice," for example, did not liberate and unify the students, but rather worked as "repressive myths," fracturing the class and inadvertently replicating traditional power relations (Ellsworth 307).

Ellsworth's article and her answer to the many scathing letters of response printed in a later issue of the *Harvard Educational Review* serve as a useful reminder to idealistic teachers and also to idealistic theatre producers. The rhetoric of liberatory pedagogy echoes that of liberatory theatre, as both call for social change through a transformation of the student/spectator.[1] Theoretically, through an active engagement with a dialogical, interrogative text (meaning the classroom or the theatre production), the model student/spectator comes to understand how knowledge is power and how history is a fiction created in the interest of power blocs. She then sees the necessity of radical social change, and herself as an agent of that change.

But Ellsworth argues that this theory fails to acknowledge, first, that students enter a class always already ideologically-constructed, and second, that the institution of the school can never completely discard its status as an ideological state apparatus. Similarly, theatre theorists and practitioners are recognizing that, however liberatory production choices may hope to construct liberated, progressive audiences, spectators arrive at the theatre with spectating practices already in place. Reception is consequently understood as a negotiation between the spectator and production text, both always within the local context.

This essay explores one such negotiation, between students in an Introduction to Theatre class at the University of Wisconsin-Madison and a University Theatre production of Marlane Meyers' *Etta Jenks*. I want to suggest that the open theatrical text and the open pedagogical context failed to provide pleasurable, radical readings of the production, but rather frustrated students in their typical search for right answers and clear meanings. Students' comments underline the gap between theories of emancipated spectators and the realities of "unskilled" readings, and point to the need to rethink those concepts.

Studying the ways students talk about theatre can illuminate assumptions of both theatre and pedagogy. As Henry Giroux writes, "Language in all of its complexity becomes central not only in the production of meaning and social identities but also as a constitutive condition for human agency" (19). In this essay, I want to foreground the knowledges that academic theatre people take for granted, and to demystify the project of critical pedagogy in theatre studies, so I am what anthropologist James Clifford calls the "'hybrid' native," the "informer" who travels· and who translates, who is both inside and outside (*Traveling* 97).[2] My method is ethnographic, in Clifford's words, a practice of "powerful 'lies' of exclusion and rhetoric" (*Introduction* 7). I quote students and analyze their comments from my own contradictorily invested perspectives, both as researcher/outsider and as insider/"native." I assistant-directed the play; I participated in the institutional production of (legitimate) knowledge through teaching. My subjects—my students—are "othered" by their outsiderness to theatre, to this particular production, and to institutionally sanctioned ways of reading.

The playtext *Etta Jenks*, written in 1986, follows a typical naive young woman who goes to Hollywood to become a film star. Unable to get a job, she decides to act in a pornography film to raise some money for an audition tape. In a series of episodic scenes, Etta succeeds in pornography, tries unsuccessfully to change careers, becomes a producer, and eventually hires a killer to dispose of her ex-boss after he apparently has her friend killed in a snuff film. In the final, ambiguous scene of the play, Etta is cleaning out her office, perhaps quitting the pornography industry, perhaps just moving on.

Etta Jenks reads like a quirky, somewhat simplistic anti-pornography play. The playwright specifies that the characters should be "mutating into animals," except for Etta and two brothers who befriend her, who are both disabled and virulently anti-pornography (Meyer 116). The male characters are cruel and Etta seems trapped, unable to extricate herself from this immoral world. Although the play does not psychologize the characters, each has a monologue that blames childhood abuse for his or her involvement in pornography.

The production, directed by Jill Dolan, complicated the written playtext's anti-pornography message.[3] It used cross-gender casting, double-casting, and casting-against-type to discourage actor-character conflation, to point out how gender is performative, and to problematize the stereotypical notion of pornography as a male-dominated, male-supported business in which women are only victims. For example, a dark hairy man was cast in the role of a porn actress who typifies innocence and ignorance; he/she gets pregnant. The same actor also played the pimp who tries to pick up Etta at the beginning of the play. A blond, blue-eyed, fair-skinned woman was cast as the pornography king.

The production also focused on strong acting choices, especially for the women. All of the actors employed a Brechtian acting style, presenting their characters rather than embodying them. The slick, industrial set, and the costumes, furniture, and props were marked as comfortably middle or even upper-class. The intention was to offer an image of women as active agents of their own desire, and to undercut stereotypical ideas about women sex workers as coerced.

To make clear associations between the theatrical performance and the production and consumption of pornographic images in contemporary culture, Dolan, the two dramaturgs, and I created a lobby exhibit, the "Museum of the Gaze," and a pre-show, the "Pornography Do's and Don't's Midway." In the theatre lobby, traditionally a safe and neutral space, we covered the walls of the semi-circular, alley-like lobby with words—headlines from the National Enquirer, ad copy, quotations from feminist theory texts, articles about pornography, relationships, and gender from a variety of magazines and newspapers—and with images—photographs from pornography magazines, covers of fashion magazines, advertisements for Victoria's Secret, the Gap, movies, and cosmetics. Removed from their usual context and reframed, the images revealed surprising similarities. It was, for example, virtually impossible to distinguish a Penthouse pin-up from an advertisement for bras.

The walls were complemented by events and performances in the lobby. An actor carried a huge dildo and some rubber rings, encouraging spectators to "Step right up and toss one on." Spectators could call a number for "phone sex," and hear a tape on which all of the explicit words were bleeped out. Actors posing as "roving reporters" circulated through the crowd to ask spectators their opinions of pornography, and volunteers from the Madison AIDS Support Network answered questions and distributed free condoms and safe-sex information.

The lobby displays and activities aimed to blur the boundaries between representations that are considered pornographic and those that are acceptable, to trouble a clear, commonsense definition of pornography. It also put spectators in an active mode of reading. Both the production and the context encouraged spectators to talk about the play, to talk about pornography.

Talking about the play was, of course, the very agenda for the discussion sections of Introduction to Theatre that I taught. Because of (what seemed to me to be) the openness and ambiguity of the production, I thought this would be a good opportunity to see how critical pedagogy might be working in conjunction with a critical theatrical project.

I do not want to suggest that the introductory-level student's untrained eye innocently perceives the "real" reception of Etta Jenks.[4] The fact that students are required to see the production and write a paper about it disciplines their readings. As Nancy Comley writes:

> In an academic setting, students almost always read for someone else, usually a teacher who stands above them literally, but certainly figuratively, in a power hierarchy in which the teacher is the holder of the "real meaning" of a literary text, as well as the dispenser of grades. (180)

However I try to subvert this arrangement—the students set the agenda, they sustain a conversation—my position as teacher saturates the situation with power. Students' responses often indicate their desire to please me, to read the production "correctly" even as I tell them there are no right answers. However, the students' candor (or in some cases, their frustration) exceeds their diligent efforts, often because they simply have not (yet) learned what the correct answers are. They read theatre through commonsense expectations about "theatre" and about the university.

An instructor's stereotypical image of a section of Introduction to Theatre includes only one African-American student, one Asian student, one self-declared feminist, a few outspoken women who don't refer to themselves as feminists, one self-declared ultra-conservative, a few unself-conscious humanists (who see their position as natural, neutral, objective, and true), one student from New York or Chicago who has attended a number of Broadway plays, one student from northern Wisconsin who had never seen a play before, and one student from a nearby town who has performed in high school plays. There are usually about half men and half women, a few seniors, but mostly freshman and sophomores with undeclared majors.

This description is not meant parodically or scientifically, nor to suggest that this is an extremely diverse group; each person could be placed in a number of differently constituted categories. However, these are the ones that appear to be salient in class discussions. Identity becomes a place from which students justify their interpretations. And when they do, these are the identity labels they call up.

Interestingly, in the case of *Etta Jenks*, students seldom leaned on their identity positions of gender or race, or on their politics. I expected, for example, that the women students might be more sympathetic toward Etta and more critical of pornography. I expected the more liberal students to appreciate the production's anti-censorship slant. But I was wrong. All of the students, whatever their gender, race, or politics, were equally judgmental of Etta, or found the production funny or boring, or felt frustrated having to write a paper. Taking advantage of different (and for me, unexpected) spectatorial opportunities, they did not grapple with their gender or racial identities, but with morality and theatricality.

Students' responses to the production fell into two general categories: comments that illustrated their uses of the production through their interpretations of it and comments that rejected the production altogether. Several used *Etta Jenks* to think about gender, theatre, pornography, and morals. Rejection of the production also served a useful value, to reinforce what they already understood as representation from seeing other plays, television shows, and movies. Both modes of reading relied more on context than text, more on conventional spectating strategies than the critical practices preferred by the production.

Students were fascinated by the cross-gender work, and by their own frequent inability to read gender apart from sex. They enjoyed comparing the different female performances of men and praised the women for their believable, accurate portrayals. Although the actors did not attempt to hide their bodies or to do realistic gender impersonation, the traditional theatrical conventions of mimesis induced spectators to look for visible accuracy. For the students, the cross-gender work did not foreground gender as performative but rather as a visible verification of sex. As one student said, "It was a woman's perspective playing a man, and certain things were so funny. Like James, he's such a smart ass. I liked seeing a woman doing a guy who was so cocky." Here, gender was reduced to sex and essentialized. The performance did not cause student spectators to see how gender is a costume or a gesture, but instead told them that the female actor understood the essential attributes of men and could perform them.

Students also used the cross-gender casting to work out their ideas about feminism. For example, many students thought that the women played the men "better." To explain why, one woman said, "This may be a feminist viewpoint, but I think that women spend more time living in a world of men and watching men and figuring out men." At this remark, the rest of the class nodded in agreement. In a mainstream humanities class, openly acknowledging power discrepancies between men and women is construed as "feminist."

Students' insistent individualism was apparent in their readings of Etta. Twentieth-century western spectating practice primarily relies on identificatory modes of reception that underline a character's psychology. Remarks about Etta used a psychologized discourse, in which the character was described as a real person with choices and agency. While I saw the production as a condemnation of any capitalist industry's abuse of its workers, the students read it as about a woman who was morally depraved, weak, and inconsistent. Etta's strength, determination, and high-class clothing contradicted commonsense notions and media-proliferated images of the pornography worker. But students did not rethink stereotypical notions of sex workers; instead, they blamed Etta for selling out. One student said, "Her boyfriend—Burt—he was the real hero of the play. He wanted to get married, have kids and a house. He was normal." Again, rather than question her own assumptions, the student used the play as an assurance of her sense of "normalcy."

The carnivalesque lobby and the pre-show events, intended to promote spectators' movement and activity, tended to "shock" the students. They used the lobby to draw their own lines and to position themselves defensively as imperfect spectators. As one student said, "I had never seen anything like that. It was not just on stage—it was in a place where people did not expect to be watching."

When students "escaped" the roaming actors to the bolted-down seats in rows in the auditorium, they detected their own differences from other spectators who came, as one student said, "on their own free will" and enjoyed the lobby. They also often felt that their reactions during the production conflicted with the audience around them. One student explained, "I was sitting by a lot of students who didn't want to be there. I heard other people laughing and I wanted to be sitting where I could laugh too." He wanted to be included in the pleasure of the event, to distance himself from other students who refused those pleasures. Another student felt alienated by a group of feminist spectators who she felt positioned themselves as insiders and laughed too hard. She said,

> I get frustrated when people try to be too much of an activist just
> because they're in Madison, just because they're here. When the play
> was trying to make an obvious cut-down of women, it wasn't a funny
> issue, but it was like they understood, and they were laughing because
> it was preposterous. I found it kind of annoying because I was thinking
> about it on a serious level of how awful it was.

I see this student as a budding feminist who wanted to read the production more
literally then ironically. In the context of Madison, with its reputation for
political radicalism, and within the bound community of the theatre event,
students worked out their own political affiliations through reactive differences.
Their comments contradict the assumption of some theatre semioticians,
including Anne Ubersfeld and Keir Elam, that theatre audiences respond
homogeneously (Bennett 76). On the other hand, students' awareness of the rest
of the audience confirms Ubersfeld's and Elam's emphasis, as Susan Bennett
writes, on "the audience as a social phenomenon" (75). Also, as folklorist
Richard Bauman points out, the social event of theatre was, for many students,
the primary focus and organizing principle of their experience (27). Because
Bauman studies performance reception in context, he extends the boundaries of
the occasion of theatre. While he is interested in the significations of the
theatrical choices within the performance, he also values the meanings of
apparently extra-theatrical details. From my perspective as both the assistant
director and instructor, it became clear that students were less struck by the
directorial choices and more by the very experience of "going to the theatre."
    Many students simply refused to engage with the production at all. Their
reasons point to conservative, conventional expectations of performance. One
student commented on the casting of Etta:

> At the beginning of play, I thought Sherry was Etta. She fit the
> stereotype. The actress who played Etta—she looked more like a
> waitress. She didn't look like she should be...

Her voice trailed off, there was laughter in the class, and embarrassment. The
student did not want to talk about the actor's body, but she refused to see the
actor, in her body, as a pornography star. The student continued:

> You have this idea of what people in pornography look like. The
> actress who played Etta just did not fit. Nothing fit after that. The play
> was not interesting any more. I do not know why. It was like having a
> witch in 'Snow White' and the witch was beautiful.

Rather than reimagine what a pornography star might look like, rather than let
the production confound the stereotype, the student rejected the actor's portrayal
of Etta, implying that the visual image of the sex worker occupies as stable a
place in the cultural imagination as a fairy-tale witch. The student described her

impression as a stereotype; she recognized it as representation, but still insisted that this representation could only reinforce what she already knew.

Students also rejected the production because they felt it lacked emotional engagement. Many noted the dispassionate tone with which the actors described stories of physical abuse and incest. For example, "If any of the sides of the issue could have been portrayed with more emotion and more depth, people would have been more sympathetic." All of their comments reveal assumptions about representation and theatre: that it will have a clear argument (which presumes that there will be winners and losers); that it will be emotional (which means causing the audience to empathize with one side or the other); that the actor will become the character; and that there will be a seamlessness between words and tone, between language and gesture.

Through these discussions, I repeatedly asked myself, Why were these students untouched, unmoved? Why did they read ambiguity as dispassion? Literary theorist Volosinov writes that "in order to observe the phenomenon of language, [...] the speaker and the listener must belong to the same language community—to a society organized along certain particular lines" (46). *Etta Jenks*, as producer of language, and the students, as listeners, did not belong to the same language community. The play produced anti-realist signifiers which the students interpreted as failed (realist) choices. Several students made remarks like this: "I expected it to be more of showing that this woman was being totally exploited and how porn was in her life and she kind of just went along with it." When the production's meaning was more ambiguous than their expectations, they refused to think about it.

Much critical pedagogy presumes a conservative academic institution and a reactionary dominant culture. *Etta Jenks*, however, complicated the formula by disrupting the university's typically conservative role and by providing spectators with the (potentially) active pleasure of decoding a complex production that was itself resistant. However film theorist David Sholle reminds us that spectator activity does not necessarily equal resistance, and that resistance is not necessarily progressive (89).[5] The students' responses exemplify his point. Students' perceptions generally showed much interpretive activity. They were extremely active spectators. In many ways, they resisted the production. Their interpretations, though, were, I think, not progressive theatrically or politically. They did make their own meanings, but they repeatedly avoided the production's semiotic complexity and its political contradictions. Conventional expectations, based on the institutionalized markings of the event as high art, the theatrical genre markings, and the topic of pornography were unshakable. Entrenched conservative reading practices prevailed, and the production became, in students' words, confusing or boring, and as I see it, virtually unreadable for them.

Conservative educators might argue that the discussions prove that students need to be taught how to be spectators. The very project of education, as argued by Bloom, Bennett, and D'Souza, aims to stratify levels of cultural capital through cultural literacy.[6] Most students, accustomed to a traditional pedagogy, imagine themselves as passive receptors of knowledge and want to acquire more cultural capital. In my class, the students and I struggled over the value of such capital. We struggled over meaning, and we struggled over access to meaning. They wanted a more traditional pedagogy that would have given them tools to read *Etta Jenks* "right." They insisted, in accordance with Bloom, that if I taught them Brechtian theory before they saw the production, they would have been better, more prepared spectators, and they could have read the production in line with our choices. In other words, they would have been diligent spectators.

Pedagogical theorist Peter McLaren writes:

> Empowerment of the self without regard to the transformation of those social structures which shape the very lineaments of the self is not empowerment at all but a sojourn into a version of humanistic therapy where catharsis is coextensive with liberation. (172)

In the case of introductory-level students and *Etta Jenks*, I believe that my giving them the intellectual tools would have provided them with a moment of classroom catharsis when they answered "correctly," when I was pleased, and when we all agreed. However, as MaLaren points out, simply empowering individuals without changing social structures does not really empower people. It makes them feel empowered and thus works like catharsis, ultimately dissuading them from trying to make structural change.[7]

The production of *Etta Jenks* (theatrically and I think pedagogically) wanted to avoid espousing a correct reading. Critical pedagogy is a radically progressive project, where the classroom is not a place where knowledges are dispensed by teachers and consumed by students, but rather a site for the production of new knowledges grounded in students' practices.

I don't see *Etta Jenks* or my students' discussion of it as a failure, though. I would suggest that my students had certain theatrical and political needs, which they met through their interpretations of the production. I think the discussions showed the inextricable connection among cultural forms and practices, including theatre, education, and politics. They showed how, as theatre scholars, practitioners, and educators, we need to see our enterprise in relation to the everyday, in relation to conventions, in relation to students' needs. The question remains how those needs might shift. I continue to ask how theatre and pedagogy might together reconstruct active and progressive student spectators.

Notes

1. Example: Luke and Gore, Giroux, Henricksen and Morgan.

2. I am indebted to Vicki Patraka for calling my attention to this image.

3. For a discussion of the production, see Dolan.

4. Other spectators, such as upper level Theatre and Drama students, professors, local feminists, and so on, used the production completely differently from the students whose responses I discuss here.

5. Recently, many cultural theorists have problematized the assumption that all spectatorial activity is resistant and progressive. See, for example, Morley.

6. On cultural capital and its relation to economic and educational capital, see Bourdieu.

7. Interestingly, McLaren's theatrical allusion echoes many feminist and Marxist critiques of realism that note how oppressive social structures are elided by realism's obsession with individual psychology. Still, other feminist theatre critics argue for realism's efficacy precisely because of its accessibility through conventional spectating practices. Ironically, the reception of Etta Jenks "proves" that side of the feminism debate.

Works Cited

Bauman, Richard. *Verbal Art as Performance.* Prospect Hills, IL: Waveland Press, 1977.

Bennett, Susan. *Theatre Audiences: A Theory of Production and Reception.* New York: Routledge, 1990.

Bourdieu, Pierre. *Distinction: A Social Critique of the Judgment of Taste.* Trans. R. Nice. Cambridge: Harvard UP, 1984.

Clifford, James. "Introduction: Partial Truths." *Writing Culture: The Poetics and Politics of Ethnography.* Ed. James Clifford and George E. Marcus. Berkeley: U of California P, 1986. 1–26.

———. "Traveling Cultures." *Cultural Studies.* Ed. Lawrence Grossberg, Cary Nelson, and Paula Treichler. New York: Routledge, 1992. 96–116.

Comley, Nancy. "Reading and Writing Genders." *Reorientations: Critical Theories and Pedagogies.* Ed. Bruce Henricksen and Thais E. Morgan. Urbana: U of Illinois P, 1990. 179–92.

Dolan, Jill. "Gender, Sexuality, and 'My Life' in the (University) Theatre." *Presence and Desire: Feminism and Theatre Studies.* Ann Arbor: U of Michigan P, 1993. 99–118.

Ellsworth, Elizabeth. "Why Doesn't This Feel Empowering? Working Through the Repressive Myths of Critical Pedagogy." *Harvard Educational Review* 59.3 (August 1989): 307–19.

Giroux, Henry. *Border Crossings: Cultural Workers and the Politics of Education.* New York: Routledge, 1992.

———, ed. *Postmodernism, Feminism, and Cultural Politics: Redrawing Educational Boundaries.* Albany: State U of New York P, 1992.

Harvard Educational Review 60.3 (August 1990): 388–405.

Henricksen, Bruce, and Thais E. Morgan, eds. *Reorientations: Critical Theories and Pedagogies.* Urbana: U of Illinois P, 1990.

Luke, Carmen and Jennifer Gore, eds. *Feminisms and Critical Pedagogy.* New York: Routledge, 1992.

McLaren, Peter. "Schooling the Postmodern Body: Critical Pedagogy and the Politics of Enfleshment." *Postmodernism, Feminism, and Cultural Politics: Redrawing Educational Boundaries.* Ed. Henry A. Giroux. Albany: State U of New York P, 1991. 144–73.

Meyer, Marlane. *Etta Jenks. Womenswork.* Ed. Julia Miles. New York: Applause, 1989. 115–74.

Morley, David. *Television, Audiences, and Cultural Studies.* New York: Routledge, 1992.

Sholle, David. "Reading the Audience, Reading Resistance: Prospects and Problems." *Journal of Film and Video* 43.1–2 (1991): 80–89.

Volosinov, V. N. *Marxism and the Philosophy of Language.* Trans. L. Matejka and I. R. Titunik (1930), Cambridge: Harvard UP, 1973.

Wolf, Stacy. "Talking About Pornography, Talking About Theatre: Ethnography, Critical Pedagogy, and the Production of 'Educated'

Audiences of *Etta Jenks* in Madison." *Theatre Research International* 19.1 (1994). 29–36.

Romancing the Stones:
Teaching Introduction to Theatre in the Age of the Soundbyte

Patricia Flanagan Behrendt

In 1991, Ronald Willis noted that "no course in the theatre curriculum is more susceptible to the coupling of fuzzy-minded idealism and cynical execution than Introduction to Theatre" (143). While his words characterize the problems posed by a course intended to introduce college undergraduates to the complex discipline of theatre, they perhaps inadvertently reflect the growing dilemma of many theatre academics and theatre programs faced with extinction if they cannot effectively articulate and justify their importance to the university curriculum. The anxiety and confusion surrounding this core academic course is paradigmatic of the anxiety and confusion which characterize many academic theatre programs across the country. With this in mind, the following essay both considers the Introduction to Theatre course in relation to the broad educational concerns that trouble the undergraduate curriculum and proposes a realistic profile of many of today's undergraduates, a perhaps disturbing profile but one which is indispensable in generating effective teaching strategies in theatre programs of the twenty-first century.

For several years, I thought that the subject of the Introduction to Theatre class was "theatre" and, furthermore, that the problems of teaching "theatre" centered logically around finding teaching strategies that suited the subject. I now understand, however, that the problems that we face in teaching this course are the same problems that relentlessly plague undergraduate teaching across the curriculum. What we share with other disciplines and, particularly, with other introductory courses are the large numbers of undergraduate students who are unprepared to learn—who are unskilled in listening, in reading, in speaking, and in writing, skills integral to an appreciation of the complexities of theatrical art.

The problems of teaching introductory material center not around what we teach but around who we are and, principally, around whom we teach: the audience for our subject. Of the concept of an audience, in general, Herbert Blau writes, "how we think about an audience is a function of how we think about ourselves, social institutions, epistemological processes, what is knowable, what is not, and how, if at all, we may accommodate the urge for collective experience" (28). A similar problematic vision applies to the students in our classrooms. How we think about our students reflects how we think about ourselves; how we think about knowledge and knowledge acquisition; and how we, as individuals, feel about our own relationships with others. Our own needs are inevitably played out to some degree in the way we manage a classroom. Furthermore, as faculty, we age with each year that passes while the students that fill the Introduction to Theatre classroom remain, like Dorian Gray, forever young. As theatre faculty, we are often comfortably convinced of the relevance of the role of theatre in public discourse and in culture and may resent the challenge to that complacency increasingly represented by students who often suspect and openly argue that live theatre can only aspire to the effects achieved in television and in film. Perhaps the best analogy for the pedagogical uncertainties that characterize the Introduction to Theatre course are the typical Introduction to Theatre textbooks, which often are a kind of Pandora's box of history and production practice peppered with slick images from Broadway shows, far removed from the students' experiences, and with photos of actors recognizable to students primarily for their roles in popular movies and television. Major concerns like these are outweighed, however, by the fundamental learning deficits many students bring to the classroom.

Despair over the fact that undergraduate students possess so little general knowledge on which to build permeates the undergraduate curriculum. In some schools, the sciences faced this problem by instituting remedial, non-credit courses to correct deficiencies. We have no such options in the arts where the materials that we teach are assumed, somehow, to transcend the need for fundamental knowledge and for fundamental language skills. In the last few years some educational theorists have insisted that we must avoid the paralysis that accompanies the realization that students know less and less upon entering college and, furthermore, that we must resist any temptation as educators to expose and to confront students' fundamental problems, since doing so might damage their self-esteem. Some advocate a teaching model designed to help students to discover and to become empowered by what they know. The typical model revolves around a discussion format in which students generally are encouraged to apply intuitive understanding and life experience to situations in novels, plays, and works of art in general. This inclusive, non-confrontational classroom model has feminist origins in a rejection of the patriarchal paradigm in which knowledge appears to flow in one direction: from teacher to student (Belenky 217). Although free-flowing discussion is important to the classroom experience, and usually boosts teaching evaluations, many of my colleagues recognize that any attempt on the instructor's part to introduce discrete materials, such as dates and historical references, into the discussion quickly meets with student disinterest. The problem of student resistance to learning fact-based materials remains entrenched regardless of the classroom rapport established through open discussion.

Furthermore, efforts to introduce culturally diverse materials into classrooms filled with predominantly white, middle-class students frequently produces not just disinterest but outright resistance. For example, in a 1992 study describing their experiences in developing a multicultural theatre course, Meg

Swanson and Robin Murray noted that one of the "principal discoveries was that many white majority students are highly resistant, occasionally even hostile, to the inclusion of the works of people of color within the curriculum" (105–6). While traditional decorum prevents prolonged or outspoken public criticism of the students' lack of preparation and initiative—despite shocking government reports on the declining effectiveness of the American school system—many of the private complaints voiced by instructors about teaching focus on the often combative resistance to learning that characterizes so many classrooms.

While it is important to discover and to reinforce what students know, coming to terms with the realities *of what they do not know and why they resist knowing* has far greater implications for our ability to teach. The first consideration in teaching Introduction to Theatre has nothing to do with what we would like the students to learn about production practice, theatre history, dramatic literature, or the aesthetic joys of an art form. Teaching is no longer about what we think our students should know about our favorite subject. Perhaps it never was. Students no longer come to the classroom, as many of us did as undergraduates, with a *willing of suspension of disbelief,* guided then by the perhaps naive but powerful premise that the material is worth knowing. The first consideration of teaching now is the nature of today's students; for how we think about them *is* a function of how we understand epistemological processes, what is knowable and what is not, and how, if at all, we can achieve a collective experience. But how do we discover and explore the students' deficiencies without intimidating and, perhaps, humiliating them? How do we help students to want to *know more* than what their feelings, intuitions, and prejudices alone tell them about their world? For if we do not undertake an honest assessment of today's university students and their attitudes toward learning, we cannot hope to achieve any kind of collective learning experience.

With these concerns in mind, as part of my teaching preparations, I gather as much information about the students as I can through questionnaires on a variety of subjects, which the students answer anonymously. Over the last three years, I have begun to focus on this material to create teaching strategies primarily in the form of exercises that make students more receptive to class materials which they would otherwise typically reject, such as those dealing with research, facts, and dates. The questionnaires fall into two categories. One type solicits information about how students manage time. The second type usually probes the students' understanding of an issue that arises in the class which is usually, but not necessarily, related to the material. Understanding how students manage their time is essential to understanding their thinking patterns and the hierarchy of values to which they subscribe as individuals and as groups. Profiling students assists in understanding why some materials are difficult to teach, while others are more accessible. More importantly, the profiles can be used to develop approaches to materials that take into consideration the thinking patterns and values of the *student* rather than of the teacher. For example, imagine the implications of the following information gathered from 400 questionnaires distributed in the Introduction to Theatre classrooms at the University of Nebraska in the spring of 1993. For the purposes of this study, I have selected information from three basic categories including work, television, and reading habits, respectively.

Questions concerning work habits outside of the university reveal the following: 60% of the students work at a variety of money-making jobs on an average of 12 to 15 hours a week; 5% work 30 to 40 hours a week; 5% choose not to work at all. Most of the remaining students work seasonally or are in the process of looking for work. Of the 60% who work 12 to 15 hours a week, most confirm that they are not paying, in fact, for tuition and books. They are what I call the "velvet trap" students who work to pay for extra creature comforts— such as fashionable clothes, entertainment, stereos, cars, and VCRs—to which they have become accustomed since high school. Many of these students worked nearly full-time jobs in high school to support spending habits that had quickly become a higher priority than high school course work. Many avoided college preparatory courses in high school because the demands of those courses cut into the after-school hours available for work. In most cases, parents still provide the basic unit of financial support, including such necessities as housing, food, clothing, and car insurance. While most of these students conclude that they would do better in college classes if they worked less, they admit that the "extras" are more important than a letter grade. In fact, many believe that they would only improve by a half of a letter grade in any given subject if they gave up their work hours entirely. This belief is largely a self-serving rationale, rather than one based upon experience. For years I assumed that students who offered long work hours as excuses for falling asleep in class, for poor attendance, or for missed assignments were working out of financial necessity. In other words, I made the leap to the sympathetic conclusion that if they were not able to work, they probably would not be in class at all. Through questionnaires, however, I have discovered that, in many cases, long work hours are offered as an excuse for poor performance when the student need not work at all. In fact, many students have developed a value system, workable throughout the high school years, which prioritizes work hours and devalues study time. By leaping to the conclusion that the student *must* work, I frequently appeared unnecessarily sympathetic to the student's situation. My naive sympathy merely reinforced the student's value system—built upon short-term goals—and, in fact, belied my own value system—built upon long-term goals. As a corollary with regard to student attitudes toward the learning environment, it is interesting to note that 80% of the students admitted to cheating on a minor test, quiz, or assignment in the last 6 months; the same 80% admitted to some form of cheating on a major exam or final project in the last 6 months. Cheating was defined as substituting the work of another person for your own.

Questions concerning television habits reveal that 60% of the students keep the television on for an average of 3 to 5 hours a day; 33% have it on for 7 to 8 hours a day, though many claim to be focused actually on another task; 5% watch no television. Ninety percent of the students actually have televisions in their rooms for entertainment and, some say, for companionship. By extension, 80% claim to see 30 to 50 movies a year including video rentals. Finally, 96% have not read a book—that was not required for a class—in the last year.

The implications of these critical percentages point specifically to the problem of language skills and to the devaluation of the fundamental role of language skills in the educational process. Most students have a highly fragmented lifestyle that not only undermines but denies the importance of reading and reflecting on course materials. How many students will go to great, if not bizarre, lengths to rent a video of a play rather than read it for class? Furthermore, students who do not read cannot write effectively because they are not visually familiar with the syntactical relationships of words and phrases as they appear in print. It is virtually impossible for students to reproduce in their own writing words and language structures with which they are not visually familiar. Likewise, students have trouble taking good notes from lectures—*not necessarily because* they don't understand what is being said, *not because* they can't write fast enough—but because some of the words that they hear in the classroom are words or phrases that they have seldom, if ever, seen in print. As a result, often students record poorly spelled words and phrases in their notes which they cannot recognize later. Furthermore, because students do not listen or read avidly and willingly, they do not recognize oral and written language cues that signal what is important and what is not in a given text.

In the age of visual technology and special effects, a paradoxical problem confronts theatre educators with regard to the act of reading dramas. While we take for granted the imaginative act of visualizing characters, actions, and environments as we read, many students come to us without the ability or the skill to visualize what they read because they have never been taught to do so. These are the students who cannot remember the names of characters, the events of a plot, the locations of events, or the ideas contained in a text.

The more we explore how our students regard and experience language, the more effective we can become in the classroom, for example, by taking time to teach the students how to analyze a paragraph from the textbook for the thesis sentence and supporting material and by teaching them to make use of the same structures in their own writing; by asking students to volunteer to define and spell words that emerge in class discussions; by asking students to read information aloud from their notes so that one can clarify mistakes. Class exercises in visualization as part of the reading process build better readers while they illuminate theatre aesthetics. Exercises that analyze paragraphs in the text for the verbal cues that point to important information are, likewise, analogous, for example, to studying directorial devices or visual cues that create focus in a scene.

Investigating students' language skills alerts us to ways of handling more complex language problems which have even more significant implications for the teaching environment. For example, during a class discussion this spring of *A Raisin in the Sun*, the terms "political correctness" and "affirmative action" were introduced into the conversation by students. Part of my teaching strategy during each undergraduate class hour is to keep a list of terms and concepts—both pertinent and not necessarily pertinent to the material—that emerge in the discussion. Often at the end of the hour, I ask students to write down, anonymously, what they think those terms mean. What they write is a better indicator of what occurred during the class than my residual perceptions. Furthermore, what they write gives me the opportunity to design class material that will address misconceptions and misinterpretations.

The terms "political correctness" and "affirmative action" are examples of general terms I have asked students to define. One of the students wrote, "I think that political correctness is truthful information about government released in the media." Another wrote, "Political correctness is knowing about your political party and what they stand for." And another said that political correctness is "acting or speaking in a way that accurately represents our government and its beliefs." Of affirmative action, one young man wrote, "Affirmative action is based on the communist notion that everyone should only have so much; remove merit based promotion—the idea on which this country was founded." Ominously, one young woman said that affirmative action is "free benefits for minorities and reverse discrimination." While some of the students indicated in some way that affirmative action was aimed at preventing discrimination against specific groups, none mentioned women in relation to the policy. In fact, most defined it as "taking strong or firm action."

Notice that the language used by the students is just as confident, relatively articulate, and above all, just as assertive as it is inaccurate. On the surface the class discussion of the play constituted a satisfactory class hour. In fact, however, the students' definitions of the terms, which I read after returning to my office, reveal that beneath the veneer of thoughtful interaction that characterized the class were pockets of confusion and distortion, as well as hints about attitudes that students may harbor. Having this information puts an instructor in a more effective position to plan follow-up exercises and discussions intended to address misunderstandings, misinterpretations, attitudes, and general perceptions in an informative and nonjudgmental manner. Nonthreatening, anonymous exercises of this type create in many students what I call a *need to know* which may not exist prior to the class discussion but which often results in students who return to class actually having researched a definition they then want to share with everyone.

Interacting with the students through questionnaires and exercises which the students answer anonymously frequently reveals the degree to which we assume that they understand common terms and concepts. As we internationalize our curriculum to broaden our students' exposure to diverse cultures, for example, we should ask ourselves what the average undergraduate understands about the concept of cultural tradition. It is illuminating to ask students to write a paragraph that explains the term "Western cultural tradition." Doing so led me to the further realization that most students have such a poor background in geography that many often have no real understanding of basic references to parts of the world that we may mention casually in class. Therefore, when we approach any subject or drama from the Western cultural tradition, I begin by asking the students, anonymously, to sketch out on a sheet of paper what they can recall about the configuration of Western Europe. At the same time, I have a slide of the map of the world ready for viewing immediately afterward. This is a most sobering exercise for both instructor and students. The realization that most students cannot visualize the relationship of the major countries of the European continent must make us reconsider our assumptions about what students know when they enter the classroom.

It is not our knowledge about teaching that produces informed students; instead, it is knowledge *about* students that informs the teaching process. Many students have little frame of reference for terms, concepts, and ideas which we may believe are within the realm of general knowledge. Inquiries that reveal the educational backgrounds of today's students force us to view the problems of teaching theatre in relation to the problems faced by undergraduate teachers across the curriculum. First, many students often reject dates, historical information, and research because they have no framework of learning that gives meaning to factual information. Second, the language skill level of most students prevents them from understanding many verbal and written language cues that signal important information in a given text. Only by assessing the values and lifestyles of today's students can we envision the ways in which our discipline can contribute to the learning environment. Understanding the needs of students forces us, as educators, to reevaluate what the study of theatre can contribute to undergraduate education in the age of electronic images and virtual reality. It is through perceptions that link theatre educators to the concerns and teaching missions of other academic programs that the academic theatre can envision and secure its place in the university community. An ability to articulate the needs of students rather than the needs of theatre programs will characterize academic theatres across the country that survive into the twenty-first century.

Works Cited

Belenky, Mary, Blythe Clinchy, Nancy Goldberg, and Jill Tarule. *Women's Ways of Knowing*. New York: Basic Books, 1986.

Blau, Herbert. *The Audience*. Baltimore and London: The Johns Hopkins UP, 1990.

Murray, Robin, and Margaret Millen Swanson. "Towards a Multicultural Theatre Course." *Theatre Topics* 2.2 (1992): 105–11.

Willis, Ronald A. "Introduction to Theatre—Who Does It Serve? What Does It Contain?" *Theatre Topics* 1.2 (1991): 143–47.

Teaching Theory to Undergraduates
—from Methodology to Ideology

Sarah Bryant-Bertail

Several times over the past three years, I have taught a required undergraduate course called "Play Analysis" at the University of Washington. The following is an imaginary conversation with someone—a lost student perhaps—who wanders into the classroom by accident a few minutes early on the first day. I stand with my syllabi and notes ready, and have just written the name of the course and my own name on the board. This person asks questions and expresses assumptions that students have had about the course and that I have asked myself.

What kind of a course is this? What is Drama 302, Play Analysis for undergraduates?

It is just what the title suggests. Students learn to analyze plays. For drama majors it is a required course, and for others it is a humanities elective. It's also an official writing course. Here, take a syllabus. Look there under "aims of the course"—

—What do you mean, analyze plays? I thought this was the director's job. Doesn't everyone want to be an actor? Sure, they have to learn their parts and create their characters, but they know how to read the play already, don't they?

Yes, but this course teaches them to get more out of what they read. It is important for actors too, and for directors and designers, for anyone who deals with theater. Let me just quote from my syllabus, where the aims of the course are explained: "Students gain skill in analysis of texts and performance through learning about contemporary critical theories; and they put these theories into practice through writing papers, oral presentations, and class discussions. They also are introduced to a variety of plays and performances in their historical contexts."

Contemporary critical theory? That sounds more like a graduate seminar to me. Why should you teach theory to undergraduates?

Because they need to know what the currents of thought are in the world today. Because theory gives them a more interesting and complex view of dramatic texts and performances. Because otherwise they think they confront texts directly—for example, they believe in the origin and ownership of meaning by the author.

What's wrong with confronting texts directly—and what do you mean the ownership of meaning? Doesn't the author know what he was writing about, what he wanted to say—sorry, he or she, I should have said.

That is too complicated to explain right now, but it's the basic idea of deconstruction, which is one of the theories I'll be teaching. The problem is, if students really believe that the author has final say over what the play means, then they'll believe that they themselves can never have access to the right meaning. It's empowering for them to realize that meaning is historical, and is not owned by the author.

But do the students really have more power? Don't you as the professor still have power over meaning? Don't you decide whether their interpretations are valid and invalid?

Of course I have power over students. I make up the syllabus, and I am the one who evaluates them. This is my responsibility. Yet I try very hard not to disqualify their interpretations, or better, readings of a play, but to encourage them to use all the different critical approaches, to be open-minded and not afraid of what they might find. Each theory is complex enough to allow many different readings of a play. I prefer the term "reading" to "interpretation," because reading is an ongoing process, whereas the idea of interpretations implies a right and wrong looking for a capsule meaning that can be wrapped up and swallowed.

However, some students dislike the idea of theory, because they think it is irrelevant to plays. Theory means dissecting the play and it feels like a violation, like overkill, if the play is analyzed too much. And students still suspect that a theory is not valid if the author didn't intend the play to be read in this way.

Students think theory is irrelevant, but the reality is that they themselves are using theory all the time and are unaware of it—that is, they have certain attitudes about reading and understanding a play or being a spectator that seem so natural to them that they can't see that it *is* a theory.

So what is a theory in your definition—that is, a conscious one?

A theory is a system of assumptions, a certain set of issues, an organized knowledge that one can acquire and apply to plays, performances, to film and television, and ultimately to life. With theories we can analyze or explain specific sets of phenomena. Practically speaking, I divide theory into two functions: the methodological and the ideological. For this class, I have worked out a sequence that proceeds from one to the other, the purpose being first to give students some basic rather neutral methods of analysis, which they can connect later with ideological theories. The ideological theories are not organized around analytic methods but focus on certain human subjects and social processes—for example, the working class, women, gays, or people of color. In using theories to analyze, one can illuminate aspects of the work that otherwise would not have been seen.

But when you say illumination of aspects of the work, aren't you assuming that the work is an object with some parts hidden and some obvious, but still an object?

It would seem so; "illuminating the aspects" might imply that there is only one true, complete object—but if theater is an object it is only so in the cubist or dadaist sense. That is, illumination is the process of understanding—and the process itself is the work of art.

Isn't that the same as saying that there is no art object per se, nothing "out there" but our perceptions of it. Aren't you coming close to complete relativism—are you saying that nothing matters but our different subjective points of view—and that anything goes?

Well, no, the work does not "dissolve" into points of view—as in Norman Holland's idea of five readers' readings. There certainly *is* a work—or rather, works—"out there," if we take a work as seeming definite at a certain point in history to specific people. But that specificity is exactly what we need to explore in its complexity, not to dissolve into something general called the universal meaning. As for subjective points of view, this is all we have, but some points of view do more justice to the work than others. That is, no theory is "true" in an absolute sense, but theories are more or less *valid* in particular cases.

So would it be possible to take any theory and apply it to any play?

Theoretically, anything is *possible*. However, some theories did fit a particular work better than others. You could use it. But, what would it bring you? It would be uninteresting if there is too little in the work to go on. A theory is valid only and always in particular, because it can deal with more of the play or performance than can other theories. It is more valid if it can account for more of the work's complexity. No theory has universal validity, and theory should not be used to master the work, to reduce it to an example.

If we learn all about these theories, will we be able to understand every work?

It is not a question of understanding every work, or every aspect of one work, because this implies again that we can master the work, stand above it and see its totality from an outside standpoint. However, we can get a sense of the work as a complicated design, a nexus in Bakhtin's sense, where many discourses intersect at specific historical moments. The reader or spectator brings his or her own historical context with all its conscious and unconscious assumptions to that work. Theory, then, should not be thought of as something external that one lays over a pure work of art, but rather as ways of illuminating how the play or performance speaks to us.

So is theory like a foreign language—if we learn it, we can understand what someone from another country is saying, and we can unlock their world?

Never completely, no more than we can unlock our own. Our world and the world of the work cannot be entirely distinguished in any case. It is not only that the other world speaks to us—the conversation is not one-sided. We can also speak to and *through* the works—and they will speak back to us, whereas they were closed fortresses before, or they seemed so obvious that they were not interesting enough to converse with.

In this imaginary conversation, I have given voice to several reservations that my students have about theory, and I have voiced my positions as temporary answers. I sometimes share my students' reservations, and also have a few of my own. For example, one reservation is that I am still somewhat uncomfortable teaching Freudian psychoanalysis. I don't "believe" in some of its assumptions enough to use it in my own scholarly work. Yet, I also believe that one can neither understand many issues in contemporary theory nor understand twentieth-century theater without having studied Freud's theories of the unconscious and the dream. Another kind of discomfort comes from knowing that I *do* believe in the potential validity of other theories that I teach, such as semiotics, deconstruction, and even structuralism if one does not essentialize it, as well as the more openly ideological theories of Marxism, feminism, gay/lesbian criticism, and post-colonialist criticism. This discomfort is also a fear that I may not be giving students enough freedom to dissent.

Yet I still am convinced that theory is freeing to students who have been, on the one side, imprisoned and paralyzed by the belief that the work belongs only to its author and to an unreachable origin, and on the other side, "liberated" with the idea that since any reading is as good as any other, it does not really matter what they think. Nowhere is our Anglo-American bias on behalf of common sense more evident—and more limiting—than in a class of undergraduates, most of whom have never had a course in literary or dramatic theory. Most undergraduate literature courses do give them at least a smattering of theory, but often it is only whatever they happen to run across in doing their research papers.

Indeed, many professors of literature, not to speak of drama, never expressly teach theory nor tell students their own theoretical assumptions. This also enhances the effect of mystical distance that helps sustain the authority of the professor. This situation, at the universities I know, has not changed much since my own undergraduate days as a double major in theater and English. Then only one course in literary theory was required of English majors and none for drama majors. This one course struck terror in our hearts. Then as now, students often reacted with definite resistance and a sense that someone was asking us to state our beliefs and values which were then found inadequate. Perhaps this helps explain their tenacious clinging to common sense or, as Paul de Man once noted in an article of the same name, their "resistance to theory." His words on the subject are worth quoting:

> The resistance to theory is a resistance to the use of language about language. It is therefore a resistance to language itself or to the possibility that language contains factors or functions that cannot be reduced to intuition. But we seem to assume all too readily that, when we refer to something called 'language,' that we know what it is we are talking about, although there is probably no word to be found in the language that is as overdetermined, self-evasive, disfigured and disfiguring as 'language'... (161)[1]

When de Man speaks of "language," he uses the word in a broad sense, just as he does "reading" which to him is what we also do when confronting a painting or other plastic art. The "text" thus also includes language that is nonverbal. Theater, of course, consists of verbal and nonverbal languages and thus many kinds of "texts." De Man, like Bakhtin, as well as Barthes and other post-structuralists, does not posit "reality" in opposition to "texts," but defines texts as a nexus of conflicting discourses.

I see it as a crucial pedagogical task to confront my students' resistance to theory. In an important sense this very resistance can be and often is a source of energy in the classroom and perhaps is even necessary in making the transition between learning passively and using actively. Most of the rest of this chapter will be a sharing of the methods I have used to help students make this transition from passive to active. The course in play analysis, as explained above, begins with the methodological and moves towards the ideological approaches, and the plays are chosen so that each one of them could also be used in connection with the following week's theory. At present, the class begins with structuralism and *Oedipus Rex*, both of which will be remembered the following week when students read *Desire Under the Elms*. O'Neill's play will in turn not only be seen as an example of psychoanalysis, but in the week after that, when we are on deconstruction, it can be seen as a new kind of mythic structure with patriarchy as the unacknowledged center of power and women—and matriarchy—as the marginalized other. The absenting of women allows patriarchy to become central. Likewise Brecht's *Mother Courage*, read first in relation to Marxism, also later becomes an example of deconstruction as stage practice. Feminism is followed in the syllabus by gay/lesbian criticism, a sequence that reflects the history of these two movements that have so many issues in common. Since I began teaching gay and lesbian criticism a year ago I have called on my colleague David Roman or upon my teaching assistants to help introduce this approach because, as a heterosexual, it seems unethical for me to claim the voice of authority in a business-as-usual manner. Indeed, since students themselves are able to introduce each theory as it comes, and since many gay and lesbians sign up for the group on gay/lesbian theory, those with life experience have usually had the first authoritative word on the subject. By the time we have come to post-colonialism, the last approach, the students can clearly see that the construct of polarities, of an arbitrary system of difference which first emerged within the context of structuralism eight or nine weeks before, is vividly relevant to the post-colonial political situations students can see all around them in our multicultural society. I have found that as the weeks pass, the operating principles (though not the technical terms) of structuralism and semiotics are gradually and imperceptibly adopted into practice by the students as a resource, a mode of analysis that they are so comfortable with that it recedes from consciousness—not entirely forgotten[!], but faded into routine like the first steps one takes in learning to drive. As the reader may notice, in beginning with Oedipus and structuralism and moving through *Desire Under the Elms, Mother Courage*, and sometimes *A Streetcar Named Desire*, to feminism, gay/lesbian theory and post-colonialist theory, certain thematic threads are created. Notably there is an ongoing critique of the father (especially the great white Western one) and a concurrent focusing on errant mothers, daughters, and sons, especially those of underprivileged class and color. This might be evidence not only of my conscious politics but also of the energy created by my resistance to Freudian psychoanalytic theory.

With the goal of letting theory empower students to speak for themselves and to let works speak to them, I have developed a number of practical classroom techniques: small group discussions and reading scenes of the plays aloud helps students find a void—in a class of 35 to 40 many feel too intimidated to volunteer during a general discussion. There are also two speaking requirements: at the beginning of the quarter students sign up for groups of two to five who will be responsible for introducing one particular theory, with each student speaking a few minutes and taking one aspect. The presentation can also involve performance and can be as creative as they like, the only requirement being that they manage to cover some fundamentals of that approach. Of course, the teaching assistant and I are available for advice, and students almost always ask for outside sources to read, besides the assigned articles that the whole class reads. This approach allows students to become experts in one field, so that others come to them for advice: in a sense, they own this theory—both authority and responsibility are taken by them. The final project is also a group presentation combining performance with critical analysis. For this, students may either form a group on their own, or be placed in groups according to their interests. The final presentation can take whatever form they agree upon, and can involve an existing play, film, or television work, or a work of their own conception, as long as it deals with some of the theories studied in class. This element of the course has been especially successful and popular with students, and at its best it brings what has been learned into focus and relevance for them.

One of the most memorable of these final group projects, by way of example, was a trial scene wherein the Little Mermaid sued the Disney Corporation for depriving her of her voice and of her subjecthood, for bringing her "mental anguish and the loss of income due to gross stereotyping." Besides the Little Mermaid in a red wig and sea shell bra, there were also two female lawyers, one defending Disney in patriarchal, social-Darwinist, capitalist terms and the other accusing in feminist-Marxist ones. The affable, chauvinistic Prince was called to the stand, unhappy with his wife's political activism. A male judge presided over the proceedings, and a video machine continuously and silently played the Disney film behind the actors—thus setting up a Brechtian epic estrangement effect as well. Among other crimes, Disney was found guilty of erasing from the story all the positive female role models in the Mermaid's life: namely her grandmother and the sea witch. Instead, the film ends with a foaming sea battle between her father, the good white-bearded King Tritan (a Neptune-like patriarch not in Anderson's original story) and the evil white-haired Sea Witch Ursula, who had become the villain of the story. The Sea Witch is finally vanquished by the Prince. He relates his deed to the prosecuting attorney as the scene of the same sea battle also plays on the video screen behind them:

PROSECUTING ATTORNEY: Can you tell us how you killed Ursula?

ERIC: (As the prince tells the story, we see the scene from the movie on the monitor.) Well, she was about to destroy Ariel, and she had already turned King Tritan into a polyp. I got into a sunken ship which had been raised by the churning waters. (Pointing to the monitor) See, there I am with my bulging biceps. I commanded the wheel, and I thrust the broken cutty sark into her belly.

PROSECUTING ATTORNEY: You impaled her with the ship's frontal appendage?

ERIC: (Proudly) Yes. (Nagel)

Despite such moments, which make all the work of the course seem worthwhile, there are still some students who resist to the end, obviously not at all convinced that any of this has been worthwhile. In addition, some of the techniques outlined here may be more effective in a smaller group than with a class of 35 or 40. The techniques and curriculum are submitted to ongoing rethinking and revision, and in many ways, I still feel daunted by teaching this course. It is far easier, and it seems more "organic," to teach one theoretical approach all quarter in connection with a more prescribed approach. For instance, in my course on epic theater, Marxism and Brechtian theory appear easier for students to accept, as do the theories of Artaud in the class on the European avant-garde theater, or feminist theory in connection with the "Women in Theater" course. Here there is a more recognizable cumulative effect of learning. In short, the students seem to have less resistance to the theory in such courses—although another undoubtedly influential factor is that these courses are elective, in contrast to the Play Analysis course which is required.

Yet, the very risks and frustrations of the Play Analysis course are also part of its excitement. As students themselves have remarked, a certain element of danger is there, not only in the diversity of students' fields and ethnic backgrounds, but in the fact that for many women, or gays and lesbians, or Black, Asian, Chicano, or Native-American students, the material gives them a sense of finally being represented. Other students, such as the white fraternity boy and former football player from an upper-middle-class suburb of Seattle, are thrown into a kind of culture shock as they recognize that there are gays and angry women and people of color all around them. In this student's own words, "I can't believe the things I learned about in this class. I realize now that I've had a pretty sheltered life. I came here straight from Bellevue High School, I'm in a fraternity, I'm a senior about to graduate, and yet this is the first time I've ever heard about some of this stuff. I never would have guessed the people who are gay in this class—it was a shock when I realized they were there all the time and they didn't even hit on me!" This was the kind of moment memorable to all teachers, where material learned in a class had been applied to life itself.

However, to temper such victories, it has also become evident to me that most undergraduate students have no idea of where we teachers of drama—and especially of history and theory—stand in relation to theater or to higher education as a whole. After a very successful group presentation and quarter, one bright African-American student asked how I had decided to become a university teacher. When I answered that it was a difficult thing to be hired at the university level, with many competing for very few jobs, and that I felt fortunate to be teaching at the University of Washington, he was surprised, and said he had always assumed that colleges and universities had trouble finding enough professors willing to teach—especially (he implied without saying) theory and history. Presumably, in the eyes of a majority of students, all the valuable jobs are out in the "real world" of professional theater, in hierarchical importance: acting, playwriting, directing, designing, and working backstage. In fact, most undergraduate students do not know how the practice of theater is structured inside or outside the walls of the university, nor do they have a sense of where actors, for instance, stand in a broader historical or cultural context, even though so many students aspire to act professionally. For this reason alone, it seems evident that they need more theory and history rather than less.

A few years ago Barry Witham, my colleague at the University of Washington, co-authored a short paper with his then teaching assistant John Lutterbie, on using Marxist theory to analyze Ibsen's *A Doll's House* (76–80). This useful article, which I have assigned to students many times, appeared in an anthology of essays on teaching the play. The authors describe an undergraduate course also called "Play Analysis," the ancestor of the course I have described. Witham and Lutterbie noted then that the students' "resistance to theory" first needs to be broken down, and the authors suggest thinking of the various theories as different lenses which one may put on to see the play in new perspectives. Then years later the metaphor is still useful, and the resistance is still there. Yet, I submit that this resistance is a necessary part of the transition from passive intuition or common sense to active engagement, to taking power and responsibility to one's own encounter with the work of art and the theory.

Note

1. The Newton anthology is a very useful one for students because it contains lucid introductions and short essays by the original authors on most of the major critical theories. Its only drawback is that the editors often cut the examples out of the critical essays, which makes them much more dense and difficult to read, even for graduate students.

Works Cited

de Man, Paul. "Resistance to Theory." *Yale French Studies* 63 (1982): 7–17. Rpt. in *Twentieth-Century Literary Theory: A Reader*. Ed. K. M. Newton. New York: St. Martin's Press, 1988. 161.

Nagel, Emily. "The Case of the Little Mermaid." Class Presentation. 12 June 1991.

Witham, Barry, and John Lutterbie. "Marxist Approaches to Teaching *A Doll's House*." *Approaches to Teaching Ibsen's* A Doll's House. Ed. Yvonne Shafer. New York: Modern Language Association, 1985. 76–80.

Deconstructing the Design Process:
Teaching Scene Design Process Through Feminist Performance Art

Raynette Halvorsen Smith

Introduction

Can a pencil really control a designer? A number of years ago when I was a design student, a teacher had our class do an exercise which seemed to demonstrate that it can. We were to begin sketching a preliminary design idea in the same manner we had done many times before in our training—with only one difference—he would provide the drawing instruments. In the first exercise we were given a very sharp hard-leaded pencil. What emerged were very detailed and delicate designs. When we were handed large markers, bold and dramatic drawings emerged. With each successive drawing tool we used there was not only a dramatic change in the drawing technique employed, but a dramatic shift in the design idea expressed in the sketch.

The intent of this drawing exercise was to broaden our available repertory of drawing techniques. But it also became a startling demonstration on the extent to which technique could and was shaping the content of our design work; the pencil was controlling the designer to a much greater extent than we had imagined.

As a scenic designer and a teacher of scenic designers, I find it increasingly more difficult to ignore the extent to which the process and technique of design controls what can or cannot be expressed on stage. The newly emerging focus on process demonstrated outside of theatre, in venues such as performance and installation art, challenge the unspoken assumptions about the process of designing scenery—and how this process should be taught.

Unlike the visual arts, the fundamental technique and process for the design and production of scenery has not significantly changed for close to a hundred years. As most widely practiced, the scenic design process has become frozen, steeped in tradition—tradition so pervasive that we have become blind to it. While scenery has taken on the veneer of style changes in "looks" borrowed from other disciplines such as architecture, painting, and sculpture, at its core it has remained unchanged since the practices outlined early in the century by Craig, Appia, and Robert Edmond Jones.

It is interesting to note that most of avant-garde theatre practitioners in this century stripped away scenography, or indeed eliminated it entirely; Grotowski "gave it back" to the painters and sculptors to create his Poor Theatre. Artaud dismissed scenery as "decoration," preferring the more kinetic qualities of light and props for his "spectacles." It is as though the practice of scenography had become so rigid that it had to be totally obliterated to build a "new theatre."

The failure to reassess critically the process in which scenery is conceived and produced has retarded the evolution of the art. The underlying assumptions that have marginalized the role of process can be seen in the methods by which designers are trained in this country. These methods assume that the creative act has three distinct and separate components: technique, process, and content.

Customarily, technique refers to the specific skills required to achieve a desired effect (rendering, drafting, model building, etc.). Process is viewed as the way those skills are strung together—how an artist works (production meetings with preliminary sketches and so forth). And finally, content is the artistic intent or message of a work contained in the finished design (the "concept"). We regard technique and process largely as though they were neutral—detached from the content of scenic art. We give the design student the "tools" of technique and process which he or she can supposedly take away to "construct" his or her own art. Student work is criticized in terms of "what works" and "doesn't work," to avoid treading on the student's "right" to control content.

The manner in which the design is realized also puts these assumptions about a neutral process into practice. Consider the simple element of time. We approach collaboration as ritual. We play out our well rehearsed roles with good reason. It is all a designer can do to try to meet the deadlines and to stay in budget, much less rethink the entire process by which these goals are to be accomplished. However, the pressure of hurdling through the design process to opening night narrows the scope of what can be created. The time component of process acts to control the content of the work in ways that are not overtly intended. Sure, we all know we could have done something more or different "if only there was a little more time." We do not think to challenge the lack of time built into our process as a form of censorship, that these methods might routinely exclude certain types of artistic expression in scenic art.

The most dangerous implications of our unconscious process are far more subtle. They are dangerous to the art of scene design because they can escape the designer's attention and function to undermine the intended content of the work. Unconscious process is dangerous to the teaching of scene design because it denies the political content inherent in artistic process by treating it as neutral. The denial of political content in process acts to covertly censor and marginalize some forms of individual artistic expression. To look at how traditional design process can privilege some artistic voices while censoring others, to uncover the assumptions of traditional design process so they can be openly confronted by the artist (and the student) requires a shift in critical strategy, a deconstruction of the design process.

Deconstruction

The term "Deconstruction," as used here, refers to an adaptation of the critical approach first developed by French philosopher Jacques Derrida. It is most familiar in the form in which it has been most widely applied, in literary criticism. In an essay entitled "Deconstruction, Postmodernism and the Visual Arts," Christopher Norris explains some of the key aspects of Derrida's complex theory as they relate to the visual arts: "To 'deconstruct' a text is to draw out conflicting logics of sense and implication, with the object of showing that the text never means what it says or says what it means." He further explains that to deconstruct is to read texts "very much against the grain of their overt meaning and intentions" (7).

In this context, to deconstruct the design process means reviewing it "against the grain" of "overt meanings or intentions," in search of embedded "unconscious" intentions or meanings. Once these unconscious meanings have been teased out from the camouflage of traditional practice, their impact upon design work can be assessed and a reconstruction of different processes can be explored that will serve new kinds of artistic expression.

One way to look at traditional scenic design process "against the grain" is to locate a contrasting process. Feminist performance art is one of the most, if not the most, radical movements in the arts in this century, yet it is closest to theatre in its form. However, the processes used in creating performance art are in many ways polar opposite of the methods used in theatrical collaboration. The symbiotic relationship between the content of feminist performance art and the process of its creation underlines the importance of a critical look at the contribution process makes to the meaning of art.

The intended content of much feminist performance art would be neutralized by grafting on traditional theatrical design process. Such a comparison reveals the real danger of separating design process as neutral and separate from design content—its potential to marginalize, or worse, silence and oppress some types of artistic expression, while privileging others in spite of overt intentions to the contrary. Traditional scenic design practice teaches indifference to the philosophical and political meanings embedded in the way designers work.

The Text as "Authority" versus the Self as Text

The traditional—and current—design process in theatre starts with the script. In theatrical collaboration, the script is viewed as the source of "truth," the authority for the production. The scenic designer's function is to serve the script in a tradition that dates back to Edward Gordon Craig and Adolph Appia. Craig wrote, "It is idle to talk about the distraction of scenery, because the question here is not how to create some distracting scenery, but rather how to create a place which harmonizes with the thoughts of the poet" (22). In America Robert Edmond Jones took this idea further when he stated that, "If the designer's work has been good, it disappears from our consciousness ..." (27) and, "Get the personal *you* out of your work, who cares about *you?*" (41). The ideal then is performance and scenography amalgamated into a seamless whole supporting the script.

Designers have been complaining about this role of servitude to the text ever since, although to little avail. For example, in 1940 Mordecai Gorelik commented, "Current dramatic reviews and books on drama are overwhelmingly concerned with the playscript alone. In practice the fundamental belief is simply that dramatic production exists to illustrate a story written by a dramatist...." (17). In his book *The Stage Is Set*, designer Lee Simonson complains that the progress of theatre must wait upon the dramatist: "In the modern theatre, as in every other, the beginning is in the word" (464).

In view of this tradition of privileging the script, it comes as no surprise that a new theatrical form, one that favors the visual over the textual, emerged from outside of the theatre, born instead as a reaction against constraints in painting and sculpture. From its beginning, feminist performance art has stood as the antithesis of Jones's ideal of the designer's subservience to the larger vision of the poet, with the words often coming after visual imagery or music, or sometimes not at all.

Performance art emerged in the 1960s concurrently with the women's movement. Early feminist political protest—the 1968 demonstrations against the Miss America Pageant, bra burning—was not conceived as performance art but surely served as a model for such early performances. As Moira Roth points out in *The Amazing Decade: Women in Performance Art in America 1970–1980*, through activities such as consciousness-raising, women "individually explored and collectively validated the substance of their lives" (16). She goes on to state, "As early feminists recognized that what had previously been designated (and, accordingly, often dismissed) as merely individual experience was, in actuality, an experience shared by many others, they developed the concept that 'the personal *is* the political'" (16). Quite the opposite of Jones's "Who cares about *you?*"

The "authority" and the "truth" of the poet as envisioned by Craig are also directly challenged by the feminist insistence on sexual difference. If we accept that experience as a female in this culture is quite different from that of a male's, this difference can no longer be denied under the pretense of a unified "mankind." If there is no gender-neutral "mankind," then on what is concept of production "unity" based?

It would seem that an easy solution to this problem of sexual difference could be found in the emergence of the feminist playwright. However, occupying the position of the poet, as "the authority," as a vessel for "universal truth," while attacking that role neutralizes the feminist playwright's argument. The very form of her attack from the position of "the authority" is contradicting the content of her work, which stands in defiance of that authority.

In autobiographical performance art, which has encompassed much feminist work, the performer is the subject; the words are hers, the representation is directly of herself, and the environment in which she performs is of her own making or choosing. Colleagues in theatre have criticized this focus on the self in feminist performance art as "self-indulgent" and "idiosyncratic." However, the performer can also be viewed as brutally honest about the limits of the "truth" she can present. Performance art, founded in its denial of traditional art forms, is claiming no "universal aesthetic." The singular voice of the performance artist does not correspond with the singular voice of the playwright. She claims no "unified truth" or authority, but only the expression of the immediate reality of her experience.

Theatre of the "Dominant Idea" versus Theatre of "Undecidability"

After analyzing the script, the next step in the traditional theatrical design process involves the director. In the twentieth century the growing independence of the director has made it possible for a production to take on a personal stamp. Thus has emerged, dating back to Craig and Jones, the "theatre of the dominant idea" (Walton 102). The director's "concept" for the production serves to coordinate all the aspects of the production, acting, costumes, scenery, lighting, and sound, into a unified whole. So the set designer's work must not only "harmonize with the thoughts of the poet," but also with the director and all other members of the artistic collaboration. We have long believed that this unity in look gives a production its coherence. Traditionally, one the hallmarks of a poor design is that it disrupts the unity of the production.

In performance art, unity gives way to a quality that Henry Sayre has labeled *undecidability*. Rather than strive for a unified whole,

> … meanings are explosive, ricocheting and fragmenting throughout its audience. The work becomes a situation, full of suggestive potentialities, rather than a self-contained whole, determined and final. (7)

> If pluralism can be defined as the many possible, but more or less equal, "solutions" which arise in answer to a particular aesthetic situation or crisis, undecidability is the condition of conflict and contradiction which presents no possible "solution" or resolution. (xiii)

Examples of this quality can be seen in the work of performance artist Karen

Finley. Everything in her performance seems calculated to keep the audience in a state of imbalance and uncertainty. In a piece entitled *We Keep Our Victims Ready*, she enters and starts to greet the audience, then announces she must leave to go to the bathroom, blurring our understanding of when the performance actually begins. She is costumed in sexy lingerie, but immediately mocks this seductive image by pouring jello into the bra. Each image she presents is a contradiction; the "candles" she lights on a birthday cake are actually little American flags. She begins reciting her poetry in a deep trance-like state, but is interrupted by the slightest cough or sniffle in the audience. Then she interacts with her audience by throwing candy and T-shirts. During the performance I attended at the Sushi Performance Gallery, a fight broke out in the street below the performance space. She went to a window and screamed at the participants. Visibly upset, she then left, ending the performance. The ending was as blurred as the beginning.

Harmony was definitely not the goal of this performance. In fact it was attacked whenever it appeared. We were constantly sent conflicting messages: Woman as sex object/not sex object, the candies were props/not props, the actions were real/not real, and so on. This is a direct attack on the notion of "universal truth" and authority assumed by artistic homogeneity. Finley's thesis is that the patriarchal system is disintegrating, "And that's the reason why these people are very fearful of us." "These people" have recently included the National Endowment of the Arts who attempted to cancel her grant, underlining how threatening her attack on the traditional aesthetic order can be perceived to be.[1]

Aesthetic Harmony versus Collage

Returning to the theatrical design process, in the next step after collaborating with the director, the designer starts sketching to find a "look" or style to reflect the director's concept. Once again the goal is to unify line, texture, color, and mass to harmonize with *the idea*.

In contrast, in feminist performance art the visual effect sought is more closely allied with collage, directly challenging the harmony implied in "taste." As Donald B. Kuspit states,

> Taste involves keeping a restraint on technique, insisting that only the traditional media are sure sources of art. Collage destroys the very idea of a medium, of any one "pure" mode of art. With collage, art is nowhere and everywhere; it becomes a freewheeling way of dealing with random material, emblematic of fragmented experience. (140–41)

Performance artist Laurie Anderson's work is self-consciously interdisciplinary and utilizes the technique of collage. In her piece entitled *United States*, she combined projected hand-drawn pictures, blown-up photographs taken from TV screens, and truncated film forming huge projected backdrops. Anderson used a vocal synthesizer to change her voice to that of a robot's.

Every image was appropriated and manipulated in a creative process that had a deliberate political intent. Notes Kuspit:

> The collage replaces privilege with equivalence, definitions of artistic being with deconstructions of artistic becoming, unity with energy. (130)

> The difference between collage and contemporary attitudes about appropriation is that in collage the force of the collision between high art and low remains oppositional. Rhetorically, it seems reasonable to use words such as "undermines," "subverts," or even "deconstructs" in order to describe how, in collage, the intrusion of mass culture operates upon the site of high art. (Sayre 20)

The Military or Industrial Model of Process versus the Ensemble

Another factor dramatically affecting the design process in traditional theatre is the organization of the artistic staff. It is no accident that this organizational structure closely parallels that of the military and industry. The idea behind this kind of hierarchical structure is to fuse the energy of the many into a singular concentrated force. In the military, any show of individuality is considered a breakdown in discipline. This is echoed in theatre practice where any detection of separate individual artistic expression in the production product is considered a threat to the "willful suspension of disbelief," a distraction that weakens the impact of the performance.

The organization of the theatre staff also resembles the industrial model. The term "design process" carries within it the implication of a design product. The process mimics that of commercial production; the playwright initiates the "product blueprints" (i.e., the script), which are then interpreted and refined by the director and subsequently the designers, and sent to the shops to be built. The scenery then becomes finalized in the process of technical and dress rehearsals into a product. Although performance in theatre is dynamic, it is objectified in its repetition. Each theatrical performance strives to duplicate an accurate rendition of opening night, when the process has been deemed to have reached completion.

In contrast, a characteristic of performance art has been the adamant denial of the product, or object in art. Visual artists consciously turned to the "theatricality" of performance to abandon the idea of the static art object. In presenting the art object as a relic from the artistic period labeled modernism, Henry Sayre has stated:

Theatricality may be considered that propensity in the visual arts for a work to reveal itself within the mind of the beholder as something other than what it is known empirically to be. This is precisely antithetical to the modern ideal of the wholly manifest, self-sufficient object; and theatricality may be the single most pervasive property of post-modern art. (20)

In performance art, the meaning of a work is not viewed as a stable commodity. Art-as-object reflects a belief in empirical reality the performance artist seeks to undermine. The belief in an empirical reality is opposed by feminists as representing a commitment to patriarchal reality. Absolute reality is seen now as a set of positions; objectivity traded for subjectivity. Karen Finley's performance, by design, is never quite finished; it is perpetually in process and will never be duplicated in exactly the same way twice.

The Watching Audience versus the Witnessing Collective

The same quest for universality that acts to homogenize the production team in theatre is reflected in the designer's treatment of the audience. The introduction of electrical stage lighting left the audience sitting in the dark so as not to distract from the reality the designer was painting with light on stage. The privileging of the singular viewpoint in the unified production assumes an objective reality that will be received directly by a homogeneous audience. This denies not only the plurality of the theatrical collaboration, but of the audience as well.

Early feminist performance art occurred outside of the conventional theatre. A close relationship with a mostly female audience was critical to the confessional quality of autobiographical performance. As each new performance space was explored—parks, streets, galleries, homes, to name just a few—a different performer-audience relationship was also discovered similar to street theatre and happenings. The small group of supportive individuals was a critical component of these performances; they were an integral part of the piece. The quality of "witnessing" in autobiographical performance art would be lost on a lighted stage in front of the masses sitting in darkness.

Conclusion

By now, it must seem that I am advocating the replacement of the current theatrical collaborative design process with the process of performance art. Certainly much of the traditional process I have been examining has already been challenged in the theatrical avant-garde by artists such as Artaud, Grotowski, and Schechner. The point is not replacement but rather careful consideration. We have a responsibility to ourselves as artists and to our students as developing artists to consider the meanings, philosophical and political, embedded in the methods we use to create. I do not advocate the total abandonment of the traditional design process, but only to treat it in our own art and in our teaching of design as one process among a multiplicity of existing and possible processes.

I realize this is a risky business. Our students may learn to deconstruct and resist the design processes we present to them. This reaction places the teacher in a new position—the position of having consciously to locate his or her personal relationship to the art, and to overtly convey this position to the students so that they can sort out its personal relevance (or irrelevance) to themselves. To do this the teacher must represent him- or herself as an idiosyncratic individual rather than the "authority" on "the truth." This postmodernist strategy is challenging when the forms and processes of the institutions in which we must work (both theatre and higher education) are still very modernist. However, if we are to give more than lip service to "cultural diversity" and "cultural democracy," then our techniques and processes must be revisited along with the content of our theatre art.

Note

1. One could argue that Karen Finley is her own director, and that there is a unity of production centered around her body. This is true, but there are important differences. She certainly directs her actions, but so do the environment and the audience. Because she does not rehearse, we are also left with the undecidablity of how much of the performance is under her control.

Works Cited

Craig, Edward Gordon. *On the Art of the Theatre*. New York: Theatre Arts Books, 1957.

Fox, Howard N. *Metaphor: New Projects by Contemporary Sculptors (Acconci, Armajani, Aycock, Ewing, Morris, Oppenheim)*. Washington, D.C.: Hirschhorn Museum and Sculpture Garden, Smithsonian Institution Press, 1982. Cited in Henry M. Sayre, *The Object of Performance*. Chicago: U of Chicago P, 1989: 9.

Gorelik, Mordecai. *New Theatres for Old*. London: Dennis Dobson, Ltd., 1940.

Jones, Robert Edmond. *The Dramatic Imagination*. New York: Theatre Arts Books, 1941.

Kuspit, Donald B. "Collage: The Organizing Principle of Art in the Age of the Relativity of Art." *Relativism in the Arts*, ed. Betty Jean Craige. Athens: U of Georgia P, 1983.

"The NEA Five." *New York Times*. 22 July 1990, H5+.

Norris, Christopher, and Andrew Benjamin. *What Is Deconstruction?* New York: St. Martin's Press, 1988.

Roth, Moira, ed. *The Amazing Decade: Women and Performance Art in America 1970–1980*. Los Angeles: Astro Artz, 1983.

Sayre, Henry M. *The Object of Performance*. Chicago: University of Chicago Press, 1989.

Simonson, Lee. *The Stage Is Set*. New York: Harcourt, Brace & Company, 1932.

Walton, J. Michael, ed. *Craig on Theatre*. London: Methuen, 1983.

East Decodes West:
Russian Formalism and the New American Dramaturgy—Critical Theory to Creative Process

Paul C. Castagno

I.

For the past five years I have been studying the dramaturgies of the playwrights Mac Wellman, Len Jenkin, and, to a somewhat lesser extent, Eric Overmyer and Connie Congdon. These four playwrights are significant since they offer new dramaturgical approaches to the art and craft of dramatic writing. Through analyses of their plays, I have been able to establish certain working paradigms that I have then applied in the teaching of advanced playwriting courses. Moreover, my "action research" in the new dramaturgy informs the criticism and literature courses that I teach.[1] In fact, these models are construed out of necessity, since the litany of playwriting texts unhappily persists in the Aristotelian mold, even as playwriting's "cutting edge" defies and redefines "what constitutes a play?"

In theatre practice, "action research" is a kind of problem solving in which research is directly applied to meet an immediate need within a specific context. Addressing a lack in the practitioner's skill, experience, or even methodology, action research utilizes interdisciplinary approaches to tackle short-term problems cogently and decisively. Thus, it is particularly apposite to the classroom, where the instructor must meet the ever increasing demands of a diverse, multicultural curriculum, or in performance, where a particular style may cease to be effective when circumstances change. For instance, a director who continually works with inexperienced actors has developed, perhaps from necessity, an autocratic style. Now commissioned to direct a group of equity professionals, she becomes conscious of the real need to alter her leadership style. This leads her to pursue an understanding of transactional analysis techniques which she applies successfully in the rehearsal process. In the development of a new play, the playwright and dramaturg are stymied by an unclear passage of text. An improvisational dance unlocks and clarifies what could not be verbalized, thus freeing the writer to a host of hitherto unseen possibilities. When applied as in the above examples, action research involves three basic steps: 1) the recognition of a real and immediate need; 2) an intuitive capacity which prompts the teacher or artist to appropriate ideas and practices from disciplines or sources not directly related to theatre; 3) the resultant opening of options and creative outcomes.

II.

I will demonstrate how appropriation of the critical theory, Russian Formalism, can provide the stimulus for creative applications. The basis of the methodology is the critical application of Russian Formalist terms and concepts to the language devices of the new dramaturgy. Once the student has an understanding of the working applications in various examples from the plays *Dark Ride*, *Albanian Softshoe*, *Tales of the Lost Formicans*, *On the Verge*, and others, a model is established that provides a foundation or point-of-departure for actual playwriting exercises.[2] These exercises are designed to "open" the playwright and dramaturg to new possibilities in structure, language, and character. For those more interested in theory and criticism, these paradigms can illuminate or unlock difficult critical concepts by providing these plays (or their parts) as exemplars of a particular device. In the more expansive and cross-cultural realm that now serves the larger need of diversifying the curriculum, these exercises demonstrate the value of a meeting between East and West, between proto-revolutionary Russian literary theories and the cutting-edge American playwriting practices found in an increasing number of non-canonized playtexts. In the process of decoding the contemporary, we are translating the arcane past anew, refreshing a difficult modern theory in its fusion with that which is seemingly so postmodern.

While each of the above playwrights has developed a distinctive voice, some overall characteristics are evident. Generally, there is no sense of narrative linearity as is common to most realistic drama. Mac Wellman's Obie Award winning play, *Sincerity Forever*, repeats entire interactions word for word through the voices of different characters. Len Jenkin's *Dark Ride* challenges the spectator to situate the story line within a multilayered, constantly shifting structure. In both cases, textual devices reorient our focus and involvement away from the narrative. In her article, *Presence and the Revenge of Writing: Re-thinking Theatre after Derrida,* Elinor Fuchs posits that, "Like a moebius strip, *Dark Ride*'s frame and framed narratives cannot be logically distinguished, and the conventional distinction between performance and text is unsettled as the performance draws its textuality to our attention" (Fuchs 168).

In another sense, rather than motivationally-oriented character choices causally related to plot structure, the new dramaturgy disrupts continuity through spontaneous language shifts that alter the world of the play: through historical time as in Overmyer's *On the Verge* or Jenkin's *My Uncle Sam*; through interstellar space in Wellman's *Albanian Softshoe* and *Whirligig*; by creating worlds within worlds as in Len Jenkin's *Dark Ride* or *New Jerusalem*; or through the bifurcation of character-identity as in Congdon's *Tales of the Lost Formicans*; and the transformations between characters and objects as in *Tallahassee*, a collaborative effort written by Wellman and directed by Jenkin, which was created and performed in December 1991 at the Atlantic Center of the Arts. *Tallahassee* offers some extraordinary transformations as characters turn into vegetation, lawn furniture, parking lots, and musical notes.

The new dramaturgy inverts the Aristotelian hegemony whereby character determines diction. In these plays, diction routinely controls or determines character choices. In *On the Verge*, three nineteenth-century women travelers speak not from individual choice but by osmosing (involuntarily) the future:

> **MARY:** Something else is happening, obviously. Something even more astonishing. Not only are we advancing in time, not only are we encountering the future with every stepC(Beat) Ladies, we are beginning to know the future! (Beat) It is entering into our consciousness. Like mustard gas. Whatever that is. Wait a moment. I'll tell you. (She osmoses.) Oh. Oh. Oh. Unfortunate simile. I withdraw it.
> **ALEX:** We are absorbing the future! Through osmosis! (I.13:36)

This "osmosed future" is in the form of a language, external to the historical context, which literally propels characters through time. Language is clearly not internally motivated, nor can it be seen as an "imitation of an action" from real life. Moreover, Overmyer's use of language obscures character individuation— who is saying is incidental compared to what is being said, or to the affective poetic rhythm, or to the strangeness of language without context. Overmyer defines his use of language as neoclassical in the sense of being rarefied and removed from the quotidian (New Directions Panel 2). Similarly, Mac Wellman's iterative devices in *Sincerity Forever* remove the possibility of character-specific dialogue, a dictum of traditional dramaturgy. As a result, the rhetorical as well as the psychological determinants of character are absent. Wellman's "take" on character is worth quoting:

> One of the most striking features of American dramaturgy is the notion of "rounded" character. This creature of theatrical artifice with its peculiarly geometric—nay! symmetrical—aspect is so like an object from a math textbook; and one finds it so frequently on stage (and nowhere else) that I have dubbed it the Euclidean Character. Every trait of the Euclidean Character must reveal an inner truth of the same kind about the personality in question; each trait must be perfectly consonant with every other trait. (Wellman 1984 62)

As an antidote to the character-centered "theatre of good intentions," Wellman counters in the preface to the anthology, *Theatre of Wonders*, that from the perspective of the new dramaturgy the "vision of drama comes first of all from language creating plays with a life inimitable, and not imitating" (Wellman 1985 x). Indeed, noteworthy for their ability to do things with words, these playwrights have been coined "the language playwrights" (Robinson 32, 33). Because of their emphasis on the autonomous properties of language and the use of non-motivational plot devices and treatment of character, I have chosen to critique the new dramaturgy with the techniques of Russian Formalism. While a useful critical theory, Russian Formalism is most often neglected in the critical curriculum, since it can be most difficult for students to grasp,[3] particularly if the instructor is unable to provide relevant, cogent, and on the spot applications. Similarly, the practices of the new dramaturgy might seem gratuitous or impenetrable if not seen in Formalist terms. At the 1991 ATHE Conference in Seattle, Paula Vogel, playwriting instructor at Brown University, indicated to me that Eric Overmyer, Mac Wellman, and she consciously applied the techniques of Viktor Shklovsky, one of the founders of the Russian Formalist School, in a playwriting workshop they formed in New York during the late 1970s. Eric Overmyer corroborated his debt to Formalism in a recent missive to me, describing *ostranenie* (see below) by saying "I think it explains what I'm trying to do."

Historically, the Formalists addressed the deviant and innovative aspects of language as *la critica moda*, particularly in regard to the transrational language of Italian Futurist Poetry (Matejka 9). Russian Formalism emerged in the first two decades of this century as part of the same pre-revolutionary ferment in Russia that had spawned Kandinsky's creations in painting and Meyerhold's in the theatre. Like the Formalists, both Kandinsky, who is widely recognized as the father of abstract painting, and Meyerhold, who sought an autonomous theatrical language, shared the central notion that the arts must *not* be contingent upon a representational or referential one-to-one relationship with real life.[4] In 1915–16 the Russian Formalist movement became widely recognized with "the founding of The Moscow Linguistic Circle and the Petersburg Society for the Study of Poetic Language (*Opojaz*)." Roman Jakobson was most influential in the Moscow group, as were Victor Shklovsky and Boris Eichenbaum in the Petersburg contingent. Although the movement persisted into the early twenties, the leaders of the new Soviet state demanded a literature (socialist realism) that would reflect the orthodox values of the state. As a result the Formalist movement splintered into various camps, the directions taken by Bakhtin and Jakobson being most notable. Eventually, many of the tenets of Russian Formalism were assimilated and modified by the Prague Structuralists. Thus, from the standpoint of an instructor in critical theory, Russian Formalism offers an excellent premise or point of entry into the major movements of structuralism and semiotics.

Essentially, Russian Formalism is concerned with the means and functions of poetry rather than theme or interpretation. Formalists isolate the "artfulness" and articulatory aspects of poetry from its relationships to history, political backgrounds, or biographical influences—focusing solely on the literary qualities, or "literariness," of a given work. Literariness is best articulated through devices that "create interest through *defamiliarization* and in the literary devices that succeed one another as each successful mode of literary structure becomes stale." Indeed, "such an emphasis on the importance of structural devices undercuts the importance of characterization, the characters themselves being simply devices." The project of Russian Formalism is to focus upon aspects of an individual work or the relationships between works[5]—foregoing a set methodology that attempts to classify and generalize (Matejka 4). These limited aims of Russian Formalism result from its pre-eminent concern with the idiosyncratic devices in the literary work. Thus, Russian Formalism defines the ends or functions of literature as within the work itself, rather than as an improvement of the individual, society, or the emphasis of some thematic value.[6]

III.

Several Formalist techniques and characteristics are evident in the particular plays. The primacy of "poetic language" celebrates its autonomous qualities over language that serves as a means of communication (practical language) (Matejka 14). Poetic language may function to foreground sound value (the articulatory aspects of words) by emphasizing the rhythmical or alliterative function and arrangement of words into "phrase units" (Matejka 10). Krystyna Pomorska "insists that the works of the Opojaz scholars eloquently show that their interest was focused upon the nature of sound and sound patterns in literature" (Pomorska 27). Nowhere is articulatory foregrounding more apparent than in Act I of Connie Congdon's *Tales of the Lost Formicans*. Within the frame of a short French scene the speech patterns of the characters echo the transrational, linguistic strategies of the Futurists:

> **CATHY:** (To herself) Cha-erks mumrf geentrats. Dog eyem ho.
> **JUDY:** Kab ti kate dluk I heewa I.
> **CATHY:** Tner-rerf-fid see eebyaim.
> **JUDY:** ?Tuff tawn me eem illet ooya nak. Tuff eelatote my. Tuff my.
> **CATHY:** To touba eerow tnode. (I.4)

Shklovsky suggested that "the enjoyment of the meaningless transrational word, the articulatory side, a sui generis *dancing of the speech organs,* causes most of the enjoyment of poetry." (Pomorska 30) Congdon's linguistic strategy defamiliarizes the word as signifier both visually and phonetically, whereby signified "meaning" and sense of narrative are momentarily erased.

Some of the anomalies of the new dramaturgy can be approached through the Formalist device of *ostranenie*—or "making strange" (Medvedev and Bakhtin 61). *Ostranenie*, which influenced Brecht's concept of alienation, suggests a dislocation in agreement, function, or context such as, between the word and object as in Overmyer's *On the Verge*. The result of this "deautomization of the word" is its "abstraction from semantic context"; it forces the spectator to see, not to know (Medvedev and Bakhtin 62). In *On the Verge,* everyday objects such as eggbeaters are transformed both functionally and historically in a virtuoso play between the object's expected and actual use:

> (They hold up their artifacts, including the egg beaters and buttons.
> FANNY and ALEX have been wearing their egg beaters like pistols.)
>   [three lines later at the end of the scene]
> (FANNY and ALEX rotor at one another.) (II.14:41,42)

A moment earlier, the act of naming objects is undermined as descending objects, described as "fallout from the future," are labeled in bizarre and unfitting ways (II.14:40). Overmyer's self-conscious use of *ostranenie* as the "dominant" language and formal device of *On the Verge* continues as Cool Whip conflates with Noxema:

> **MARY:** Hello, what's this? Manioc? (She takes a spoonful of Cool Whip.)
> **ALEX:** Noxema.
> **MARY:** Have you tried it? (She smears some on her face.)
> **ALEX:** Mmm. The texture is indescribable.
> **MARY:** (Takes a big bite—savors) Why this is sheer heaven, Alexandra. (II.20:64)

At times, the arbitrary relation between word and object is demonstrated in a more mundane albeit informative manner; for instance, Fanny insists that cream cheese is neither cream nor cheese (I.5:13). Ultimately, Overmyer's comic defamiliarization of objects replaces the need for or the possibility of continuity and closure, and assumes a "form-quality" of its own—one which substitutes for plot in the traditional sense of a linear, conflict-driven action. In *On the Verge* the accumulation of devices creates the work:

> **MARY:** Terra Incognita, by definition, could not be otherwise. I have a theory. One that explains the unknown objects. The *strange words in our mouths*. The *references to persons unknown* that spring to mind. Spring to mind. It is spring in our mind ladies. A New World! Blossoming! Within and without! ... Not—as we usually do in savage lands, moving backward into the past, into pre-history—but forward, into the future! A New World, within and without! Beckoning! [italics mine] (I.13:35)

Perhaps, Overmyer's "Terra Incognita" becomes a kind of metatheatrical assertion of an "inimitable" theatrical world, one "beckoning" toward future experimentation in the possibilities of language for the stage.

Overmyer uses the technique of *ostranenie* to create a special perception about a thing, to promote a new way of distancing over-familiar recognition. In *Tales of the Lost Formicans*, Congdon splits characters into human/aliens, allowing the audience to "see" rather than recognize the absurdity of much human behavior. By utilizing this double-identity Congdon focuses our attention on the "strangeness" we take for granted in our everyday lives:

> **CATHY/ALIEN:** The cushions of the chair are covered in a substance made to mimic the epidermis of the sitter, but treated to hold a sheen which is kept polished by friction of the buttocks against the surface. The significance of the hole in the backrest is unknown to us at this time. It was, perhaps, symbolic: a breathing hole for the spirit of the sitter, or even the ever-present eye of God. (I:1)

The alien "other" allows us to "see" the chair beyond its limited function, offering an example of the theatre's capacity to transform the mundane object into an object of fascination and wonder.[7]

The alien's wondrous way of seeing things anew is part of the delight of *Formicans*, and a measure of Congdon's distinctive theatrical voice.[8] But for those playwrights whose voices may be rutted in the prosaic mode, the following exercise is helpful in opening the semiotic and imaginative possibilities inherent in the device of *ostranenie*.

Examples:

> Read Congdon's *Tales of the Lost Formicans*
> Read Overmyer's *On the Verge*

Playwriting Exercise:

1. Write a short monologue in which a character describes a common object as if for the first time. Character could be an alien, foreigner, child, one suffering from loss of memory and so on.
2. Or like Overmyer's characters, they might arrive from another historical period—time travelers.
3. Imbue the object with talismanic qualities.
4. Posit the opposite to generally recognized value or function.
5. Describe the negative space created by the shape of the object.
6. Attempt to address the "whyness" of the design in imaginative and transcendent language.

In a classroom or workshop setting it may be helpful for the playwright to conceal the identity of the "described" object. Only after the monologue is read do other participants attempt to identify the object described. In this sense, everyone's imaginative resources are focused and even stretched. Since the responses are "right-sided" rather than critical, this exercise can work wonders in bringing a positive, relaxed atmosphere to a workshop or classroom situation.

IV.

A Formalist audience from experiencing a sense of closure or continuity by short-circuiting the cause and effect mechanisms that characterize traditional dramaturgy. By impeding the linear narrative flow the synchronic moment of perception is foregrounded. At this point, the understanding of what is familiar or recognizable is hampered, or better, it is challenged. For spectators nurtured on the comfortable conventions of traditional forms, which allow for tracking a discoverable narrative or the peripeties of character development, the challenges of the new dramaturgy can be problematical—even insurmountable. Yet, Shklovsky averred, and Wellman would attest, that "the perception of art manifests not the law of least effort but the law of maximal effort" (Steiner 50). (As an instructor of a Wellman play you may wish to repeat that statement often to the class, as a means of inspiring recalcitrant students to overcome their resistance or apathy to a dramaturgy which at times seems impenetrable).

For spectators and critics who attended the world premiere of Wellman's *Albanian Softshoe* at the San Diego Repertory Theatre, the arbitrary character and plot shifts brought a number of negative responses (Schoen). While Wellman's stage directions clarify his intentions for the reader, spectators had to wait and struggle through the beginning of the second act for the crucial discovery:

> Nightfall on Iapetus, the eighth moon of Saturn. The ringed planet is visible in the distance. Applause for the puppet show. OLD WOMAN bows. The puppets bow. Their little theatre is a miniature replica of the first act set. The puppets are miniature versions of the characters presented there. So, Act One has been a show for the amusement of the characters of Act Two, the dwellers of the ice-moons. (23)

By compelling the audience to perceive Act One as a puppet show Wellman impedes narrative continuity. The developments of characters and situations experienced in Act One's suburban setting are severed at the act curtain. Act Two opens with a group of alien misfits commenting on the show they have just seen (Act One), in which the apparently normative "human" characters, from our perspective, are now reduced to puppet caricatures. The metatheatrical *device* of the puppet show foregrounds the voyeuristic artifice at the core of theatrical experience. Yet, according to Walter Schoen, the production dramaturg for the world premiere of *Albanian Softshoe*, critics and audiences would not accept the dislocation between acts (Schoen). What had been "set up" for the "payoff" in traditional dramaturgical terms was impeded, forcing the audience to focus upon the *device* rather than the anticipated closure of content and form. Thus, for San

Diego audiences the sense of impeded form became a frustration, not a challenge, and a number of spectators demonstrated their outrage by exiting directly across the stage during the course of the second act.[9] (Perhaps, this may suggest that defamiliarizing strategies in theatre, unlike literature, embrace the fullest range of the performance to include the audiences' spontaneous egress across the stage during performance). While Wellman's theatrical goals may seem recondite, he asserts that his plays are "not an argument for obscurity or incomprehensible dramaturgy, but only a plea for recognition of the fact—long ago a truism in modern music and poetry—that each work of art is unique and must be allowed to take on a unique and expressive form" (Wellman 1984 64). Nevertheless, San Diego audiences were frustrated or even insulted by the device of impeded form, believing that Wellman had played them for dupes, or as the "butt of the joke," as Schoen lamented. Where clientele are accustomed to Wellman's work, at the Brass Tacks Theatre in Minneapolis or Primary Stages in New York, productions have generally been favorably received. Wellman's play, *The Murder of Crows*, which opened in Dallas during November (1991) and Primary Stages in the spring of 1992, actually confused critics by its move toward a more tractable narrative.

V.

The Formalist technique of *skaz* can be appropriated to suggest an approach to the actors' performance of the new dramaturgy, in this sense expanding the range of Russian Formalism to another element of the performance text. Supplanting the hegemony of Stanislaviskian "action theory" whereby the actor seeks to incorporate underlying objectives and obstacles as the heartbeat of the character's through-line, *skaz* promotes the narrator's manipulation of phrases and speech devices, thus shifting emphasis from the story to the narrator's style of presentation.[10] *Skaz* erases subtextual motivation by focusing the actor's intention upon the articulatory or rhythmical aspects of language, and to the gestic potential of words or phrase units. The texture and the surface of language "motivate" the choices of the performer, similar to the way in which variant sounds and audio feedback "motivate" the extrapolations of a rock guitarist. The technique of *skaz* can be particularly fruitful when applied to the monologic sections in the plays of Jenkin and Wellman, which require a distinctly non-method approach from the actor. Wellman posits that this may present some difficulty as "any writer who is produced with any frequency at all must sooner or later come to terms with the obdurate and implacable dogma of method acting" (Wellman 1985 65). In the appropriated sense that I am using the word, *skaz* can free the actor from the requirements of internal motivation, thus foregrounding autonomous artful or theatrical potentialities (Matejka 20, Bakhtin 182).

For instance, in Wellman's *Whirligig*, the external choices of delivery rather than her subtextual "action" provide a more positive means for the actor to establish the sense of a momentary evanescent world. Five pages into Scene One, two space travelers continue their conversation at a rural bus stop:

> **GIRL:** Girl-huns, ponies, night, sigh!
> > *pause*
> Murder, mayhem, slaughter of innocence, rock 'n roll. Death. Death, departure, pilgrimage, Mecca, Moluccas, sea-green. Robespierre, revolution, raunch, ranch, Ronald Rubout. Death, destruction, blast force, crater, lime pit, deathstar, wipeout....
> > *pause*
> Girl-huns, feathers, foxtails, spurs. (5)

In this monologic passage which proceeds for two more pages, Wellman uses the poetic technique of "nouning," whereby the serial juxtaposition of nouns creates new potential relations in our perception of language. The result describes what Wellman calls the "radioactive effect" of language. The metaphor aptly foregrounds not only the instability of language and meaning (see exercise below), but also focuses the spectator on the actor's choices of phrasing and articulation. Moreover, nouning in Wellman's *Whirligig* invokes a kind of inter-galactical voyage through language space as the Girl-Huns verbal pyrotechnics literally project the audience to distant planets (and other "places") far from the dreary bus station. An exemplar of what he describes as the language of gesture Wellman asserts the notion that, "particularly in the theatre, words should be objects flying around the room" (Wellman 1992 49):

> Scene 2: Aboard the spacecraft, the GIRL HUNS. We see only their eyes, They sing their songs and accompany themselves on plucked bowstrings
> **GIRL HUNS:** Turn our backs and forge ahead ... (repeat over and over and ...)
> **GIRL HUNS:** Plinth ... Mitake Mura, Dikan'ka, Elmer, Hektor, Doctor Spock, Roswitha, Pia, Wolfiana, Erda, Helio, 1935X, McCuskey, Wild, Whipple, Zu Chong-Zhi, Zulu, CrAO, Sy, Toro, Kacheuvskaya, Fanny, Voloshina, Wirt, Bistro, Scobee, Durer, Vondel, Niepce, Reddish, Karin, Kron, Goto, Tuulikki, 2009P-L, Sawyer Hogg, Thusnelda, Gorgo, Yrsa, Valeska, Hamburga, Vesta, Marlu, Winchester, Jole, Brunsia, Manto, Monachia, Hippo, ... Bonsdorffia, Shane, Shaposhnikov, Gondola, Fulvia, and mythic Grayways [name of bus company]
> The blackest of blackouts
> End of play (II.2:29)

The following exercises offer a point of entry into what may be unfamiliar dramaturgical territory. Since the impact of nouning is most noticeable in its articulatory aspect, this interactive exercise in dramaturgy should prove helpful.

Example: Read Wellman's *Whirligig*.

Dramaturgy Exercise:

1. Read aloud the above example of nouning.
2. How does nouning create the sense of travel or movement for the spectator? For the characters?
3. How is Wellman "making strange" by his juxtaposition of proper names such as Doctor Spock, Zulu, Hamburga, with other more or less acceptable space names? How are words affected by their proximity to other words?
4. What effect does word juxtaposition and proximity have on meaning within the play?

Playwriting Exercises:

1. Freely associate names that are associated with given rooms, spaces, or businesses, time periods, or cultural phenomena.
2. Use slogans as well as nouns.
3. Set a timer to four minutes and do not lift pen from paper during this word barrage.
4. Attempt to free the "self-censor"—any tendency to censor your writing. This is a free-writing exercise.

Variation: Allow characters in a scene you are now working on to associate freely in the above fashion.

a) How does this practice inform your writing?
b) Does it open the characters' voices in any way?

The nouning exercises are attempts to free the student from normative syntactical choices. Indeed, that much of our daily life is consumed with lists, and nouning is really a dramaturgical activation of this impulse. Most rote learning is achieved through the memorization of facts on lists. Playwrights must continually strive to "do things with words." This exercise and the one that follows demonstrate how words can operate within narratives in an exciting, vital way. The playwright should not neglect the spatial effect nouning and proper names can have on the sensory imagination of the spectator.

VI.

While Wellman has been called "recklessly obscure," his syntactic strategies focus the presence of the text, creating language juxtapositions rather than what Marc Robinson calls "realism's laborious linearity"[11] (32). The new dramaturgy liberates language from realistic conventions such as exposition with its demands for "filling in" past events and offstage actions. As the need for motivational development becomes superfluous, character psychology and historicity are erased or rendered insignificant. Representational conventions are fractured in several ways; one motif common to Overmyer, Wellman, and Jenkin is the notion of "travel" (Robinson 33). So pervasive is this notion that it might constitute a new subgenre within the realm of the new dramaturgy—the journey play. For instance, the journey strategy in Len Jenkin's *Dark Ride* supplants linearity through the Formalist device of "content-in-form."[12] The play begins with a translator discussing his difficulties with a particular section of text:

> **TRANSLATOR** reads: "Margo lies back on the couch in her apartment and opens a book. She turns the pages slowly until she finds her place. Her lips move slightly with the words she reads, like a child […]"
> SCENE SHIFT: MARGO now appears, reading aloud: Chapter Nine.
> At the Clinic....

The scene at the hospital continues until MARGO reads aloud to her friend from a postcard sent by her absent lover, the THIEF. MARGO's utterance from the THIEF's postcard "outskirts of some city, for miles alongside highways" serves as a segue to the next scene. The phrase is repeated by the THIEF as the Scene shifts to the:

> Outskirts of some city, for miles alongside highways, feeding out into suburban streets, and I'm walking […] after three days on the road I figured I better […] I figured I better get inside somewhere, I figured I better eat something. I'm in America, coming into town […] O.K. Now I'm really hungry but it's a long way between neon, and then I see one coming, a red blur in the distance, and I see another one, and its a revolve, turning and turning, and it says THE EMBERS. We Never Close, So I Go in. I'm here. Jukebox. (Scene 2, 3, 4)

At this point a waitress appears and seats the Thief. The Thief has "called" the new scene into creation at the point when he says "THE EMBERS." A dramatized scene in dialogue form follows in a restaurant.

Instead of cause-and-effect linearity, the "form–quality" of the shifting narrative motivates the emergence of new content. "Content-in-form" is clearly foregrounded in *Dark Ride*. This is a radical shift from most realistic dramas in which the effect of form is recognized only at a subliminal level.[13] Jenkin notes to the director in the Dramatists Play Edition:

The director and performers should be aware that *Dark Ride* is a weave of tales, of scenes within scenes, like the facets of the diamond. That a scene is within a book, or a picture, or in someone's mind makes it no less "real" in terms of staging. The "real" point of view is a shifting one (47, 48).

Jenkin provides us with multiple narrators, whose dramaturgical functions are to "call" scenes into being or to intervene within active dramatic sections, in order to disrupt the action, and move the sequence elsewhere. After characters finish role-playing as narrators, they either return to the action, move to another area, or disappear altogether. Thus, each sequence of the action is literally wrapped within a given narrative, formal device. While this may appear complex and intricate, in practice it is really quite straightforward. In the exercise below we will explore the most prevalent of Jenkin's narrative techniques—"the call," or invocation—essential to understanding the concept of "content-in-form" in his playwriting. In the call, the narrator's function is twofold: 1) establish the basic story or subject matter of the play—usually from memory, dreams, or fantasy, 2) call forth the dramatized scene. The call occurs at the end of a narrated story or passage, and is generally positioned in the penultimate sentence or phrase of the speech. This placement allows the other characters to enter and assume actions while the narrator finishes the speech. At that point, the narrator either enters into the dramatic action, moves to another area of the stage, or exits the scene.

Example: Read Jenkin's *Dark Ride*

Playwriting Exercise:

1. Begin with two characters in a scene. One character picks up a letter, a postcard, a photograph, or painting of someone they are in relationship with, or have been in close emotional involvement with.
2. At the point where reference is made to the "other" character—the other appears at another place on the stage.
3. The character in (1) reads a direct quote from the "other" character, the last lines of which this other repeats, and the transition is made to the next sequence.
4. The first two characters disappear as the "other" enters a building, the house of a lover, a church or any other place depicted in the monologue. This narration represents the call for a new dramatized scene to begin.
5. Dramatized scene dissolves as new narrator character appears and returns to the characters in (1); we find that the scene just created was a fantasy or daydream in the character's mind.

Jenkin's use of proper-name signposts represents a predilection he shares with Mac Wellman for lists, proper names, and their combinatory powers. These referential markers transport the spectator through journeys of the imagination, while demonstrating to the reader one of the reasons Wellman and Jenkin have received acclaim as "language playwrights." Words serve a spatial and temporal function, language imbues the stage with protean characteristics.

VII.

While my analysis of these plays considers the new dramaturgy within the realm of Formalist aesthetics, I in no way wish to marginalize other approaches.[14] Chaos or complexity theory is helpful in understanding some of Wellman's devices, particularly iteration, which he uses extensively in *Sincerity Forever*. In an article in *New Theatre Quarterly*, I utilized Bakhtin's theory of dialogism to discuss its intervention in the monologic dramaturgy of both Wellman and Jenkin. In a larger sense, I have found the linguistic theory generally known as "Discourse Analysis" to be very helpful in teaching effective dialogue practices, better than the dialogue exercises to be found in the standard playwriting texts. Discourse analysis studies and unlocks the hidden codes of dialogue, allowing the strategies to be understood fully, then creatively applied. Rather than inhibiting the playwriting student with another "left-brain" theory, in practice I have found that exercises gleaned from discourse analysis now open the student to the affective strategies and performative qualities of dialogue, clearing away the transactional, psychological weight that labors so much dramatic writing. As such, the metacommunicative function of dialogue can be integrated and subsumed within the larger realm of dialogue practices. These discourse analysis strategies provide both the instructor and playwriting student with a different "take" on material, then enable a potential "move" through exercises and scene work, and lead ultimately to a new "tool" which enhances conceptualization skills and crafts[wo]manship.

The techniques of Russian Formalism can be helpful in unlocking some of the pervasive tendencies of the new dramaturgy, particularly when their present usage is modified somewhat toward specific applications. For instance, in the translation of Russian Formalist devices to new dramaturgical practice, specific terms such as "nouning" or the "call" emerge as helpful tools for critics, dramaturgs, and playwrights. As part of their mission, the Formalists had expressed an interest in the creation of novelty in texts throughout the history of literature. Shklovsky's famous principle of the "canonization of the junior branch" is most apposite to an assessment of the new dramaturgy:

> I'm interested in suggesting paths of inquiry, I don't think you can make
> a perfect play in a class, except by luck. I just try opening the doors to
> new kinds of writing. (Beeber 26)

Notes

1. As a Lilly teaching scholar in 1990–1991, I attended two national conferences in which the concept of action research was explored.

2. While these exercises are based upon the quotes or sections that precede them, it is preferable to read the entire play before attempting the exercise.

3. After I presented an earlier version of this paper at an ATHE Conference in Seattle, three instructors of critical theory lamented this fact to me.

4. Like Meyerhold, the Formalists initially supported the Bolsheviks' ascent to power, and the anticipation of experimentation in the arts. By the mid-twenties, however, most of the Formalists had rejected the official demands for social realism which posited a pro-proletarian message served up in a strictly realistic format. Autonomous art had been supplanted by committed art, or art with a political, pro-Soviet agenda.

5. The focus on aspects of the work distinguishes Formalism from the larger structuralist project which attempted to use language as the structural model applied to investigating other disciplines, to study the relations between elements in a given work, or to see structuralism as the unconscious activity of the mind. (Levi-Strauss) which consists of imposing forms upon content (Harris 379–80).

6. I am not using Michael Kirby's approach in *Formalist Theatre* since it ignores the historical foundations of Russian Formalism and makes little distinction between Formalism and structuralism.

7. The Prague Structuralists were the first to explicate the generative capacity of the theatrical sign. Bogatyrev posited that the same stage item stands for different signifieds depending on the context in which it appears. His colleague, Jindrich Honzl, determined that there were absolutely no fixed representational relations; any stage vehicle can stand, in principle, for any signified class of phenomena. See Keir Elam, *The Semiotics of Theatre and Drama* (London: Routledge, 1980) 12–13.

8. Perhaps the most culturally telling aspect of Congdon's "voice" in *Tales of the Lost Formicans* is evident in her treatment of male characters. The male characters are in effect rhetorical strategies of incoherence. Jim, the grandfather figure has had his memory "short-circuited" by the aliens, and suffers from Alzheimer's disease; Eric, 15, is rendered in terms of hostile profanities which he spouts relentlessly, and Jerry, about 30, is identified by

non-sequiturs, repeated "wows," and his subsequent fear of speaking. In this play, the male really becomes "other," defined by his inability to communicate with the women characters. Congdon offers no psychological "rounding" or dimension to her male characters.

9. According to Shoen the major exit was directly behind the stage area and thus the egress point for the most bold of the disenchanted spectators.

10. "Narrator" in the sense of a performer's extended direct address to the audience. The character's "frame" may be obscured by techniques such as "nouning" (see below).

11. Here, Robinson is positing the linear motivational development that coheres the structure of realistic plays. "Laborious" is used in the well-made play sense, whereby through the continual rehashing of well-worn plot lines, or techniques such as foreshadowing, plays are too often predictable or lifeless. In this sense, realism suggests the sense of structure.

12. Content-in-form posits that formal aspects are apparent rather than hidden. One is expected to "see" the artifice.

13. One needs only think of Freytag's cardiographic approach to playscript analysis, or to any number of prescriptive texts on playwriting which posit methodologies for constructing a play. The mastery of the craft, in those cases, means that the crafting should not be overtly apparent. Form is, in a sense, "backgrounded."

14. In fact, essentially formal devices such as Wellman's nouning could be considered as subversions of traditional dramaturgical formulae, thus carrying with them an implied, ideological disclaimer of traditional dramaturgical methodologies. The question of what makes a play, has been readily served up in a number of playwriting texts, almost all of which base technique on Aristotelian or 19th-century models. Implicit in the new dramaturgy is the re-addressing of this central question, what makes a play? I am currently working on a playwriting text (working title: Playwriting Techniques of the New Dramaturgy) that squares this question by opening up the possibilities of what playwriting can be.

Works Cited

Beeber, Neena. "Dramatis Instructus." *American Theatre*. January, 1990.

Castagno, Paul C. "Varieties of Monologic Strategy: The Dramaturgy of Len Jenkin and Mac Wellman." *New Theatre Quarterly* 9, 34.

Congdon, Constance. "Tales of the Lost Formicans," *American Theatre*. 1989.

Elam, Keir. *The Semiotics of Theatre and Drama*. London: Routledge, 1980.

Fuchs, Elinor. "Presence and the Revenge of Writing: Re-thinking Theatre after Derrida." PAJ. 1989.

Jenkin, Len. *Dark Ride*. New York: Dramatists Play Service, 1982.

————. *My Uncle Sam*. New York: Sun & Moon Press, 1986.

Kirby, Michael. *Formalist Theatre*. Philadelphia: U of Pennsylvania P, 1987.

Matejka, Ladislav, and Krystyna Pomeroska. *Readings in Russian Poetics*. Ann Arbor: U of Michigan P, 1978.

Medvedev, P. N., and M. Bakhtin. *The Formal Method in Literary Scholarship*. Baltimore: The Johns Hopkins UP, 1978.

Overmeyer, Eric. *On the Verge or the Geography of Learning*. New York: Broadway Play Publishers, 1986.

Schoen, Walter. Personal interview. 1990.

Steiner, Peter. *Russian Formalism: A Metapoetics*. Ithaca: Cornell UP, 1984.

Wellman, Mac. *Albanian Softshoe*. Unpublished manuscript, 1989.

————. "Figure of Speech." PAJ. Spring, 1992.

————. "Sincerity Forever." *Grove New American Theatre*. New York: Grove Press, 1993.

————. "Theatre of Good Intentions." Symposium on New Writing for the Theatre. Minneapolis, February 1984.

————, ed. *Theatre of Wonders*. Los Angeles: Sun & Moon Press, 1985.

————. *Whirligig*. New York: New Dramatists, 1988.

Part III: Empowerment and Democracy

Rhonda Blair

The keynote of the essays in this section is the empowerment of students to function as conscious, independent artists, scholars, and citizens through the study and making of theatre. With the goal of preparing students to take responsibility for themselves, their art, and their own social engagement, the authors explore ways of expanding students' analytical and perceptual skills by engaging them experientially with theatre research and practice. Threads that run through a number of the essays are, (1) a belief in the necessity of helping students realize the assumptions that underlie their views of theatre, (2) the direct relationship between historical/theoretical materials and their own lives and, (3) how grappling with such materials within the context of theatre can deepen their awareness and strengthen their ability to have an impact on situations affecting their lives and creativity.

In "The Value-Added Classroom: Plato, Aristotle, Mapplethorpe, and You," Gary Jay Williams describes helping students see how theories are permeated with immediate cultural values and that applications of theory—explicit or implicit—have direct consequences for artists (see also Sarah Bryant-Bertail's essay on this subject). In teaching theatre criticism within an M.A./M.F.A. program, Williams requires students to engage the cultural contexts and ethical implications of their readings in theory by posing specific assignments and questions, and by examining classic theories in light of current situations in the arts; his purpose is to bring students to confrontations that require them to be accountable for their own aesthetic and ethical choices. Through engaging criticism from perspectives that contextualize and integrate the personal, Williams raises students' awareness about cultural values' embeddedness in critical operations and how a given critical stance serves particular political ends. By confronting students with the ways that aesthetic, moral, and cultural responses to art intertwine, Williams challenges students to understand that they are personally implicated in the making of culture and politics, and that each one of them has a responsibility to participate consciously in that making.

Sam Abel's "Learning History by Doing History: Alternative Approaches to the Undergraduate Theatre History Course" talks about teaching undergraduate students to understand that theatre history, and the writing of history in general, is mutable, constructed, and ambiguous. This essay propounds a post-positive approach to theatre history and asserts that teaching theatre history is not about teaching "facts" or "truth," but about teaching research and analytical skills. Abel describes using factual information in the service of "the central purpose of a liberal education, the development of independent, responsible intellectual and moral thought," in short, preparing people to participate responsibly in democracy. Challenging the lecture-based chronological survey course and the idea that history is chronology, Abel describes reorganizing courses to require students to become historians themselves, by creating theatre history "laboratories." With his emphasis on the discussion of historical materials and the dynamics of historiographic interpretation, Abel's method steadily guides students toward an active, critical engagement with contemporary social, political, and cultural conditions, and to understand that they themselves participate directly in the making of history.

"Voices from Life: The Dialect Life Study and Everyday Life Performance" emphasizes the performative. The essay focuses on the individual performer and strategies for deepening and broadening his or her awareness of the range and complexity of human identity. Marion Hampton offers strategies for expanding student actors' understanding of subjectivity and the specificity of the individual through literally duplicating real people's voices. Hampton describes how dialect-focused life study work is a ground for developing both empathetic understanding and a democratizing impulse in student's approach to performance. Besides demanding that students develop acute listening skills in order to create monologues out of closely-observed interview material, this work democratizes the students' sense of voice by concretely demonstrating that standard speech is simply a control medium and not a "right" way to speak. By learning to apprehend and appreciate their subjects' uniqueness more deeply through listening, watching, and enactment, students are more able to embrace difference and diversity in their work and expand their sense of human identity, expressiveness, and possibility.

The Value-Added Classroom:
Plato, Aristotle, Mapplethorpe, and You

Gary Jay Williams

For our required graduate course in drama criticism,[1] I had always tried to help our students situate the readings culturally, from Aristotle through Artaud. These were not disembodied voices, I stressed to the students in our M.A. and M.F.A. programs (who were mostly white, in their mid-twenties, and from middle-class backgrounds). More than aesthetics was at issue. Nor were these readings a rack of ready-made maps. However, each semester, too much of our journey seemed to be an air-conditioned bus ride through the monuments, comfortable, untroubling. If it's Tuesday, it must be archetypal criticism. Seek your bliss. Next week, postmodern irony. Only the feminist readings occasionally engaged students in ways that countered their expectations that the academic classroom was a value-free place where, in disinterested discourse, one sampled aesthetic systems like sherries or tried on critical schools like slogan-stenciled t-shirts. The experience of the course was not eliciting much awareness of the values implicit in critical operations, nor helping students to identify their own, to explore and test their own convictions and pleasures.

By the end of such a semester, most students could micromanage some standard critical concepts, but I had little evidence that they had begun to understand the cultural backgrounds and ethical implications of the readings, little evidence that they could better identify their own sensibilities, no evidence that they were better prepared to make their own critical choices. Notwithstanding the passionate voices in some of the assigned readings, students seldom seemed aware of how high the stakes can be. Nor were they going to know because they heard it in a lecture. These things, I decided, must become course objectives, as important as their "grasp" of concepts.

Further, I concluded, the course work should be designed to bring students to confrontation points that would require them to exercise, and be accountable for, their own aesthetic and ethical choices. Undoubtedly, the mission would reflect my own poststructuralist view that no criticism is purely literary, purely aesthetic, morally neutral, or politically innocent. Even so, the objective would not be to seek conversions to feminist, postcolonialist, new historicist, or cultural materialist approaches. The course should help students become more aware of the cultural values embedded in critical operations, including their own. It should give them the difficult experience of trying to balance this concern with aesthetic ones. They would need to read some structuralist and poststructuralist theory about the culturally constructed subject, but they would need more than abstract theory if they were to explore the implications of this. Part of our subject would need to be their own experiences with art, aesthetic and moral. Part of the experience of the course would need to be the critiquing of some of these experiences by their fellow students in an open forum. In this way, I hoped, most would begin to recognize the artificiality of the boundaries the academy (and the media) often draw around literary criticism. In such a process, some students might learn to better articulate and defend the traditional values they held; some might move toward new positions; and some might experience some painful conflicts between allegiances. I hoped that most would begin asking who is being served by a given kind of criticism and whether they felt represented. Perhaps they would come to question how a popular savant, who preached archetypal mythology on public television, could hold personal beliefs that amounted to racial bigotry. Such goals had implications for our admission policies. If a variety of cultural perspectives were to be heard, our students should come from a wider social spectrum.

When in 1989, the storm broke here in Washington, D.C., over the Corcoran Gallery's cancellation of the planned exhibit of "Robert Mapplethorpe: The Perfect Moment," an exhibit partially funded by the National Endowment of the Arts, I seized the moment. The Mapplethorpe/NEA controversy became an important part of the students' critical practicum in identifying the cultural values implicit in criticism, including their own, and in the related problem of developing aesthetic judgment.

This did not mean abandoning all Western thought before Stephen Greenblatt. It did mean some fresh critiquing of some of it. We began with Plato's *The Republic*, Aristotle's *Poetics*, and Longinus' *On the Sublime*, the classical representations of three Western critical paradigms. We did some traditional contextualizing—Plato amidst the splintering, ruling factions in Athens and the death of Socrates, and Aristotle amidst Alexander's consolidation and Hellenization. Then, in the next stage of discussion questions (distributed in advance), I stressed that they needed to define and express concisely the essential critical priorities and procedures of each classical critic. I asked them to make careful distinctions among these priorities and procedures and took care not to lose them in a grove of glosses. I ended the study of Plato, as I suppose many teachers do, with questions about the place of literature and the arts in our American culture in the recent past and present. We discussed cases of censorship, expurgated Shakespeare, book-banning, canonical reading lists, and curriculum revisions, mono- and multicultural. I asked them for their positions on some particular cases, but did not yet press hard. We ended a methodical study of Aristotle's formal concerns asking where cultural, ethical, or gender values inhere in his discussion of the pleasures proper to tragedy. What are his attitudes toward women? Does he assume a homogeneous culture? How are women constructed in the plays? What are the assumptions embedded in Longinus' conviction that sublimity is that which "pleases all and always"? Who is being served in these formulations? I showed them some connections between Aristotle and New Criticism.

We then turned to the heated controversy over the NEA-funded Mapplethorpe exhibit, photographs by the artist recently dead of AIDS. I required them to examine a well-illustrated catalogue of a recent Mapplethorpe exhibit. I provided them a Kinko's course packet of news stories, speeches from the Congressional Record, statements by John Frohnmayer, then the NEA director, and editorials of all stripes. To this packet, they began to add their own materials as the term went on. In subsequent semesters—the NEA debate raged for over four years—I adopted Richard Bolton's collection of such materials in his *Culture Wars* (New York: New Press [Norton], 1992), an inexpensive paperback (and this also relieved me of copyright clearance work). The issues materialized quickly for these students of theatre, as they realized that future theatre funding was being affected by the critical assumptions in play, in Congress and in the media. I began pressing them harder for positions on hypothetical issues. Suppose you were directing Romeo and Juliet for young audiences and your sponsors asked you to use the edition of the play that suppressed some of the more prominent sexual language in the play. (Such an edition had been published by a major American publisher in the mid-1980s.) Would you defend Shakespeare? How? Suppose you were on an NEA peer panel reviewing the application of a white photographer who sought funding for an exhibit of his photos celebrating white America, photos in which you believe the photographer's animosity to Jews and Blacks is evident. Would you fund the exhibit? At the end of this unit, I required each student to take a position on the main question, "If you were a member of an NEA peer panel, would you fund the Mapplethorpe exhibit?" Seated in our customary circle, the students presented and defended their positions to each other. My role was one of facilitator, not final authority. Appreciations of Mapplethorpe's formal virtuosity alternated in these discussions with repulsion at some of his photos, such as that of a bull whip in a rectum or "fist-fucking." Students felt keenly the pressure of taking a position and being accountable for it. Inevitably, their discussions would evolve from considerations of tax-subsidized art to questions about the extent to which aesthetic, moral, and cultural responses could, or should, be separated in evaluating art. If it was unacceptable for the religious right to seek to influence NEA funding, was it acceptable for those interested in the rights of women and gays? At times, there was tension and discomfort (although, on the whole, I wished that more students were willing to risk staking out positions). In one uncomfortable session, some members of the class were methodically defending the position that aesthetic and cultural responses were separable. A young woman burst out in good-natured exasperation, "I think you are all into some really heavy denial." Laughter dissolved the tension, and a key issue became more than a critical abstraction; they experienced the difficulty of it and saw each trying to work through the dilemma. Throughout the course thereafter, criticism had a less impersonal face, whether we talked of Samuel Johnson or T. S. Eliot. After this unit, I thought the class prepared for this take-home examination question:

> How would each of the critics below evaluate the exhibit of Robert Mapplethorpe's photographs? Which, if any, would fund it through the grants from the tax-supported National Endowment for the Arts? Your answer should make clear the critical priorities of each, and, for the first two, should explain what procedures each would follow.
> 1) Plato
> 2) Aristotle
> 3) You

Answering this question required some analogical reasoning, as I explained in the instructions, particularly in dealing with Aristotle. A photograph cannot be a tragedy. Nor did the question require them to be experts in photographic art. If they had assimilated Aristotle's priorities and procedures, they ought to be able to speculate on the kinds of questions he would ask.

Plato, most students were sure, would never allow Mapplethorpe in his utopia, given his priority of the stable state, best served by the rational philosopher king, who alone has access to absolute truth. For Plato, mimetic artists are "thrice removed" from the truth as well as provokers of dangerous, womanly emotions. A Mapplethorpe would never be among those artists acceptable in Plato's republic; Mapplethorpe's purpose was not to create hymns to the gods and famous men. Occasionally, a few of the better students recognized the respect for the power of art implicit in Plato. A few ventured imitations of Plato's Socratic style.

As to Aristotle, most students were sure that he would define terms and classify, enumerate the formal elements of the different genres of photographic prints and determine the pleasures proper to each. He would speak of simple and complex compositions, of magnitude, order, and consistency. He would explicate the internal relations among components and devote most of his attention to serious, not amusing work. Yes, inevitably, a few literal-minded students would have Aristotle looking for a beginning, middle, and end in a photograph. Students were uncertain and divided about Aristotle's final judgment on Mapplethorpe. The better ones pointed out that, while Aristotle does mention depravity of character and the morally hurtful, his foremost subject is artistic correctness.

For most students, harder than applying Plato or Aristotle, not surprisingly, was defining their own positions on the Mapplethorpe issue. A few took the quick escape hatch of a defense of freedom of artistic expression.

After the exam, I offered my own position supporting funding, expressing my confidence in the general likelihood that art itself often offers complex representations of cultural tensions and is neither essentially subversive or recuperative. I suggested that Mapplethorpe's work, with its immaculately formalized images, seemed, in some photographs, to be defying the viewer to separate the elegant composition from the sexual, usually homoerotic subject. These images did not allow the viewer to merge silently the erotic and the aesthetic, as heterosexual males are accustomed to doing, for example, with female nudes by Reubens or Gauguin. Mapplethorpe's art seemed designed to catch the viewer in a tension between his or her aesthetic and moral responses and to make sure the viewer could not suppress the knowledge of that tension. Mapplethorpe seemed to be critiquing traditional attempts to separate art and morality, and this in the historical moment in our culture in the late 1980s when there was an acute, new public awareness of homosexuality and the AIDS crisis.

I devised other course work to help students define and develop their own critical sensibilities. There were, of course, assigned readings in which they encountered feminism, cultural materialism, and post-colonial studies. They were to keep a journal during the semester, recording their ongoing engagement with issues related to the course. I specified several journal entries of essay length on which they were graded. They were to write two essays on their experiences as spectators at theatre events of their choice, events that either challenged their expectations about theatre or entailed some strong reaffirmation of their values. In these essays, they were not to concentrate on performance evaluations but to explore their critical expectations and responses, and they were to relate these to issues raised in class readings and discussions. Another assigned essay was to develop out of a similar experience of their choice with a museum exhibit. On one occasion, some students wrote about the Maryland Historical Society's landmark exhibit, "Mining the Museum." In it, African-American installation artist, Fred Wilson, showed the ways in which early American art and conventional museum installations of it have virtually erased African Americans and Native Americans. (Where museums are not so accessible for such experiences, there are well-illustrated catalogues, such as that for the Museum of American Art's controversial exhibit, "The West as America," which critiqued the myths and images of America's settlement as a triumphant narrative of white man's progress and prerogatives.) Students also chose exhibits on ancient Athenian art and on women in Renaissance engravings. Grading the journal essays was difficult; the question I needed to keep before me was whether or not a student was moving toward a bibliography of readings in various schools of criticism and to a better understanding of the criteria implicit in his/her responses to works (or the responses of other critics). I also required one relatively formal essay, in which students were to apply to a play of their choice the methods of the critical approach of their choice. The parameters of all these essays were spelled out in the course syllabus and a supplemental bibliography of readings in various schools of criticism.

On the first day of the course, I had asked each student for a credo, a short essay on his or her beliefs about the kind of theatre he/she preferred. What did they want from their experiences in a theatre? What did they find intolerable? I returned their credos with many comments, usually asking for more precise ideas and more examples. I asked them to turn in a revised, more lengthy credo at the end of the course, in which they were expected to better define their positions and to do so in relation to some of their course readings and experiences. I did not expect fully formed critical positions in a semester, of course. However, in their revised credos and their other essays, I did see some evidence that students were better prepared to be accountable for their aesthetic and ethical choices in their encounters with art. At times, their journal essays and credos did dwindle into solipsism, which was my worst fear, despite my stated requirement that students were always to relate their experiences to issues raised in our readings and discussions. At times, a few students would lay claim to the moral high ground, on the left or the right. The one semester course was, of course, a somewhat artificial arena. Nevertheless, all of this seemed, and still seems, worth risking in order to help students better identify the aesthetic and cultural ethical issues in criticism, to help them better understand the stakes and better define themselves.

Note

1. The course work described here was developed in a criticism course for second and third-year graduate students in the M.A. and M.F.A. theatre programs at the Catholic University of America in Washington, D.C. The students' relative maturity was an asset for the handling of some of materials and moral issues, but the processes seem manageable for upper level undergraduates.

Learning History by Doing History:
Alternative Approaches to the Undergraduate Theatre History Course

Sam Abel

Those of us who teach undergraduate theatre history courses face daily the hurdle of how we can bring the past of the theatre to life in the classroom.[1] How can we take the litany of dates, names, and disparate trivia which constitutes the raw material of theatre history, and put it in a context that will make it real and meaningful for our students? How can we evoke for our classes the images we ourselves see (or imagine) of how actors of earlier eras moved on stage, the way past audiences responded to performances? How can we give them not only the data about theatres of the past, but also convey the gut sense that defines theatre as an aesthetic experience? How can we build for them the links between the past and the present?

Even more difficult is the problem of how to convey these ideas to undergraduates in light of the recent upheavals in the way historians construct theatre history. In the welter of complex and often seemingly contradictory post-positivist approaches to the study of history, where once-certain assumptions are challenged and historians cast profound doubts on the very nature of historical "truth," time-honored approaches to basic education no longer work. How do we make this material interesting, or even explicable, to students who bring no previous knowledge of theatre history (or even general world history) to our classroom? How can we teach students a basic narrative of theatre history when we reject the adequacy of linear, chronological narrative to encompass what we mean by history? Is it even possible to devise a post-positivist undergraduate theatre history survey that does not violate the theoretical underpinnings of historiography? As teachers, can we engage our students in an approach to history that we, as scholars, no longer accept as valid?

Most responses to the problem of making history "come alive" in the classroom fail to address these issues. Instead, discussions of theatre history pedagogy usually address a very different question: how to make the classroom environment come alive. As we plan our classes, we think about how to keep our students awake: how to create engaging assignments, deliver amusing lectures filled with colorful anecdotes, making sure to show lots of exotic slides and cutaway models. However, these techniques, vital as they are to a classroom where students will want to learn the topic, do not address the issue of how we can make the history itself both vibrant and theoretically valid, more than any array of questionable "facts," more than a requirement to be surmounted. In order to engage our students' minds, and to bring the undergraduate theatre history class in line with current knowledge, we must first abandon the belief that our job is to pass on to our students the received "truth" about our subject. Instead, we must use our basic-level courses to teach students *how* theatre history works, how history is a living process created by historians, not a static set of facts about the past. Only then will our efforts to enliven our classes amount to more than a song-and-dance aimed at artificially resuscitating fundamentally lifeless material.

As teachers, we have a moral obligation to teach what we believe to be the nearest approximation to the truth (or, in the post-positivist world, to the *truths*) of our subject. Equally clearly, we do our students a disservice by pretending that the intellectual world is as it always was, Professor Bloom notwithstanding. We cannot teach our students what the interior of the Globe theatre looked like, or how Greek actors moved on stage, as if we ourselves possessed that knowledge. Even so, as soon as we attempt to depart form the traditional, positivist approaches to teaching history, there are few alternative instructional models to follow. Once we abandon the position that we as teachers are in full command of our subject—once we admit that we do not know everything about theatre history, and that we can only present limited ways of knowing that history in the classroom—we must perpetually try to reinvent the pedagogical wheel. Furthermore, as we experiment with new classroom techniques, we risk leaving our students utterly baffled in the wake of our own uncertainty, discouraged from pursuing a difficult body of material when we tell them that the information they must memorize is not really the "truth."

The problem is not simple to resolve. First, post-positivist historical methodology is not an easy set of concepts to grasp; its assumptions are alien to most undergraduates. I cannot send a group of sophomore students off to do a quick reading of Foucault over the weekend, and expect them to follow a discourse on the archaeology of knowledge on Monday morning. Second, the postmodern debate is still in full swing, and it is not at all clear what the upshot of the process will be, and what, ultimately, a revisionist theatre history text (or texts) might look like. It is difficult to survey a subject when you do not have a clear view of the landscape. Finally, post-positivist methodology obviates settled answers to historical questions, and rejects the notion of single, stable texts. How do you teach a methodology that rejects previous historical assumptions to students who have never learned those assumptions in the first place? In addition,to those of us trained to teach to a formal syllabus, in which we subdivide a well-defined body of knowledge into its constituent parts and present them sequentially, the concept of building a self-deconstruction syllabus, which teaches that its very organization is ultimately invalid (or at best only a partial view), is truly a dizzying prospect.

Ultimately, all of these questions lead back to a more fundamental issue: why do we teach theatre history to undergraduates in the first place? Certainly not in the hope that most of our students will become theatre historians, or even that they will use this information as a basis for professional theatre careers. Relatively few of our students will go on in the theatre. Instead, our course must aim at the development and stimulation of the thinking human mind. Rather than teach facts, the basic theatre history course should (as should all undergraduate courses) inspire ideas; it should teach students not what to think, but how to think, and allow them to test various modes of thought. Along the way, we must of course also convey a certain amount of factual information, as raw material for study, but this information is secondary to the central purpose of a liberal education, the development of independent, responsible intellectual and moral thought.

The traditional theatre history survey course, which presents theatre history as a unidimensional chronology, has ceased to address the needs of our undergraduate students. In presenting a single-minded approach to theatre history, it limits rather than expands our students' range of intellectual skills. In assuming a stable base of knowledge about theatre history, it falsifies the nature of our historical knowledge. We need to find new ways to approach this material, if theatre history is to remain a viable subject of study for undergraduate students. In this essay I will first outline some of the problems raised by the traditional undergraduate theatre history survey course, and then propose some alternative approaches. I will also relate a few personal experiences in my struggle to find a better way to teach theatre history to undergraduate students.

Theatre History and Chronology

In recent years, the methods of studying history in general, and theatre history specifically, have undergone radical transformation. Under traditional positivist assumptions, history is seen as an objective science where the task of the historian is to collect data, to sift out significant from insignificant material (judgments based on "objective" study of the data), and to convey the resulting historical narrative in as close a manner as possible to the way things "actually happened," in the chronological order of their occurrence. Above all, the historian is supposed to maintain an objective stance, and not impose personal views on the historical events. Recent thinking about history has challenged both the possibility and the value of this approach. The new historiography questions the possibility of the historian's objective stance, arguing that all historical narratives are constructed, and necessarily reflect the viewpoint and cultural biases of the historian. Historical narrative depends on whose story is being told, and who gets to tell the story. Moreover, contemporary historiography has expanded the definition of history beyond linear chronological narrative, into more diverse approaches, including explorations of spatial and synchronous construction of historical data.[2] For post-positivist historians, chronology is only one element of a complex historical fabric, where numerous social, political, and economic forces intersect to determine the function of theatre in a given place and time.

While these developments have exploded traditional thinking about theatre history, the traditional undergraduate history survey continues to reflect the older mode of thought. Within the frame of the survey course, the instructor may choose to address some of these contemporary issues, as facets of the chronological narrative, but they remain secondary to the sweep of the linear progression of the course. No matter how much the instructor questions traditional historical thinking, the fundamental structure of the lecture-based chronological survey course reinforces traditional thinking, telling students that, ultimately, history really is chronology. This message is certainly sent by the popular undergraduate theatre history textbooks. These books follow the parade of well-defined periods of Western theatre history: Ancient Greece; Ancient Rome, in less detail than Greece; Early Medieval, Late Medieval; Italian, English, and Spanish Renaissance; French Neoclassical; Europe in the Eighteenth Century; Romanticism; and "modern" theatre from Ibsen to the present. However, as Thomas Postlewait has argued, these period divisions are, at best, artificial, and while periodization is necessary to historical study, a slavish restriction to a single set of categories limits possible historical interpretations.[3]

The appeal of the chronological format is strong. First of all, it is comfortably familiar and easy to follow. Chronology remains the most obvious way to organize history, at least in a survey course, and it is certainly the structuring guide which students bring with them from high school. Indeed, if we want to tie theatre history to a more familiar world history, we are virtually locked into traditional period divisions, based on the politics of national boundaries and governmental upheaval not matter how little these events may have to do with the theatre. If we want to discuss (as we usually do) how theatre has developed from the "primitive" past to the "triumphant" present, we remain tied to chronology. It makes no sense to teach Renaissance theatre before classical theatre if we want to discuss how the latter inspired the former. This kind of cultural Darwinism is reassuring, conveying a sense that "we're getting somewhere," that history has a purpose, and that we have learned from the past. All in all, the chronological model is very easy to live with.

Historiographically, though, the chronological outline is fraught with problems. First of all, it is inherently dull. For most students, the course consists of memorizing long list of unfamiliar names, mostly in foreign languages. Depending on the zeal of the instructor (who, having lived with these names for the bulk of her career, sees no difficulty in picking them up), this task can become overwhelming, overshadowing any other material in the course. The chronological survey takes on the character of a marathon, with the only goal being to get to the end, somehow, before collapsing into an exhausted stupor. The disheartened student is told, by way of consolation, that there are only a few more historical periods to "get through" before the end. As soon as academic material is looked upon as something to be gotten through rather than some to enjoy or confront, it dies for the student intellectually. The instructor may effuse over the material, and liven lectures with racy anecdotes, but nothing will change the essential tedium of the course.

Of course, much of the factual material is information the instructor does not know, and never will know, especially for the more ancient historical periods. In the chronological survey we tell our classes, in effect, to sit still, while we relate all the facts students need to know about theatre history, and then we spend the next ten to fifteen weeks, if we are honest, saying how little we really do know. We know a great deal about Shakespearean production at the Globe, except what the interior of the theatre looked like; we have interesting evidence about Greek actors, except about how they moved and how their voices sounded. So this string of information not only risks being dull, but it cheats our students of the promised payoff. This is not the best strategy for engaging our students intellectually.

More importantly, although the survey course purports to cover all of theatre history, this image is illusory. No year-long course, much less a one-semester course, can cover all of theatre history, or even a significant portion of it. Assuming for the moment that the historical units covered in the standard model represent the bulk of significant theatre history (a highly dubious assumption), any survey can only scratch the surface of the available information, and can pay only lip service to the controversies that surround the most ambiguous issues. An entire course could be devoted to argument about the Greek theatre building or the Medieval pageant wagon; in the survey these must be reduced to the briefest generalizations. Students are often left thinking that an old theory, long discarded by historians, is an accepted truth. Indeed, even in areas of supposedly settled fact, the available information is so vast that any individual course can only include a tiny fraction of it. Further, because there is so much to cover, there is rarely time to address the issues of historiography and social analysis which underlie these facts. It is little comfort to students to be told that they will get to these question in a higher level course, which they probably will never take, if it is offered at all.

Just how valuable is all this information to the undergraduate? For the student not majoring in theatre, it is often difficult to justify taking the course. Even for students intending a career in theatre, the litany of names and dates has limited value, since in reality they will forget most of this information soon after the course is over, especially if exams encourage "cramming." Practicing theatre historians absorb their broad base of factual knowledge through constant exposure over many years of intensive study, not in a "once-over-lightly" survey course. The best that can be expected from a student in such a course is a reasonable facility for name recognition of the major personalities and terms of theatre history, a skill that may prove useful at cocktail parties, but which cannot be said to constitute an understanding of the history of theatre.

Rebuilding Courses

If the reliance on chronology is so problematic, what else can we do? Are there other ways to approach undergraduate theatre history that address these concerns? Over a number of years, I have experimented with several alternative models for an undergraduate theatre history syllabus. In particular, I have searched for ways to wean this course away form a strict reliance on chronology, and to find a balance between presenting facts and discussing their implications. I have looked for ways to convey basic information, while at the same time putting that information in the context of current theories of historiography, so that my students have the tools not only to learn facts, but also to explore the volatile nature of historical information, especially in a field as inherently elusive as stage performance.[4]

I would be disingenuous to claim that I have found the single solution to these complex problems. My explorations have taken varied forms, some looking relatively like the traditional course structure, and others departing more radically form the norm. In each case I work from a common set of beliefs about what beginning students ought to get from a theatre history course. First, I believe that at the undergraduate level there is no predetermined body of factual material the instructor must "get through" in class. Students may read a survey of the material in a text, but in class they should explore historical issues, not get a simple rehashing of the book. A substantive discussion of the problems surrounding one aspect of a period's theatre is more useful than a cursory survey of all its "facts." The instructor must, for all practical purposes, limit the scope of class discussion, but such limitations should not grow out of artificially imposed value judgments. The instructor has not failed if the students discuss Corneille but not Racine, Greek staging devices but not choreography, as long as the topics covered in class address issues that broaden the students' historical understanding.

Therefore, the memorization of factual material should play a secondary and supportive role to the real material of the course, the discussion of historical materials and the dynamics of historiographic interpretation. Factual material should never be presented in isolation, or as an end in itself, but as evidence for historical analysis. Students should have access to selected primary historical materials, to develop an understanding of how historians construct historical narratives. Course examinations should reflect this emphasis, with comparatively little (or perhaps even no) credit given for the rote repetition of names and dates. Students may be asked to remember some factual material (for example, to support arguments in essay questions) and be penalized for error, but the grading structure should not imply that facts are more important than concepts.

To implement these beliefs, I have looked for organizational strategies other than strict chronology on which to build syllabi. Rather than taking the class chronologically from ancient Greece to recent times, I have often opted for a series of topical units, each addressing a question of historical interest. In some syllabus configurations, I have used a topical structure entirely in lieu of chronology; more recently, I have interwoven topical and chronological structures in a variety of ways. For example, in one configuration I divided the course into two units, each built roughly chronologically: one discussing physical elements of past theatre production; and a second discussing broader social, economic, and religious dynamics which surround the theatre. At other times I have chosen to alternate classroom sessions devoted to discussion of basic information (with emphasis on source materials) with periods for discussion of broader social issues, to emphasize the connections between physical production and social context.

The array of questions on which to build a topical discussion of theatre history is almost endless: Who pays the cost of putting on the theatre? Who is in the audience? Why do they go to the theatre? Who makes the artistic choices? What does the theatre's visual imagery imply? What is the role of women or other marginalized social groups? What is the relationship between theatre and the government in power, or between theatre and the dominant religion? What is the lifestyle of the performers? What kind of technology is available? Is theatre considered a good or bad influence on society, and why? What kind of evidence is available about past theatres? How have interpretations of this evidence changed over time? It is, of course, possible to discuss any of these questions in relation to any period of theatre history. Normally, for each topic I choose one period that raises particularly interesting issues for discussion. For example, I might ask students to explore the questions of stage technology raised by Aeschylean scripts, or governmental power as exemplified by Jacobean court masques. While these issues often arise in chronological surveys, by foregrounding them, students learn to see history as a series of questions rather than as received fact describing a linear progression of events.

In spite of my attempts to break free of chronology, I still feel an acute need in my undergraduate classes to find a simple device by which to organize the material. Chronology, in one form or another, still presents itself as a viable method, as long as it does not become the sole structural device for the course. In some early attempts to create a course structure entirely divorced from chronological narrative, many of my students became very insecure, because this territory is still so unfamiliar to them. Even in the elite Ivy League institution where I teach, most of my students show up with remarkably little knowledge of dramatic literature, or even the basics of western history, and so I feel a strong need to fill in these holes before I can discuss the theories and dynamics of history. In employing chronology, though, it is vital to emphasize that it is one tool for analyzing history, not a synonym for history itself.

Clearly, in an introductory class it is impossible to dispense with some level of information transfer. We can assign reading outside of class to provide some information, but much class time will still be spent telling students what theatre used to be like, probably in some vague chronological order. The most important point, and the central way to dislodge the tyranny of chronology, is to place this information in the context of historiography. Rather than taking the attitude in lecture of saying "This is how theatre happened," I attempt to build all of my classroom discussions by saying, "Here are the available data, and here is how various historians have interpreted them." This latter approach takes more time than the simple historical narrative, and it means covering less territory, but it gives my students a sense of historicity: not just information, but the ability to think independently and creatively about that information. It gives them ways of knowing theatre history.

Ways of Knowing

Even (or perhaps especially) on the undergraduate level, we need to teach our students not just facts, but how historical events are distributed in time and space, and how this distribution affects the way societies respond to those events. This is an easy remark to make, but a difficult process to accomplish. Helping students to develop a sense of historicity is a complex and often unfamiliar process. It involves thinking on several levels at once: juggling the available data; contextualizing the data; and judging how the data are filtered through the minds of historical writers. This task can prove daunting, especially when a class arrives with little sense of the general world history in which theatre occurred. The theoretical problems here can be daunting; I have a hard enough time digesting the current historiographic discussions in the journal literature here myself, let alone communicating them to my students.

When I sit down to write a syllabus for a "paper" course such as theatre history, my tendency has been to begin by asking myself "what do my students need to know?" The answer can only be a string of information, leading to the kinds of bribery games to enliven the material which I mentioned early in this essay. But in my current approach to undergraduate theatre history I have formulated this question a different way. Instead of asking what I want my students to know about theatre history, what base of information they need to have when they leave the course, I instead begin by asking *how* I want my students to know theatre history. What are the thought processes that I want to develop in my students? How do I want them to understand the dynamics of theatre history? Further, what do I mean by "understanding" history at all? What constitutes historical understanding?

To this end, on the first day of the course I ask students to address the whole question of historicity, to question their own understanding of what history means to them. I start with an apparently simple exercise: working in small groups, I assign them the hypothetical task of writing the history of our theatre department for the last ten years. I ask them what sources they will use in their research, and then ask them to devise chapter heading for their historical narrative. These speculations lead to a discussion of the problems faced by the theatre historian in interpreting historical evidence, and in translating an evanescent experience like theatre into a concrete narrative. As the discussion develops, I ask them to focus on the department's most recent productions, shows many of them worked on or attended, to demonstrate the elusiveness of the historical narrative, even for events in which they themselves participated. In other words, I ask the students to function as historians.

Another technique I use to develop an understanding of historicity is to tell the same historical story in different ways, to take as it were a "Rashomon" approach to a problem. For example, I might present one reconstruction of the interior of the Elizabethan playhouse, or one theory of the origin of theatre, as if it were accepted truth, and then immediately present a contrasting theory. I then ask the class to compare the different versions of historical "reality." By setting up one reality, and then presenting an alternate view, I can give a tangible demonstration of the unstable nature of historical narrative, and a sense of how historians do their work. These techniques, by providing concrete illustrations that history is not settled fact, can go a long way to dislodge pervious patterns of thinking about history, and to replace it with a sense of historicity.

I also try to help students develop a sense of place. History occurs within space, as does theatre. Yet most discussions of theatre history shortchange the spatial dimension of performance. Models are lovely, if you have them, but not everyone does. Furthermore, the simple process of looking at a model or a cutaway drawing of a theatre space does not guarantee that a class will understand how an actor might have related to that space. Further, theatre space is not restricted to the playhouse. One frequently overlooked area is the geography of the cities where theatre happened. As Marvin Carlson argues in *Places of Performance*, we need to know these urban patterns to understand how the theatre of a city worked (10). It is much easier to understand the *commedia dell'arte* with a sense of what it feels like to walk around the streets of Venice, or of the medieval theatre with a mental picture of the walls of York. I cannot put my class on an airplane and take them to all of the sites of historical performance which I discuss, so I substitute descriptions of these spaces, along with maps and photos, personal stories—anything to make the space real to them.

Teaching historicity is a process equivalent to teaching students how to draw. Not all students will be able to develop a sense of historicity with ease; to some student, even a simple chronology will remain as opaque as solid geometry, let alone more sophisticated concepts of historical dynamics. To expand the art analogy, teaching historicity is as much as a right-brained as a left-brained activity. History is more than logical analysis; it involves intuitive responses. Here we have an advantage in theatre study. Most of our students have training in intuitive knowledge, and how intuition relates to analysis; this process is at the core of acting training. We can appeal to intuitive knowledge, to treat historical data as we do an actor's given circumstances. In effect, we can ask them to play the role of an actor or spectator in a past era. By asking students to get up and, for example, test out eighteenth-century gestural language, we let them explore history not only in their minds, but in their bodies.

The Theatre History Laboratory

In short, rather than viewing the undergraduate theatre history classroom as a place for information transfer, a place for one-way communication, we can look at the classroom space as a laboratory, where the instructor leads students in hands-on testing of historical material. In the sciences, undergraduate students perform lab work, in order to get a feel for doing science, and a knowledge of scientific methods. The lab work is not original, but it serves a vital pedagogical function, introducing students not only to the data, but to how the data are generated and interpreted. Students work in lab with a limited factual base, and they are not expected to make new discoveries (though such innovation is certainly possible). Even so, no instructor of undergraduate, or even high school, science would dream of building a basic course without a laboratory component to supplement the lectures.

In the theatre history classroom we provide few comparable opportunities for hands-on experience in doing what historians do. We give students information, and no practical experience for dealing with it. When, at the end of the courses, we ask students to turn in a term paper in which we expect them to function as historians, we are dismayed when the papers contain only rote repetitions of material presented in class, with little understanding of historiography. However, it is unreasonable to expect students to function as historians unless we first guide them through the process of what historians do. Without this opportunity, the chronological survey becomes a dead spot in the students' liberal education, especially in contrast to other introductory courses such as beginning acting, design, and technical courses, which provide such a large proportion of hands-on instruction.

To supplement the classroom exercises described above, I set aside one period a week and designate it as a "Theatre History Laboratory," similar to a lab period in science courses. In the theatre history lab, I give the class a piece of primary historical evidence, and then have them work (in full class discussion or in small groups) on finding solutions to clearly-defined problems based on the artifact. For example, I give them a Greek playtext and, using the three-actor rule, ask them to assign roles to the Protagonist, Deuteragonist, and Tritagonist. Instead of lecturing on the Fouquet miniature, I project a slide of it on a screen, and ask the class to interpret what they see. In what has proved my most successful lab class, I give the class a list of various *commedia dell'arte lazzi*, with brief descriptions, and have them rehearse and present them in groups of two or three. After each exercise, I ask the students to write up a brief lab report, outlining their results, and comparing different solutions to the problems raised by the historical data explored.

On the undergraduate level, it is important to follow the example of science lab classes, and keep the approach to historiography relatively simple. One year, rather than setting up an in-class laboratory, I asked my students early in the course to write a paper comparing two opposing historiographic views on a problem, and gave them free reign to choose a topic. A few students were able to do this assignment, but most of them floundered, because they had insufficient information to find their way through the debates and make a comparison of contrasting views. I now make sure they first have a base of information in historiographic texts (not to mention basic reference sources), before expecting them to delve into the journal literature. If we want our students to be able to do history, we need to lead them through a coherent process. No one will be able to perform complex historical analyses right away, nor can we expect our students to grasp the full range of historical dynamics the first time around.

It can be extremely exciting when we see our students engage with the material, when they discover a sense of historicity and apply it in creative ways. Success can, however, have its pitfalls. Students thus empowered start to get unruly ideas; they want to deviate from your carefully (or not so carefully) planned assignments. For example, in a class I taught on avant-garde performance, while delivering a lecture on surrealism, several of my students were one step ahead of me. During my lecture, at regular intervals, in complete deadpan, they silently exchanged newspaper-wrapped books with each other, a surreal performance which sharply contrasted with my rather staid lecture on the subject. The greatest appeal of such events is their spontaneity, but it is not unthinkable to encourage such relevant disruptions, to make the classroom into a space where a kind of historically informed theatre can happen.

In another instance, in a course I taught on U.S. theatre in the 1960s and 70s, I assigned a project in which the students would research an experimental theatre group and present their research in a formal paper. Most of the class had no problem with this assignment, as it fell comfortably in the realm of their educational experience. One particularly bright student, however, chose to examine Richard Forman's Ontological-Hysteric Theatre. The more he found out about Forman, the greater became the tension between the subject and the form of the assignment. He became so engaged with the material that he began to despair of the power of words to express anything at all; in studying Forman, the student fell into a bout of ontological hysteria. I had to overcome my own resistance to the "you must complete the assignment as given" syndrome. In the end, we had a long discussion in my office about the nature of the avant-garde, during which he presented several paintings on which he had been working. I never got a paper, but I also know that he understood the material on a level which the other students in the class never dreamed existed.

Students also tend to ask unusual and often challenging questions in the atmosphere of the history laboratory. Without a rote indoctrination into the canonical questions of theatre history, students often come up with surprising angles on the material. During a discussion of acting and rehearsal methods in the Greek theatre, one student asked a question I never heard before: did Greek actors rehearse from scripts until they memorized their lines; did they, in fact, have written scripts at all? It is a perfectly reasonable question; actually a rather revealing one, suggesting insights into the transition in Greek culture from an oral to a literary society. Yet this is not a canonical question; it is not part of the received body of facts in the standard theatre histories. I looked at her and said I did not have a clue, opening a lengthy discussion of probable solutions in light of the Greek theatrical and social situation.

It is always difficult to practice what you preach. We tend to fall back into familiar patterns of behavior; old habits die hard. Despite my good intentions, my sharp shifts in course structure, and my abandoning old notes, I find that I still revert to my old lecture patterns, repeating the same old materials, only in a different order. As in politics, it is hard to sustain a revolution in the classroom, and teaching is exhausting work. It is easier to lecture than to interact with students, especially when we are juggling classes, committee work, and a production at the same time. In addition, there will always be a split between the ideal and the actual in the classroom—we want to take students further than they will be able to go in a single course. However, if we cannot always reach our ideals, we can at least begin to give our students a sense of how historiographic analysis is dynamic rather than static, how history is a living, growing thing, as much a kind of performance as the performances which historians seek to document. If we can achieve this goal, we will do far more than give our students a base of knowledge in theatre history; we build a generation of historical thinkers who can make their own history and apply it creatively to other aspects of their lives.

We as teachers have a real opportunity to change the face of knowledge; in our dizzying high-tech world, we really have no choice, if education is to maintain its viability. The place to begin that change is with our undergraduate students. They are the ones who will construct new stories, the ones who will reassemble the historical narratives we so gleefully dismantle. Even if we are unsure of how to rework our courses, even if we feel we are swimming over our heads in uncharted waters, we must let our students know about this instability and what we think about it. The greatest service we can do our undergraduate students is to let them know that the world is changing; that if we cling to the traditional, monolithic view of history, then we will disappear in the powerful sweep of change. As responsible citizens in a chaotic, post-positivist world, students need to learn to think about how they think, and to rouse themselves from intellectual lethargy and stasis. If we can use the theatre history course to foster this kind of speculation, we will have accomplished a great deal.

Notes

1. This essay is a revision and compilation of three papers which I presented to the Association for Theatre in Higher Education over a number of years: "An Alternate Models for Teaching Theatre History in the Liberal Arts Curriculum" (San Diego, August 5, 1988); "The Undergraduate Post-Modern Theatre History Course: A First Year's Experience" (Chicago, August 8, 1990); and "Resurrecting Dead Actors, or Learning History by Doing History" (Philadelphia, August 4, 1993). Thanks to my fellow panelists and the ATHE colleagues who made suggestions, argued, and stimulated my thoughts on these issues, and to my theatre history students, who have taught me how to build a course. Special thanks to Kae Koger, who thought these ideas important enough to pursue. Thanks to Bruce McConachie for his valuable editorial suggestions.

2. A useful introduction to the variety of new historiographic methods in theatre history appears in Thomas Postlewait and Bruce McConachie, eds., *Interpreting the Theatrical Past: Essays in the Historiography of Performance.* A special supplement to the *Journal of Dramatic Theory and Criticism*, edited by Rosemarie Bank, explores some of the fundamental theoretical challenges to traditional methods of analyzing theatre history, particularly as they relate to similar paradigm shifts in physics; two articles by Postlewait in *Theatre Journal* question the nature of periodization in theatre history. Developments in literary theory have also had an impact on theatre historiography. Feminist historical methods can be seen, for example, in Sue-Ellen Case's *Feminism and Theatre*, and a more detailed application of feminist historiography appears in such studies as Tracy C. Davis's *Actresses as Working Women.* Complex economic and other social forces are explored in Case and Janelle Reinelt's *The Performance of Power*, McConachies's *Melodramatic Formations*, and Joseph R. Roach's *The Player's* Passion. Marvin Carlson develops a semiotics of theatre history in *Places of Performance: The Semiotics of Theatre Architecture and Theatre Semiotics: Signs of Life.*

3. See the two articles by Postlewait cited in the previous note. Further, there are vast gaps in the traditional model. Hellenistic theatre gets far less classroom time (if any at all) than fifth-century Athenian theatre, even though in sheer volume of production the Hellenistic theatre far outweighed the Athenian. How much attention is given to the theatre of Scandinavia, the Netherlands, or Eastern Europe before the twentieth century? In general, any period, nation, or subculture out of the mainstream of Western political power, or whose theatre lacks heavy documentation, especially of scripted plays, is treated as if it did not exist, or at least as less important than more documented periods. Given the nature of documentary preservation, the

reliance on written evidence tends to perpetuate the myth that the only important theatre is that produced by those with political and economic power. The theatre of smaller nations, of the lower classes, minority groups, and women disappears in this structure. The traditional survey can add on units about these areas (further taxing the students' ability to "get through" the already voluminous material), but the course structure still implies that these are secondary theatre forms, ancillary to the "really important" documented works of the main syllabus. Tradition dictates that the instructor must "get through" the traditional material first. Unfortunately, only the smallest percentage of students ever get a chance to learn that there is anything else out there.

4. The Theatre History focus group of the ATHE has put together a collection of syllabi for undergraduate theatre history courses, including an example of a syllabus which I have used in my classes. For a further discussion of these collected, syllabi, including my own, see the article by Jerry Dickey and Judy Lee Oliva, "Multiplicity and Freedom in Theatre History Pedagogy: A Reassessment of the Undergraduate Survey Course."

Works Cited

Bank, Rosemarie. "Physics and the New Theatre Historiography." *Journal of Dramatic Theory and Criticism* 5.2 (1991): 63–64.

———. "Time, Space, Timespace, Spacetime: Theatre History in Simultaneous Universes." *Journal of Dramatic Theory and Criticism* 5.2 (1991): 65–84.

Carlson, Marvin. *Places of Performance: The Semiotics of Theatre Architecture.* Ithaca: Cornell UP, 1989.

———. *Theatre Semiotics: Signs of Life.* Bloomington: Indiana UP, 1990.

Case, Sue-Ellen. *Feminism and Theatre.* New York: Methuen, 1988.

Case, Sue-Ellen, and Janelle Reinelt, eds. *The Performance of Power: Theatrical Discourse and Politics.* Iowa City: Iowa UP, 1991.

Davis, Tracy C. *Actresses as Working Women: Their Social Identity in Victorian Culture.* London: Routledge, 1991.

Dickey, Jerry, and JudyLee Oliva. "Mulitiplicty and Freedom in Theatre History Pedagogy: A Reassessment of the Undergraduate Survey Course." *Theatre Topics* 4.1 (1994): 45–58.

McConachie, Bruce A. *Melodramatic Formations: American Theatre and Society*. 1820–1870. Iowa City: Iowa UP, 1992.

Postlewait, Thomas. "The Criteria for Periodization in Theatre History." *Theatre Journal* 40 (1988): 299–318.

————. "Historiography and the Theatrical Event." *Theatre Journal* 43 (1991): 157–78.

Postlewait, Thomas, and Bruce A. McConachie. *Interpreting the Theatrical Past: Essays in the Historiography of Performance*. Iowa City: Iowa UP, 1989.

Roach, Joseph R. *The Player's Passion: Studies in the Science of Acting*. Ann Arbor: Michigan UP, 1993.

Training Scenic Designers for a Changing Aesthetic

Robert N. Schmidt

Trends in contemporary theatre over the past 15–20 years have broadened the range of performance style to include a vast array of performance possibilities. The association of particular styles of performance with various genres of performance no longer applies. Expectations of what a Shakespearean play, or an Italian opera, or an American musical "ought" to look like can no longer reliably dictate the product. Increased exposure of contemporary audiences to a broad range of performance from many cultures and media (from Japanese Butoh dance, to MTV, to Asian martial arts, to the televised destruction of the Berlin wall) has radically expanded the visual and performance language of the contemporary stage. The increasing demand for the work of scenic designers to integrate seamlessly with the style of these varied forms of performance also demands that designers have a greater understanding of, as well a command of, many of the skills and sensibilities previously relegated to the realm of the director.

As a result, designers in the contemporary theatre require training quite different from their predecessors in previous decades. This training requires a greater understanding of performance as a temporal-visual language which has resonance through a plethora of other art forms. We are now beginning to see an emergence of re-configured design training programs that incorporate ideologies and methods found in a variety of other fields such as linguistics, movement studies, and performance art.

In April of 1990 I had the opportunity to travel to Amsterdam as part of the American delegation to an International Organization of Scenographers, Technicians, and Architects of Theatre Conference (the international affiliate of the United States Institute for Theatre Technology). It seemed that the Dutch were in a great quandary regarding the future of theatrical designer training in the Netherlands. The question at hand was which of the two existing models for training was most appropriate and productive: theatre design taught in the art schools, or in the theatre schools? During the conference we were able to view an exhibition of the student work from both types of schools which proved extremely pertinent to addressing this question. Let me briefly describe each of the two models under discussion. The "art school" model provided students with high-level craft training in drawing, painting, and sculpture, and an appreciation for and understanding of contemporary trends in the visual arts. They had no interaction with other theatre artists—actors, directors, technicians, and the like.

None of the graduating students had ever designed a produced work. According to the proponents of this model, the designers first had to develop their own sensibilities as artists before being able to work effectively as a member of an artistic team. The student work consisted of extraordinarily beautiful and evocative sketches and models (no drafting). When I asked one student to describe to me how the performance of the piece might actually transpire within the framework of her project on display, I was met with a quizzical look and something such as "Well that's really up to the Director isn't it?"

The work exhibited by the theatre schools was quite another story. There were no sketches, much drafting, and the models were workman-like. Many of the works had been produced and therefore represented a collaborative effort with other budding theatre artists. However, the latitude of visual expression evidenced was relatively narrow and uninformed. The projects seemed interchangeable between the theatrical works they represented. A design for *Three Sisters* looked pretty much like a *Macbeth*. "Uninteresting," perhaps the ultimate insult in theatrical critique, leaps to mind. When asked about their project, one of the students from the theatre schools remarked, "Well, I don't really know how to explain it, but it's what the director asked for." It was no wonder the Dutch were in such a quandary. Their fears had been that art school training was too from the performance medium, and that the theatre school training allowed for the design work to be too easily usurped by the larger egos of other artists. To choose between a model of training which seems so disconnected from the actual performance event and one which minimizes the potential value of the visual language would be a tough choice.

There was one school, the Hogeschool of Art in Utrecht, whose basic model was that of the other art schools. Their exhibit, however, was quite unique and demonstrated a very different philosophy. The projects on display were video tapes. Each of the students had created a small environment—no more than the area within the frame of a still video camera. Within this environment they had themselves performed an improvisation of a character from an extant theatrical work. Each project ran only a couple of minutes in length. In these projects, each word, each choice of gesture, each choice of object occupying space, had never been separated from the other. The choices of costume, environment, and illumination were never made or evaluated apart from the performance itself. It occurred to me that it is, perhaps, precisely this same integration of all aspects of the performance that makes the work of Robert Wilson or The Wooster Group so intriguing. Further, the "paper project," as employed exclusively by the other art schools (as well as many of us in this country), was a pedagogical tool only suited for *advanced* training. This is because working on paper requires the ability to understand the implications to performance of design choices being made which are not easily apparent or explicable on the drawing table; in order to understand this relationship to performance, students first needed to have the experience of making design choices within a performance context (though not necessarily on a large scale).

Subsequent to this experience I spoke with a colleague who had made an informal survey of artistic directors, producers, and stage directors of regional theatre and opera companies, to find out what exactly they were looking for from young designers beyond a technical ability to draw, build models, analyze and understand a text, and meet deadlines. What was it, in the plethora of young M.F.A. graduates with such skills, that made some designers more desirable, more *hirable* than others? The answer: "a point of view" "a significant insight" "a fresh way of seeing." This, together with my own experience designing in professional theatre, made it clear that it is no longer sufficient for designers to be able to develop their work in a chameleon-like way from a director's fully formed "concept." It is now essential that designers have the tools, background, and abilities to function as co-equal artists—helping to initiate rather than merely elaborate upon the director's theatrical aesthetic, style, or "point of view" for a performance. To accomplish this, designers must be able to operate as independent, as well as collaborative, artists. They must be encouraged to develop their own artistic sensibility and to trust in it.

Those of us in design training programs who have begun to address these changes in the aesthetic as well as operational procedures of the field are now beginning to recognize some of the following principles:

1. The Theatre Designer must develop as an artist capable of creating both cooperatively and independently.

2. The Theatre is primarily a poetic, not an historic, construct.

3. Theatre, while different from the arts of painting, sculpture, video, and music, exists in the same contemporary world with them, and the lines between these disciplines are increasingly ill-defined.

4. Traditional communicative forms, such as models and perspective drawings, are inherently limited in their vocabulary and ability to express a four-dimensional art form (motion as a dimension well as the three dimensions of height, width, and depth) and must sometimes be replaced or enhanced by other media such as computer simulations, video simulations, and "real space" explorations.

5. A broader base for understanding and defining "performance" is necessary to enrich the designer's aesthetic and informational resource pool.

6. The designer must be able not only to communicate effectively with a director but, in most cases, to conceive in directorial terms. In order to achieve this, student designers require increasingly more experience with

human scale kinetic space, as well as a semiotic understanding of the interrelationship of text, gesture, space, and emblematic information.

At the University of Texas at Austin we have begun to re-structure (particularly on the graduate level) the curriculum in scenic design to address these issues. What follows is a brief description of the resultant philosophy and structure.

In the first semester of their first year, graduate students in Scenic Design take two design courses concurrently. One is primarily a "technique" course that develops communicative and exploratory skills in drafting, drawing, and model construction. This course also provides the student with a highly "life-like" example of the scenic design process and the creation of drawing and models suitable for a professional scene shop. The other concurrent course addresses issues of visual metaphor, the relationship between objects and spoken text, and the temporal quality of performance, through a series of three projects.

The first project usually involves a simple object such as a table or a chair. After a discussion (and a demonstration) of visual language and semiotics, the students begin to do semiotic reading of the objects they have chosen. They begin to correlate the combination of characteristics of the objects with what that tells them about its use, history, probable future, etc. The discussion begins with the characteristics of the object they observe, such as materials of construction, surface treatments, and overall design. Later this discussion begins to incorporate the relationship of the object to its environment, its orientation to the viewer, and issues of an artist's or "maker's" intentionality in the relationship to its various characteristics. The students are then free to adjust the object in what ever way they wish (repainting, cutting apart, combining with other objects, etc.). The class then follows up on these adjustments with additional semiotic readings, looking carefully at how the adjustments have altered the meaning of the object. Through this project the students begin to develop an acute awareness of how combinations of objects with all of their various characteristics (intended or otherwise) can develop meaning.

The second project expands upon the first by looking at the relationship between an object and a verbal text (either written or spoken). This can be accomplished by many means: giving the object a title, incorporating printed text into or onto the object or, by playing a pre-recorded tape along with the viewing of the object. Specifically we look at how the object and text are affected by the juxtaposition with the other, that is, how the meaning of the object can be changed by changing the text associated with it, and how, conversely, the meaning of the text can be altered by its association with the object. Because a spoken text is by nature linear in its construction, the projects also begin to explore the role of "sequence" in establishing meaning. That is the changeability of meaning over time.

Finally, a third project again expands on the previous two. It is to create a video tape of roughly 3–5 minutes in length. By introducing video tape, the project becomes a temporal construct. It now has a defined beginning and a defined ending. It now becomes an "event." The students' job is to begin with a video of the object they had created along with its subsequent text. They also explore the nature of sustained interest over a period of time and make adjustments in the video as a part of this exploration. Most importantly, they begin to understand more about the connection between objects, environment, text, and time, as contributing to the overall meaning of performance.

In conclusion, I do not mean to suggest that these projects are appropriate for all design training programs, or even to imply that they are firmly and forever imbedded with the program at the University of Texas at Austin. I offer them as examples of alternative ways to explore and address the elusive relationship between theatrical design and performance. Further, these are not intended to take the place of more traditional skills training in drawing, drafting, and model building. These skills remain *fundamental* tools for the designer. However, conscientious design training must also help the student develop an understanding of the more fundamental dynamics of performance in an ever more quickly changing art form.

Voices from Life:
The Dialect Life Study and Everyday Life Performance

Marian E. Hampton

In the spring of 1957, as I was finishing my first year in the M.A. acting Program at the Yale School of Drama, my teacher, Constance Welch, assigned a life study to our acting class; we were to find an interesting person to study and play that character for the class. It was a deceptively simple-sounding assignment and almost casually proposed. My character was a waitress at the Duchess Diner, where my friends and I occasionally ate, when we could afford it. The one detail I remember about the woman I studied is that she spoke of "lemon moran pie." I can't recall anything else about her, but I do remember that my performance of her was deemed both interesting and well-done, as were many of the others that day; and I remember being immediately impressed with the possibilities for transformation inherent in that simple exercise. Like all good teaching/learning experiences, that one intensified a lifelong habit of observation, which has served me well as a teacher as well as an actor.

I began introducing the Dialect/Life Study into my graduate level Voice and Speech classes several years ago, at the University of Texas, as an advanced assignment in dialects.

The depth of the portrayals my students presented both pleased and surprised me, and one of my colleagues in acting said he wished all of the students' characterizations could be as rich as these were. Interestingly enough, two students have subsequently used their life study monologues as audition pieces—one of those was in response to a professional audition in which the casting agent noted that the actor had listed Italian Swiss as one of several dialects he could readily perform. She was much impressed with his prepared monologue in a seemingly complex and obscure accent.

I confess, I had no idea of the possible social value of this project when I first began using it, other than the fact that it was an undeniably effective actor training tool as well as a great deal of fun in performance. Somewhat later I began to suspect that the intense listening to and observing of another human being was actually an exercise in developing a deep sense of rapport, of empathic understanding of a fellow human being. Still later, I discovered that another teacher of actors was experimenting with a similar process.

Anna Deavere Smith, whose award-winning performance *Fires in the Mirror* presented a multitude of characters of varying racial and ethnic backgrounds, was quoted in *The New York Times* (June 16, 1993) in regard to her newer performance, *Twilight: Los Angeles 1992*:

> Over the year I would interview anybody who would talk to me. It's a matter of me having an ear that's microscopic enough to hear a person's individuality in a moment. I'm not really an impersonator. I just try to find that distinct moment and do exactly what they did. Character appears in language.

The article goes on to say that while she was teaching at Carnegie-Mellon, Ms. Smith developed a new exercise for her students:

> Frustrated at her students' dependence on the realism of the Method, she began assigning them projects to watch and record celebrity interviews on television, like Barbara Walters questioning Paul Newman. The students, in turn, picked up the nuance and voice and body language of the interviewer and interviewee…. She was looking for what she calls "characteristic moments." "That's when people actually take control of their interview," she said. "The moment they take control is the moment I want."

The Dialect/Life Study I have developed involves several steps beginning with the choice of an interesting subject and an interview of about an hour or an hour-and-a-half, which is recorded on audiotape. During the interview, the student also observes body language, how the articulators are used, gestural language, environment and response to environment, and so forth. The person chosen must have a dialect, an accent, or otherwise idiosyncratic speech. From the taped interview, a chart of deviations from General American Standard Speech is devised, using the IPA as presented in the Claude Merton Wise book, *Applied Phonetics*. The chart presents first the General American Standard phoneme, whether vowel or consonant, then the equivalent in the subject's individual speech, and then several key words that utilize that sound.

Next, the student constructs a monologue, based on the subject's taped conversation. Here, the student exercises artistic license to construct the monologue in such a way that it flows well, has a beginning, a middle and an end, and is ultimately interesting for an audience. The student then transcribes a page of the monologue into phonetics, and she or he begins to rehearse the character.

In the process of rehearsing the character, the student will uncover challenges in tone, pitch, placement, and diction, as assuming the subject's body size and shape. A criterion for the success of the project is that the student must find a way to capture the voice of the subject without placing any strain whatsoever on her or his vocal cords. Thus, the student attempts to take on both the voice and the silhouette of his/her subject, and, in so doing, stretches the student's own voice, body, and imagination.

Obviously, the student must develop an affinity with his/her subject: these studies do not work well if they are performed with an attitude of bitterness or revenge or any negative intention. Perhaps this is because to embody another being, one must like that person enough to be willing to take on his/her characteristics. If the empathy is not there, salient aspects of the character go unremarked or unnoticed, and the final result becomes a cartoon or a caricature, instead of a full-bodied person.

This project demonstrates a connection with Stanislavski's theory of the line of physical actions in that students discover that when they change their style of physical movement and rhythm, as well as altering adjustments of their articulators, their brain processes are rearranged, enabling them to develop new synaptic connections and to get into the thought processes of the subject. To apprehend the thought processes of another produces a deep understanding of motivation and objective, an understanding that is perceived at the affective, feeling level, through being incorporated, literally, into the body. Similarly, audience members, perceiving the actor's involvement with the here and now of the character, find their own thought and emotion processes engaged.

I believe that the characterizations that result from the process described above owe their depth and richness to the engagement of all of the senses and rhetorical skills: the student must first observe, with all senses, the subject; then listen to the recorded voice of the subject, over and over again and with great care, in order to develop a chart of changes from standard speech; then construct a monologue that accurately represents the true sentiments of the character (this would be an excellent exercise for playwrights); then analyze the individual speech sounds involved in expressing this text, writing down what has been minutely observed from the recording; must practice wrapping his or her own articulators around the strange sounds uttered by the subject; and, finally, the student must so believe in and commit to both his or her subject, and the created piece of art that represents the subject, that she or he is willing to perform the work publicly to share the character with an audience.

A signal aspect of this exercise is that it develops an appreciation of the uniqueness of each subject, both the one studied and the ones observed through the eyes of other students. Research of this nature succeeds in finding the drama inherent in the lives of ordinary people. It also puts to rest the notion that there is only one right way to speak. Any dialect is as individual as the specific forces that have shaped the individual subject, and "standard speech" is no more than a rule of thumb, a tool for discovering the degrees of deviation from a control medium. Thus, cultural diversity is celebrated in a highly textured and distinctive way by finding the "culture" in commonplace speech. Such a process goes to the heart of the actor's mimetic craft, without diminishing the art and individuality of the actor. Constance Welch always used to say that we should both believe in the character *and* see the actor behind the character. In this exercise, there is a joining of actor and subject that celebrates both the particularity of the subject and the empathic response of the actor, doing honor to both and bringing delight to an audience who may find their own observational skills sharpened by the experience.

At the ATHE Conference in Chicago, in August of 1994, Robert Wills spoke movingly of the bonding experience he shared with his cast of *Vital Signs* at Pacific Lutheran University, when they told stories from their lives to one another, both in and out of rehearsal. He concluded that we all need to tell our stories and to listen to the stories of those around us, in order to develop real community. Some have said that really listening to another human being is the truest act of love. In a country and a world in which cultural diversity is at issue, a source of irritation and an occasion for violence, the development of our powers of listening is a desperate necessity. For those involved in the training of young actors, conscience-struck at the futility of churning out class after class of people trained for an over-saturated market in which only a handful will achieve the success of professional employment, a redefined teaching mission becomes critically important. As we are charged with educating the whole person as well as the actor, developing acute listening skills ought to be of the highest priority. In such a context, the Dialect/Life Study offers a useful exercise for training the actor as well as a means of enlightening the whole person. Thus, our teaching could reach out to change not only the theatre but the society surrounding it as well, adding to community through a deepened understanding of the idiosyncratic individual.

Works Cited

Smith, Anna Deavere. *Fires in the Mirror*. New York: Anchor Books, Doubleday, 1993.

"Twilight: Los Angeles 1992." *New York Times* 15 June 1993.

Wills, J. Robert. "Enabling Women to Raise Their Voices in Theatre: Directing Women in *Vital Signs*." Association for Theatre in Higher Education Conference. Chicago, 1994.

Wise, Claude Merton. *Applied Phonetics*. Englewood, NJ: Prentice-Hall, Inc., 1957.

Part IV: Dealing with Difference

Bruce A. McConachie

So many of the essays in this anthology advocate pedagogical and curricular strategies for enhancing the cultural diversity of theatre education that it may seem superfluous to have a separate section entitled "Dealing with Difference." However, there are may ways of recognizing the distinctiveness of racial, sexual, and class cultures and subcultures, and not all of these ways are equally beneficial to society as a whole and to the minority cultures involved.

The four essays in this section implicitly or explicitly embrace a notion of multiculturalism. Despite much media babble to the contrary, most Americans who are not outright racist or sexist deal with diversity through pluralism and universalism; few commit themselves to multicultural beliefs and behavior. Pluralism recognizes cultural difference but does not presume equality among groups or promote group rights. Universalism often begins in pluralism, then takes the next step of supposing that all significant cultural differences can be transcended—that all peoples, regardless of culture, can find common ground on the basis of an essential and universal humanity. Historically, the American notion of democracy is built upon a conception of universality ("We hold these truths to be self evident...") that erases significant cultural distinctiveness. Multiculturalism, on the other hand, recognizes the legitimacy of cultural diversity among groups and seeks to celebrate and preserve this variety. It does not deny that there are certain commonalities to human life that transcend cultural specificity and consequently allow us to experience and enjoy the culture of others. However, multiculturalists would insist that people of one culture will never experience an event in quite the same way as people in another. Further, multiculturalism is not inherently antithetical to all notions of liberal democracy; it is possible both to define and protect a universal conception of human rights and to guarantee the public recognition and equality of all cultures.

In "Cornerstones and Storehouses: Toward a Theatre of Diversity," Robert Skloot advocates a multicultural position for university theatre programs centered in inclusiveness and humanitarian concern. Noting that past exclusions or mere pluralistic tolerance of many of the world's cultures have made for a social and moral impoverishment of all American theatregoers, Skloot urges that we produce transcultural plays that "both inspire and enlarge understanding and feeling" for other cultures on the planet. Cindy Lutenbacher implicitly explores what democratic multiculturalism might mean for teaching an introduction to theatre course. Based in the educational philosophy of Paolo Freire, her courses at two very different schools in the Atlanta area require students to experience a wide range of cultural performances and then to use them as springboards for examining race, class, and gender differences in America. Lutenbacher forthrightly discusses the gap between her utopian goals and the realities of student life and institutional constraints. Attempting to realize goals similar to Lutenbacher's in their introductory course at a state university in Wisconsin, Meg Swanson and Robin Murray found their mostly white, middle-class students ignorant and resistant. Instead of abandoning their goals, however, they developed a new course "Playwrights of Color," which allowed them to develop more fully the historical and cultural backgrounds of the Native American, Black, Hispanic and Chinese-American plays they assigned. They report that this new course gave their students an appropriate vocabulary and greater confidence about dealing with issues of diversity in their lives.

The final essay in this section implicitly takes the discussion of multiculturalism and theatre education in a new direction. Sam Abel notes that all theatre educators have much to contribute as well as much to gain from the inclusion of gay and lesbian studies in the theatre curriculum. Abel makes specific suggestions about ways to explore and discuss the many past and present cultures of gays and lesbians in dramatic lit, theatre history, acting, and design courses. His essay concludes with a helpful list of relevant articles, books, and anthologies. In addition to discussing the social construction of gendered cultures, the essay provides a useful model for teachers of theory and performance to work together on multicultural courses.

Cornerstones and Storehouses:
Toward a Theatre of Diversity

Robert Skloot

The stone which the builders rejected has become the cornerstone.
  —Psalm 118

... even you, who knows, will have added to my store.
  —Pozzo to Didi and Gogo in *Waiting for Godot*

In western culture, the theatre began as a holy place connected to gods, affiliated with worship, expressive of civic spirit. In most ways, our postmodern world is different from that of ancient Greece—perhaps in all ways save this: that what we call human progress has only served to make life's mysteries thicker, and the thickest of all is coming to understand who and what we are. For many of us rooted in the cultures of the west, Aristotle's favorite tragedy, Sophocles' *Oedipus the King*, becomes the dramatic paradigm for the individual's search for self. At his life's end, Oedipus, the wandering, eyeless, exiled king is reconciled into the bosom of something distinctly divine, swallowed up into that which ineffably surrounds and completes. If you want to feel the exhilaration of the reconciliation and the tug of the sublime, listen to the final hymn of *The Gospel at Colonus*, the recent retelling of the ancient story as a gospel musical. In the cadences of the song, we are told to "let the weeping cease.... There is no end." Together with Oedipus, we feel restored and healed. This brief essay concerns the holy, or at least the moral kind of theatre that extends to us the opportunity of restorative experience in our world.

It is clear that a restorative theatre is only one kind of theatre, and rarely the kind of theatre we seek out purposefully. In every age, from old Athens to Off-Broadway, audiences attend the theatre for an assortment of reasons among which are these: to stimulate our imagination, to confirm our beliefs, to express our concern, to witness artistic achievement, to show ourselves to others, and to enjoy ourselves through distraction from our troubles. However, prior to all these, and necessary to them, whether at the Theatre of Epidaurus, the Teatro Farnese, the Globe, at Garrick's Theatre, Forbes's, or Harold Clurman's, we gathered in order *to participate in a community*. It is in this sense first that the theatre offers up its power and its challenge to the idea of diversity. In the words of the theatre critic Elinor Fuchs:

In a society that is increasingly in the remote control of the media, the theatre is perhaps an institution of an earlier culture. It is, after all, physical, local, communitarian and present. Its motion is centripetal. The way it draws people together, its sense of occasion, is fundamentally social. Our motion as a culture today is centrifugal. We are losing the sense of the social. (17)

It is surprising that what is fundamentally true about the theatre's social and communal essence often goes unrecognized, except perhaps for two groups of people who are, not always humorously, often spoken of in the same breath: theatre critics and political tyrants. The tyrant knows his risk of assembling masses of people to witness ideas other than his own, the most threatening of which, when presented together and richly articulated, are two: that we are not the same, and that we are not alone. By gathering together for a theatrical event we can affirm both of these ideas merely by our presence. Surely Sophocles understood this in his own day, writing about how we come to learn who we are while we are together. A modern commentator, Wendell Berry, who has spent a lifetime thinking about all kinds of social communities, adds something of value to this discussion.

The acquisition of knowledge always involves the revelation of ignorance—almost *is* the revelation of ignorance. Our knowledge of the world instructs us first of all that the world is greater than our knowledge of it. To those who rejoice in the abundance and intricacy of Creation, this is a source of joy, as it is to those who rejoice in freedom. (42)

The corollary of Berry's statement is that enemies of freedom and a pluralistic democracy are those who are convinced of and satisfied with the sufficiency of their limited understanding.

Berry helps us to understand why the issue of diversity, if it is to be meaningfully comprehended and celebrated, has become central to the university. Receptivity to diversity will occur because, at least in theory, the university's first mission is the teaching of knowledge and critical thinking about knowledge, and the amelioration of ignorance. However, over the last decade, the disagreements among academics over the issue of diversity have been fierce and acrimonious, and the amount of material produced and energy expended on it proliferates at a furious rate. Traditionalists are loathe to relinquish culture's cohesive and assimilationist function, while postmodernists advocate jettisoning ideas of "unitary" heritage (if that were even possible), and replacing them with ethnic empowerment as the primary objective in the current culture wars. Nonetheless, whatever their goals, both must confront the universal problem of the academy: the eradication of ignorance. It is here that the theatre arts have a vital and efficacious role to play, for in the community formed by theatre-going we can be exposed to cultural diversity in three sites: in the audience assembled, in the idea expressed, and in the image displayed. The work of the academic theatre is to reveal knowledge, not as units to accumulate, but as a way to renew experience through the expression of the imagination.

We have recently come to understand that traditional audiences, ideas, and images have been deficient. Audiences have long been drawn together along class lines that effectively excluded large numbers of people. The ideas and images described and subsequently affirmed (patriarchy, heterosexuality) influenced negatively what is seen in the theatre. Today, we recognize the problem as one of exclusion and absence. Missing from texts were whole peoples and experiences, and it is with this realization, the one Berry writes about, that we have become alerted to the problem of our ignorance and aware of its terrible consequences: a cultural and social impoverishment that results from the perpetuation of predetermined structures and the silencing of voices. One place to remedy the problem is the university theatre which, because of the very nature of its pedagogical mission, can assist in making the changes which must occur on the road to understanding who we are and what we can be.

I have spent the past fifteen years engaged in study of the Holocaust, the near-complete destruction of the Jewish community of Europe. One result of my contact with Holocaust materials is the bias toward seeing the event as an exclusive measure of other genocides, past and future, though none so awesome or awful, so efficient or so complete as that wrought by the German nation and its allies before and during World War II. All of us know, in part, how the Holocaust was made possible: through the continual exploitation of fear engendered by denigrating images of the intended victims, the "others," the Jews. (They were not the only group targeted.) The comparison of the Jew with sub-human creatures and, worse, what the historian Michael Marrus calls "the systematic dehumanization of the victims" (23) had the inevitable result of concentrated and efficient murder of a kind and on a scale not seen previously or since in human events. This episode in history has validated not merely the negative power of images and the terrible wages of stereotypes, but of the capacity of average human beings to commit or to be accomplices to deeds of pure evil. The theatre often reveals this dark side of human nature, but it can show us alternative modes of behavior also. Prospero's moral embrace of the monster Caliban at the end of Shakespeare's *The Tempest* is just such a theatrical and moral moment: "This thing of darkness I acknowledge mine," he confesses. Here the "thing" refers to both Caliban *and* to Prospero's own ugly authorization of Caliban's oppression.

The theatre possesses the power and the obligation to work against evil tendencies, and it can do this in two ways: by raising issues of history, no matter how painful, and by presenting images of goodness, no matter how unavailing. The theatre that reflects these strategies will inevitably engage the issue of diversity. The playwright George Tabori, Hungarian-born and now working in Germany, whose knowledge of evil came with the death of his father in Auschwitz, has said: "If we cannot see beyond the taboos and cliches and regard one another as people and not as abstractions, then you might as well light up the ovens again." Or listen to the philosopher William Gass, whose prose is more fanciful than Tabori's, but whose point, here about the community that art makes, is relevant to this discussion:

> ... and we can, comforted by this realization, return for another helping
> of that dessert, and smile at our friends whose minds are momentarily
> in their mouths where ours is, secure in our communal assumptions;
> that we share with them a moist cube of cake and a number of not
> dissimilar crumbs; that calories will not capriciously cling to one of us
> rather than another; that, in one sense, we lick our fingers with the same
> tongues. (Gass 74)

For me, artists present the manifest way for seeing "beyond the taboos and cliches." It is hard work, full of risks and not always successful, but it provides the proof of the transcultural nature of art which can both inspire and enlarge understanding and feeling. [1] Of course, this belief is not universally shared, and how we feel about it determines and is determined by very powerful political, racial, and gendered attitudes. But dismissing this belief relinquishes one weapon in the fight against cultural nationalism and ignorance, and gives aid to the unhappy condition of social animosity and fragmentation. On the other hand, accepting the idea of transcultural experience places all of us at the very center of the politics and the celebration of diversity, an idea different from "mere pluralism," as the essayist-poet Frederick Turner has pointed out:

> Mere pluralism requires no change in one's own or one's neighbor's
> perspective; indeed, it is threatened by change, especially by any
> attempt to understand and imagine, and thus incorporate, the contents
> of another cultural box. It so fears hierarchy—one possible result of
> such an incorporation—that it would prefer ignorance. Its tolerance of
> other world views could well be described as neglect or even as a kind
> of intellectual cowardice. At its worst, one could describe it as an
> abdication or a shirking of the great human enterprise of mutual
> knowledge, communication (literally, 'making one together'), and
> mutual transformation. (Turner 96)

Universities are eminently suited to carrying out the mission of diversity. First, in them is found the archives of civilization, the institutional repository of memory we call History, Folklore, Art, Women's Studies, Theatre and Drama, and Comparative Literature Departments and Programs. There, one can find the written, visual, and musical record of diversity. Yet these repositories allow for individual immersion only, except for the occasional faculty lunch, colloquium, or academic conference, and the type of enlightenment these occasions offer is essentially passive and almost exclusively intellectual, though indispensable in helping to prepare the way for the world Tabori and Berry and others I will refer to envision. The dean of American theatre critics Eric Bentley referred to a statement by the Mexican novelist Carlos Fuentes:

I do not believe that literature has an immediate partisan role to play, but I do believe that literature is revolutionary and thus political in a deeper sense. Literature not only sustains a historical experience and continues a tradition. It also—through moral risk and formal experimentation and verbal humor—transforms the conservative horizon of the readers and helps liberate us all from the determinisms of prejudice, doctrinal rigidity, and barren repetition. (Qtd. in Bentley 4)

Along with literature, this is equally the theatre's function.

Second, the university is *practiced* in the way to study and celebrate diversity publicly, communally, and actively: in the arts in general and the theatre in particular. Gathering us together to experience diversity in the company of people who are *presenting* diversity in image and idea can force an intellectual and emotional confrontation upon us. Further, as an art form dependent on the collaboration of many artists, it can teach by example collaborative enterprise, behavior which often falls victim to the jurisdictional disputations of academic compartmentalism.

In my study of American plays over the last generation, I have used the term "The Theatre of the Oppressed" to describe the many powerful examples of drama stimulated by a historical sense of exclusion and oppression, plays written by African-Americans, Native Americans, Chicanos, women, gays and lesbians, and others. These plays are attempting several complicated tasks at the same time: to retrieve and revise images, to rediscover history, to reconfirm cultural vitality, to resist assimilation and to rally and reinforce spiritual and creative energy. Of necessity, but I hope of finite duration, these plays sometimes make a virtue out of exclusion. Still, these are the plays we need to see more of and, more specifically, to produce in the university, although the challenges to doing so are formidable.

However, the commitment to diversity also contains a moral obligation of another kind. It asks us, each in his or her own way, to relinquish our belief in our cultural, sexual, or racial hegemony, and it asks us to do this whether we belong to the oppressor or the oppressed group. It asks, even *insists* that we dare to sacrifice one identity for another which is less "pure," but which, I would argue, is more capacious and ultimately more rewarding. It does not ask that we give up our history (how could I give up the Holocaust?), but only that we share enough of it to make room for someone else's, thus filling the space which is created by the transaction. Frequently, the price a commitment to diversity demands is an acceptance of the threat of cultural exposure, of the risk of yet more embarrassment or discomfort of the kind that comes with the scrutiny of the ugly part we all possess. In the theatre, negative images, so powerful in their vitality and presentness, may be painful or unbearable precisely because they are known to be historically true. But they are part of the record, and making an absence of them, excluding them because they made us uncomfortable, is no help to our search for truths, however provisional, or wholeness, however temporary.

In addition, we must also recognize the *diversity in diversity*. We must listen carefully to hear the many voices in the one voice and we must act assertively to make our voice heard above the grinding hum of hegemony. A theatre of diversity asks us to recognize the joy in our task because the ultimate reward is so great; it asks us to celebrate what Walt Whitman celebrates (in the words of the poet June Jordan): "A nation indivisible but dependent upon and astonishing in its diversity" (Jordan 197). August Wilson, one of our most splendid playwrights, said this in a conversation with Bill Moyers:

> I was writing about black America—the specifics of the play are about black America. But there is something larger at work. A painter, when asked to comment on his work, once said, 'I try to explore in terms of the life I know best, those things which are common to all culture.' So while the specifics of the play are black, the commonalities of culture are larger realities in the play. You have father-son conflict, you have husband-wife conflict—all these things are universal.[2] (*American Theatre* 55)

The university can also foster diversity because an environment genuinely supportive of the performing and visual arts sanctions the process of creation which, by its very nature, is without prejudice. As it matures, this process turns outward, seeking responses from others who can hear its innermost voice and share its powerful presence. Artistic discovery (the less reputable though identical sibling of scientific discovery) is wholly selfless despite the fact that it is based in the self. For the arts produce their increase and their flourishing, as Lewis Hyde (another celebrant of the poet Whitman) tells us in his wonderful book *The Gift*, upon the sharing of those gifts, not by the hoarding or sale of them:

> The true commerce of art is a gift exchange, and where that commerce can proceed on its own terms we shall be heirs to the fruit of gift exchange: in this case, to a creative spirit whose fertility is not exhausted in use, to the sense of plenitude which is the mark of all erotic exchange, to a storehouse of works that can serve as agents of transformation, and to a sense of an inhabitable world—an awareness, that is, of our solidarity with whatever we take to be the source of our gifts, be it the community or the race, nature or the gods. But none of the fruits will come to us where we have converted our arts to pure commercial enterprises. (158–59)

In the words of the poet Maya Angelou: "Love increases with the giving of it."

If we accept these premises about the theatre and diversity, we must wonder if the university is up to the task to create the environment for its existence.[3] As I write this, it is difficult to be optimistic about the chances for success. The condition of arts faculties at many universities concerning pay and facilities is shocking and worsening. The conditions of our professional lives have become an enormous burden, and especially unfair in the light of the mission we must carry out in the struggle to create and celebrate diversity. As our workplace deteriorates in an environment of increasing commercialization, and as our compromised status and diminished relative compensation produces a plummeting morale, an extraordinary effort led by enlightened university administrations and individual artist-teachers will be necessary before the situation can improve.[4]

Above all, this job needs doing, and there is no good reason to stay around if we do not dedicate ourselves to it. It surely cannot be escaped. A diverse theatre can be the cornerstone of our academic storehouse, our artistic home in which we will always find increase and astonishment. When the weeping ceases, we can together beat a path to the sublime. If we do not, in the words of William Gass, what awaits is dire:

> But when I notice my neighborhood being infiltrated by a foreign people who don't even know what a bidet is for; when it is not one or another of them that has done me damage, but the very mode of their being, the continued condition of their consciousness; when a considerable part of their history is an awareness of me, my guilt, my criminality, of what I have done to them; when they seem to exist only to bear witness to the fallen character of man; when they refuse to couch their consciousness in my language; when they will not even pretend to fit in—they might, for instance, at least eat the same foods, celebrate the same holidays, wear basic beige and sport spiffy armbands from Bill Blass—but continue in stubbornness to insist, while being stepped on even, on their superiority to my shoes (although, I must admit, a good many are attempting to pass, very suspicious types, these, and bear watching; once you could tell their names; shifty, several have tried to gain admission to my club); and when, in addition to all this, in addition to their presence, their food smells, their clannishness, their circumcisions, they are successfully competing with me for wealth and women and other articles of exchange, for power and other positions where one can exercise inflexibility; what then? what then?
>
> Who is this *emigre* you are complaining about? who is the fellow? is he the Chink? the Red Menace? the Turk? the Slav? the Jew? Oh no. No one special. Merely our fellow man.
>
> Ah. Well, then. The dumb bunny deserves it. Puff to you, boy.
>
> Boo-oo-oo-oom.
>
> And that is the origin of extermination in the imagination.[5]
>
> (Gass 242)

Notes

1. This is an extremely complicated issue, in part because the line between cultural exploitation and transcultural inspiration may be difficult to discern. When are cultural artifacts property? When does appropriation become ethnocentric pillaging? What is the relationship of culture to power? These urgent questions are addressed in the important Special Issue of Performing Arts Journal 33/34, 1988 ("The Interculturalism Issue"). In the interview "Lee Breuer on Interculturalism," the creator of Oedipus at Colonus remarks about his recent work: "Our idea of what is right or wrong is culturally determined. There is no universal. What I am interested in doing is to put Europe in its place in American culture, because it is only about one-third of the whole story. I am trying to work against measuring everything by European rules.... Third World art is defined as good, depending on how it approximates European standards. The only way of moving toward a universal understanding is the complete interrelationship of cultures." (60–1) I am also aware of the terrible failure of art to prevent suffering, remembering, of course, that art is not intended only for utilitarian purposes. The failure of culture to stand against the brutality and murder of the Holocaust, for example, is one of the most difficult issues to ponder. See the densely polymathic work of George Steiner in this regard and, in more anecdotal fashion, Robert Coles's The Call of Stories (New York: Houghton Mifflin, 1989). There is also the continuing controversy over the fatwa issued against Salman Rushdie, and the response of artists and governments to it. Breuer's interest in the other "two-thirds" of the world may not be as wholesome or pure as he might like it to be.

2. I am reminded of the last line of Arthur Miller's moving autobiography Timebends: "...the truth, the first truth, probably, is that we are all connected, watching one another."

3. Several books take a penetrating look at the state of American universities and prescribe various remedies for the crises in their politics and pedagogy. See especially David Bromwich, Politics by Other Means: Higher Education and Group Thinking (New Haven: Yale, 1992), Frederick Crews, The Critics Bear It Away: American Fiction and the Academy (New York: Random House, 1992).

4. As I have noted, this idea of theatre is not neutral, but is based on important political assumptions which will bring—indeed have already brought—powerful negative forces to bear on the issue. The heated national and campus discussion about broadening and diversifying the traditional curriculum is one evidence of this. A theatre of diversity means teaching different plays than in the past, or different perspectives on the same plays, which is much the same thing. This job, though, is easy compared to the

problem of producing plays of diversity, because frequently we lack the diversity, minority actors, for example, who would make these productions credible or even possible. The search for diversity is being advanced on many fronts simultaneously, and we will experience setbacks on the way to doing all that we can and must.

5. Many recent books take a penetrating look at the state of American universities and prescribe various remedies for the crises in their politics and pedagogy. For a list of these books and a historical context of the issues, see Robert Skloot, "The 'P.C. Controversy' in American Higher Education," Wisconsin Academy Review (Summer, 1994): 2-4.

Works Cited

Bentley, Eric. "Writing For Political Theatre." *Political Theatre Today*. Ed. Jane House. New York: IWE Columbia University and CUNY-CASTA, 1988. 4–9.

Berry, Wendell. "People, Land and Community." *The Graywolf Annual Five: Multi-Cultural Literacy*. Ed. Rick Simonson and Scott Walker. St. Paul: Graywolf Press, 1988. 42–50.

Fuchs, Elinor. "The Theatricalization of American Politics." *American Theatre* January, 1987. 17–24.

Gass, William H. "The Origin of Extermination in the Imagination." *Habitations of the Word: Essays*. New York: Simon and Schuster, 1985. 242–61.

———. "Representation and the War for Reality." *Habitations of the Word: Essays*. New York: Simon and Schuster, 1985. 74–86.

Hyde, Lewis. *The Gift: Imagination and the Erotic Life of Property*. New York: Vintage, 1982. 158–59.

Jordan, June. "For the Sake of a People's Poetry: Walt Whitman and the Rest of Us." *Poetry and Politics*. Ed. Richard Jones. New York: Quill, 1985. 197–215.

Marrus, Michael R. *The Holocaust in History*. New York: New American Library, 1987. 23–35.

Moyers, Bill. "An Interview with August Wilson." *American Theatre* 6.3 (June, 1989): 55–9.

Turner, Frederick. "The Universal Solvent: Meditations on the Marriage of World Cultures." *Performing Arts Journal 35/36* (1990): 96-105.

Teaching Introduction to Theatre:
Community as Pedagogy, Politics, and Text

Cindy Lutenbacher

A pedagogy is that much more critical and radical the more investigative and less certain of 'certainties' it is. The more unquiet a pedagogy, the more critical it will become.
—Paulo Freire, Foreword, *An Unquiet Pedagogy*

Why

Although I feel certain that in some perverse fashion I would love to make a case for each course I teach to be the most exciting class for which to prepare, I confess to a special spot in my heart for introduction to theatre courses. Intro seems to muster the most delightful glomerulus of students with backgrounds, expectations, needs, experiences, biases, and abilities, as diverse as high weeds in last year's ball-field. The patchwork population is exhilarating, especially as students begin to embrace difference and enter community. Furthermore, the divergences offer the best challenges to students' preconceived ideas about theatre and the world—challenges far superior to anything this professor might proffer, no matter how sagacious and Buddha-ish I may wish to become one day.

I also believe that intro to theatre is one of the courses most critical to the health of theatre. Although I believe our tasks in the introductory course are similar to those in every other course—that teachers and students together may become "more fully human" (Freire 52)—I see intro as the locus that offers the greatest freedom with which to encounter our lives and those of others. Intro is a site to ask the questions that help make sense of every other course. Intro is the place to set the framework of student-generated understanding and student/teacher collaboration in learning, a most difficult framework to set considering that our entire educational structure is based on the concept of a higher authority responsible for and critical of student acquisition of "absolute" knowledge. Oh, my.

So I take very seriously the adventure of teaching introduction to theatre.

I have had the privilege of teaching the introductory course at two very different colleges which also have a major overlap of similarities: Kennesaw State College, a ten-thousand student, four-year progeny of the Georgia State University System and located in Cobb County (now nationally infamous for its censorship of "non-family values" art), and Agnes Scott College, a six-hundred student, private four-year women's college located in Decatur. Both colleges have easy access to Atlanta, both are primarily white schools with some populations of African-American, Latino/a and Asian-American students, both colleges have a substantial population of non-traditionally aged students, and both have recent histories of racist, homophobic, and otherwise oppressive occurrences. Although both colleges have students from all socioeconomic classes, Agnes Scott, by virtue of its $12,000 tuition price-tag, collects the vast majority of its students from the wealthy elite of the South. Kennesaw, with its $1,500 tuition, attracts a much higher percentage of students who are working their way through school. Because I want to work toward an education that is created by all involved in its process, I do not practice the generic design of courses; so, in imagining the intro courses for these colleges, I try to take into consideration all of these factors of population and place.

I also try to be honest with the class about the precepts that are important to me—knowing that these are simply what I have to offer as *part* of students' encounter with theatre/life: 1) theatre is most profoundly meaningful when it arises from and is connected to a particular community of people—never art for art's sake; 2) we are all responsible—from audience to actor and all in between—for theatre, for its occurrence and for its connection to community. That is, theatre does not happen "out there" as if we are free to consume it in good capitalist fashion. Theatre is the experience of theatre-going and theatre-making, a hands-on policy, rather than the reading of printed texts; 3) the whole event is theatre, beginning and ending long before and long after the time frame between "curtains," and it includes one's own self and the community as essential parts of the event (ideas popularized by Schechner, Turner); and, always knocking on my spiritual/intellectual door, 4) a commitment to the vastness of cultures and communities engaging theatre, including the community of our little classroom.

In my ideal world, we students and we teachers would all sit down together to invent all the coursework, the problems, and the questions; to some degree, I can create opportunities for this to happen in the courses charged to me. However, under the capital-based educational structure of grades and Darwinian competition, I don't know if it is possible fully to make such a leap to a class generated curriculum. Accustomed as students are to the more passive "I-am-an-empty-bucket-to-be filled-by-the-teacher's knowledge" philosophy of education, I worry that an overnight switch to my idealized pedagogical framework would leave students clueless and frustrated. I believe we need to do our darndest as teachers to structure courses that give students chances to develop the skills for claiming their own authority for knowledge as well as their responsibility to community. My participation in intro to theatre is one small step for this womankind in creating an education of authentic liberation.

What

Thus far, I have begun my intro classes by presenting a problem that becomes one of the, if not the main, through-lines for the course. "Hi, everybody," I begin, "My name is Cindy Lutenbacher and I have a PhD in theatre and drama from Northwestern University, as well as twenty-five years of experience in writing, acting, directing, designing, managing, producing, and everything else in theatre. And I still don't know what the hell theatre is." I am not lying when I say these things. Of course I have ideas about what is theatre, and I do not conceal this fact; but I work arduously to keep all tenets of my ideas open to fierce revision. I invite the students to begin asking what elements and attributes of some event are necessary for theatre to happen, according to our own experiences and beliefs. Jerzy Grotowski and Peter Brook usually find their way into these conversations, as well as Atlanta baseball, the Lao Baci, presidential inaugurations, my Southern Baptist youth, John Cage and Samuel Beckett, pow-wows, their freshman orientations, high school graduations, *The Crucible*, *A Raisin in the Sun*, their births, grandparents' funerals, military bands, television, and the latest hot movie. A fair amount of discomfort often surfaces in such discussions: most of us are more accustomed to teachers having answers than to teachers having questions, and I suspect that it may frustrate some students a bit to be confronted with the responsibility for creating one's own responses, solutions, answers. It may be equally as frightening to have those responses both challenged and validated within the context of the class.

I work very hard to keep the class a safe place to be ignorant and, therefore, open. I am cautious not to belittle any questions or comment, usually turn questions back to the class, and qualify my own opinions with "But that's just one idea—what do you think?" Although we have vociferous discussions, rarely is there disrespect displayed between students; a gentle chide is usually all that is needed in those few instances. Students respond well to this environment, risking more and more of themselves in their performance assignments and the class discussions.

At Agnes Scott I ask the class to pitch nose first into the question of what is theatre by assigning a masked performance piece (an assignment I borrow from Dwight Conquergood at Northwestern) to be presented by the third class period. Each student makes a mask that represents herself in some form or fashion, and for class presentation, she wears the mask and either sings a song, shares a dream, or tells a story. Through seemingly the simplest of exercises, students begin to encounter some of the most integral pieces of our human and theatrical puzzle: the performative paradox of self and not-self (as affected by the mask); the potential composite pieces of presentation/representation—spectacle, actor, audience, language, story; and the power and necessity of proclaiming ourselves in community. "Nothing is completely true for us as long as we cannot announce it to the world as to ourselves" (Gusdorf 72), I quote to them, and they begin fretting over the meaning and veracity of Gusdorf's statement.

More importantly, this exercise gives the class the foundation to create its own sense of community, fragile and temporal though that may be. The class knows things about one another, things shared both intentionally and incidentally. Cultural barriers lose some of their potency; for example, last autumn one of the Japanese exchange students spoke of her homesickness, of the academic pressure she was experiencing, and of her parents' long distance comfort and support. With tears aplenty, the class began to speak of what they shared as students together; this discussion laid the foundation for expressing the differences that existed because of culture and background. Yoko's story became a watchword for the "us-ness" in that room that autumn.

Because of this exercise, students' began to speak of "community" from a place of shared understanding and vulnerability as well as from their own individual experiences of community. Students began to dig for bones in the idea that community is a critical path to knowing who we are or even that we are. It is a lot to get from one small assignment.

The mask assignment breaks ground for another essential in my small effort toward revolutionary education: de-authorization of the teacher in order to claim authority within oneself and one's community. Toward this end, my classes have several important components of group work. At both Agnes Scott and Kennesaw State, the "final" is a group presentation of a performance production concept. In groups of four to eight students (depending on the size of the class), they either choose or create a text for which to create a performance. Throughout the semester the group meets, sometimes in class and sometimes in addition to class periods, and grapples with the questions incumbent upon any performance: Why are we doing this performance? Who is the intended audience/community? Why does this particular community need this particular performance in this particular time and place? How shall the performance proceed in all its various theatrical elements (including all elements leading up to the time of presentation and following presentation) et cetera ? All decisions about spectacle, language, locale, audience/community participation, etc., filter through the larger questions of "why." In groups, students make decisions for the performance as if they were actually going to produce the performance. In the final presentation, they discuss their ideas with the rest of the class, utilizing visual aids, musical scores, and enacting scenes, in order to make their concept as concrete as possible to the class.

At Kennesaw, because such a large percentage of the students have never attended a play and do not have a clue about "behind-the-scenes" work, part of their assignment for this final project is to interview (individually or in pairs) working professionals in various theatre positions: performer, director, collective theatre member, stage manager, designer, writer, etc. I help them develop interview strategies ranging from the personal (why are you doing theatre, and how do you do what you do) to the political (what do you think theatre is good for). In the individual component of the group presentations, I ask them to incorporate and respond to the ideas gleaned from these professionals, and to note how they might or might not use these ideas were they in the particular shoes of the people interviewed. Additionally, I hope that their contact with others in the theatre community will further de-authorize me and my particular biases and expose them to the reality that there are many ideas of why theatre exists or should exist. Right now in Kennesaw's home of Cobb County, these interview questions are particularly elucidative, as Marietta's

Theatre in the Square, as well as all other arts in Cobb County, have lost county funding due to Theatre in the Square's production of *Lips Together, Teeth Apart*, which contains unseen and unheard characters who are homosexual.

The smaller classes at Agnes Scott allow for more and smaller group projects such as experiments with Boal's ideas of forum theatre. For this project, to help them focus on the power of community problem-solving as elucidated by Boal, I ask them to contain their community to Scott students and as groups choose issues germane to and potent within this community's experience. Their choices vary widely, from personal choices of vegetarianism, to suicide as a response to academic/familial pressures, to the power structures within the college. The groups, in good forum fashion, present these issues in playlets, the endings of which are unfinished, and then we try out various completions using class suggestions and class participation in enactment. By the end of the semester when it is time to complete and present their performance production concepts, students have had substantial experience not only with group work but also with the idea of theatre belonging to a community of people rather than to "art."

We also "play" this course in the larger Atlanta community. Despite the protestations of many in the Atlanta arts community, I find Atlanta to be a very rich resource in people and performance, ripe for educational exploration. It offers sufficient diversity of culture and theatrical form to be, in my opinion, a far superior direct experience for students to reading play texts, performance critiques, and descriptions. Because at Agnes Scott I am free to abandon text books, and choose to do so, I make Atlanta our text, with the experience of eight or more performances as the medium. For example, last autumn we attended/participated in: two traditional Japanese Noh plays (same evening); Czechoslovakian puppetry; African-American "church" theatre (so dubbed by Johnetta Cole) with overt political content; gay/lesbian theatre; legend-making musical theatre; white American male realism, with an attempt at genderization through casting choices; South African semi-presentational theatre with undisguised political investigation; American satire of Christopher Columbus, utilizing a variety of forms and media; presentational children's theatre; and feminist comedy sketches. This list includes only theatrical performances; I did not even try to engage in a wider definition of performance including the wealth of dance, music, and "found" theatre (such as Atlanta baseball, local bars, city council, Cobb County Commission, Saturday and Sunday church, classroom experiences, etc.).

In class discussion of each performance, we focus on the increasingly familiar questions raised at the very beginning of the course: who do you believe is the primary community of this performance? What do you think was the intent or why do you think this production was chosen and created as it was (in all its various elements)? What might the performance mean within its community? What is the source of financial backing for this performance and how much does that source depend on the marketplace for its survival? What is your experience (individual and collective) of this production, etc? Inevitably, at both Kennesaw and Agnes Scott, these discussions are fertile ground for very personal and communal investigations of racism, sexism, homophobia, classism, cultural and economic imperialism, sources of power and authority, and how we choose to invent our own lives. For example, one autumn the Agnes Scott class attended Spelman College's powerful and openly militant production of two Sonia Sanchez plays which concluded with the entire stage and audience community singing, weeping, laughing, holding hands, and collecting money to help enable children to visit their mothers in prison. In my mind it would have been impossible to experience and explore this potent evening without talking about everything from the economics of incarceration to interracial relationships, from militancy/non-violence to theatre as "church"—theatre that belongs to a community. We talked about personal anger and guilt, and the fears some of the white students felt in traveling into the West End, a part of town many had never visited before. The students in that class revealed thoughts and responses that clearly made them uncomfortable. "I couldn't believe that they wanted to hold my hand even *after* that show!" said one white student. That same class attended *The Harvey Milk Show*, and for many students the performance was their first experience of the tenderness, love, and "wholesomeness" that can exist in a love relationship between people of the same gender. "When they kissed," exclaimed a first-year student, "I didn't even gag or anything—it was just plain sweet. I don't remember why I ever thought anything else." Each "chapter" of our performance text brings its own inquiries to our doorstep and invitations to discuss not only personal issues but events, attitudes, and experiences of the campus and global communities.

I believe that my task as "leader" in these initial inquiries is simply to help create the opportunity for exploration by honoring all sincere responses, thus keeping the classroom safe. I emphasize their explorations and note that my opinions are just one of many responses. My refusing "to install the language of the professor as the only valuable idiom in the classroom" (Freire and Shor 1987, 23) is intended to enable their empowerment. For example, by the end of the term, students are posing important questions of "why" and "how" to each other and to themselves, with little to no prompting from me. With sufficient class-as-community invention, my role as "mother hen" gradually diminishes and the class takes another step in the long journey toward authorization of self and self in community, rather than looking to the teacher or another outside authority for wisdom.

The Atlanta community provides another resource for these classes: people. Even with little to no funding available, professional writers, actors, designers and directors in the area are remarkably receptive to participating in fora or visiting the class to discuss the kinds of questions we have been exploring all semester. I try to save these resources for a time near the end of the term so that students have the experience and confidence needed to engage our visitors in the tougher questions of "why" and "for/with whom" that have become the hallmark of the class. My hope is that the variety of ideas expressed in these discussions will help students learn to make up their own minds about what is important in theatre and in their lives.

In the course of a term, students write three to four individual papers as well as a written version of the collective production project. These papers are their own examinations of the various theatrical, political, and personal issues raised by the performances experienced. In preparation for these papers, I briefly present the ideas of various scholars. We talk at some length about the ideas of the whole event of theatre, as published by Victor Turner and Richard Schechner. In considering the "community" of each performance, we necessarily invite questions about the "ideal" participant, about being a "resistant reader" or an included member of the congregation, as articulated by contemporary feminist and African-American writers such as Jill Dolan and bell hooks. We talk about Mikhail Bakhtin's writings concerning the multiple voices inherent in any "arc" of communication. In response to their papers, I provide them with pages of my own questions—questions concerning audience composition, the location of the performance space in Atlanta, standard technical and artistic questions, questions about their companions for the event and their feelings before, during, and after the performance. Bakhtin begins to make sense to them.

These concepts are difficult ones, especially for eighteen-year-olds, freshly aglow from the hometown high school production of *Oklahoma*. However, I think it important that students begin encountering such ideas from the most nascent moment of their college careers, even if some of them experience confusion in writing such papers. Usually by the second or third try, most students are grappling with a host of issues: the idea of their own subjective response a critical element to the event, the lack of an absolute objective reality in performance, their own authority in interpretation, and the "wherefores" of a theatrical event in relation to a community. For an intro class I care far less about students acquiring the intellectual implements of library research and far more about their meeting up with a Buddha on the road of inquiry and wonder.

Because I do believe in the power of the past in helping to shape the present, I bring in ideas about the value and definition of performance from the western theatrical tradition. I begin with a class-long imagination journey into what might be or might have been the community inspiration and necessity to perform both the self and the history of the tribe/community. Thereafter, I discuss ideas from the fifth century B.C., Aristotle, Native American rituals, the Middle Ages, Stanislavski, African American traditions, Brecht and Boal. Other traditions and concepts find their way into the class when we encounter Noh plays and Czechoslovakian puppetry. I content myself with the belief that a meager introduction to the enormous variety of ideas concerning performance is all that is needed in intro to plant the garden for investigations. Students who find themselves drawn to theatre will meet these ideas and histories again and again.

Some Questions and Issues

All of this sounds so jolly—the focus on community and on looking to a much wider world for information and ideas for making choices and on questioning more than answering. However, there are thorny patches.

For example, how does one tell if this pedagogical strategy works. Are students learning to resist the "empty bucket" theory of education that keeps them passive and unquestioning? Are they learning (or even beginning to attain the skills needed) to claim authority in making choices in their lives? Is it possible or reasonable to expect major changes in a ten- or fifteen-week term? These are qualities that would be difficult to measure with even the best longitudinal, qualitative studies, yet are germane to this inquiry.

I believe, however, that there is evidence that for most students the seeds of self-authorization were nourished in this course. I observed subtle but important shifts both in their work and class relationships over the course of the term. For example, in their response papers I noted that most students observed with significantly greater detail in their later theatre experiences. Further, they had learned to frame their experiences in terms of what they had personally received from and brought to a performance. In later papers, students demonstrated an increasing ability and willingness to examine their own particular biases and how their responses to a performance might have been influenced by bias. By trusting themselves and utilizing each other as resources, they learned to grapple with profound challenges of theatre—just how is *this* performance operating *here*?

As noted earlier, I also observed students relying less and less on me to provide the questioning, and more and more on themselves and one another. In other classes where I have taken a more authoritarian approach, utilizing lectures and tests, I find significantly less student observation, questioning, and analysis, either individually or collectively.

As teachers we can never be completely sure that our energies are having the intended impact. However, these results suggest that students were at least "trying on for size" the ideas of self-empowerment and resistance to authority.

What about the student whose resistance takes the form of becoming more entrenched in narrow kinds of thinking? For example, what about the white student who experiences the Sonia Sanchez plays at Spelman and, after searching his/her heart, finds and defends the most racist reaction? In such instances, I have found that my best response is to simply respect the student's right to an opinion and to give him/her "air-time" and my actively listening heart and mind. I may question the student about the sources of his/her beliefs and responses, but I believe it is crucial for the individual student and for the class to respect any sincerely given response or idea. Generally the classes are far more conservative than I am, but there are nearly always some leftist students who will challenge reactionary ideas with questions and countering experiences; the same paradigm operates when the political positions is reversed. At issue is learning to question more deeply and to put ourselves in the position of another.

Inevitably I find that when students are respected, whatever their personal beliefs, they become more tolerant and understanding of those different from them, more willing to question their own stances, and more open to change.

Also at issue in the pedagogical experiment, is the creation of classroom "community" and whether or not students are really experiencing and valuing this temporal confederation. In truth, the most I hope for the students is some sense of belonging to a group of people with shared experiences, vulnerability and support. True community implies more than temporary commonality, however; it means a commitment to longevity. Given the strictures of the current design of class scheduling, I am content if students simply taste an inclusive sense of "we," one that crosses differences in background and culture.

This "taste of community" was more successfully rendered in the Agnes Scott class, partly because of the influence of Conquergood's mask exercise. (I did not use the exercise at Kennesaw, but will try it with my intro class at Georgia State this next term.) Not only did the students experience first-hand the rigors, fears, and delights of performance, they also made themselves quite vulnerable by revealing the deepest matters that comprise both theatre and our lives, e.g., longing for home, fear of rejection, fear of loss of scholarship and dreams, the joy and power of standing up for oneself, and the grief of betrayal. Throughout these performance days, students continually spoke of the courage to risk, and of the degree to which we human creatures share vulnerabilities and delights. It was, as one student remarked to another at the end of the performances, "I look at you and I see someone so different from me, but really we're not so far apart." In this case, my modeling of non-judgmental response was hardly necessary, for hearts were touched, as evidenced by shared laughter and tears, and students gave one another the support needed. Furthermore, throughout the remainder of the term, students referred not only to specific moments in these performances, but also to the understanding of "togetherness" that the performances generated.

I watched the supportiveness of students for one another manifest itself in small ways throughout the term; there was little competition between the students or between groups; when students presented their experiments to the class, the rest of the students were quick to participate and help make the presentations work; the production project groups were quite willing to share resources and ideas with one another prior to (and during) the presentations to the class; and there was essentially no backbiting between students or whining to me about someone else. These kinds of subtle but detectable manifestations were quite a change from my teaching experience with other courses at Agnes Scott.

There were, of course, some students who did not participate as fully as others. On one occasion a member of a production project group talked to me about the lack of commitment on the part of another group member; I explained that confronting the other student was very much like what a theatre troupe must do in order to complete its task. She did so, and a later check revealed that the problem hand been resolved. Students were also a bit reticent to confront the occasional "rush job" evident in classwork or participation, but the disappointment was palpable in the near silence greeting such work. Moreover, these students were aware of and disappointed in simply missing out on the fun. Rare was the student who did not make up for the hastily conceived work with a far more thoughtful next assignment. In addition, attendance was extremely high in this class, even with a fairly relaxed absence policy.

Naturally, my role in this class could not and cannot be as an equal member of the "community." I am required to assign final grades, and responsible to keep the class moving along, week to week. (I do long for an educational system designed like my own Spanish class which was created by a small group of women who wished to become fluent. Our teacher was invited/hired by us for her skills and she gives us what we ask of her.)

I know that in these classes I must first of all try to model what I hope for: deeper questioning of our lives and the world in which we live, respect for *all* sincere thoughts and feelings, and support for the personal and intellectual growth of those around me. Most students are mightily schooled in looking to teachers for leadership. To utterly abandon this leadership role in the name of democracy would leave many adrift, without yet having acquired the skills needed for claiming the responsibility for and rights to their own education. However, I nurture their leadership by giving them not only opportunities to lead, but also the very support that they eventually learn to give one another— responsiveness, questioning, sharing of resources, and caring.

What of the difficult issue of grading in this deliberately non-competitive model of the classroom? At Kennesaw, my first experience with teaching the introductory course, I followed more closely the course design of previous professors, utilizing the text that the department had already ordered and incorporating a more traditional grading system. At Agnes Scott, I used a contract system to partially skirt the problem of grades and their institutionally generated power inequities. The course involved a substantial amount of work and participation: four papers analyzing performances attended, four individually and collectively created class presentations, the group production project presentation, attendance at eight Atlanta performances, and extensive class discussions. Those who did all of the work with thought and authenticity and who participated in the classwork and discussions (in other words, those who fulfilled the contract) received an A. Grades were assigned decrementally from that point, e.g. those who did eighty-five percent of the work received a B. Those whose work showed little care or thought were given responses, questions, and the opportunity to re-do the work. In this way, students understood their own responsibility for and power to improve their final grades. I prefer this contract system because it places greater responsibility on the shoulders of the student, and less on the "empty bucket" concept of education.

I was fortunate at both Kennesaw State and Agnes Scott to have supportive department chairs. Although at term's end students might not have been able to delineate the differences between Sophocles and Euripides, they were largely engaged by theatre, were knowledgeable and openly appreciative of the work and care that goes into making theatre, and were attending even more theatre than was required by the class; a number of students even changed majors to theatre or changed to a double major. The chairpersons were delighted by these results and heartily supported a more experientially-based introductory course. Furthermore, this course was offered in a context where I continually hear from colleagues, chairs, and administrators a plea for a pedagogy that encourages critical/analytical consciousness. A course that consistently asks students to explore individually, collectively, and actively the "why" of theatre is perceived as apt response to the problem of passive students. Institutions where administrators and faculty are more concerned with presenting a "required body of knowledge" rather that with the abilities to critique such knowledge, might not be so receptive.

Some Critique

I write these words of teacherly tangles with pedagogy because I see my little experiments with the introductory class as just that—experiments, tentative and temporal responses to the need for *conscientizacao*, Freire's call for a progressive/revolutionary reflection and praxis. I am not yet satisfied. I hope that this essay will be one source among many for collegial discussions about the difficult issues and questions inherent in a truly progressive pedagogy.

For example, how might we more fully involve students in the actual construction and creation of the course? As designed, this course allows opportunity for self-expression, individual and collective creativity, and student-generated authority. Yet, the teacher has chosen the performances as well as the various activities of group work, papers, class performances, etc. How do we engage students who have little experience in theatre or in self-authorized education in the construction of their own adventure in inquiry? We know that the current system of education (as a reflection of capital-driven, competition-based, hierarchical culture) has imprinted upon us all the ideas that knowledge and authority are separate from the self, and are to be acquired from those higher up on the tree of knowledge (power). How can we, at the college level, break through those expectations and imprints (both in the students and in ourselves) to create and sustain mutually student/teacher generated education? How do we help to break hierarchical ordering of knowledge so that students do not have their natural curiosity stomped out of them by the time they arrive at college?

I worry that as long as we live in a capitalist culture we will never be able to achieve *conscientizacao* in our education, because the structure of the economy will always require some system of measuring and ranking students, pitting individuals against one another for grades, like racehorses with electric prods under the saddles. As Freire notes, "It's not education which shapes society, but on the contrary, it is society which shapes education according to the interests of those who have power" (Freire and Shor 35). Freire, Shor, and others argue that a "dialogic format" and the critical consciousness to unearth and upend the dominating ideology are the pathways to a liberating education. But are these avenues sufficient, as long as we *live* under capitalism? I do not know the answer, but I dare not give up. Oppression thrives on hopelessness.

Given these realities, how do we (teachers/students) create classes in which students are less involved with teacher approval and grades? How can our classes engage our students to be more involved with the signal issues of their lives as reflected through theatrical performance? How do we utilize the larger community even more in the curriculum? If we are going to experience African-American "church theatre," should we not engage in a fuller, more intensive exploration of this community's context? In what other ways might we look to the people of the surrounding metropolis for involvement? How do we utilize the community when our college is not located in a metropolis, but in a very sparsely populated area?

Looking further at issues of structure, does an introductory theatre course have to be solely a function of the theatre department? What if we tried an interdisciplinary introductory course with perhaps political science or anthropology, and made the class a year-long course?

In designing the intro course, I create opportunities via Atlanta performances for discussions in which issues of racism, sexism, homophobia, classism, and all their kissing cousins can surface. I try to keep the classroom a safe place so that authentic feelings, fears, and perceptions can be expressed openly. I also work to make sure that students know that my opinions are simply one person's response and that diverse thoughts are a necessity as long as they are sincere. The larger culture drenches us daily in its education for oppression. In an intro to theatre class, what are ways to open the door to a countermanding knowledge?

In what other ways can we create and incorporate the class as community, especially when the group has a diverse range of ages, races, classes, genders, and sexual orientations? How do we more deeply examine our own communities of origin to understand our need for communal expression, for "completing" one's individual truth?

Despite the diversity of Atlanta society, there are still wide fissures in the course with regard to students' experiencing the performances of our multicultural world. How do we avoid privileging western performance modes (more readily available in the flesh) over eastern, African, and indigenous people's theatre?

I don't have conclusive answers to any of these questions. Nor should I, I suppose. But these questions, and no doubt many I have not even imagined yet, are my concerns in the introductory course and in every other course assigned to my care. My hope is to further turn the soil of reflection and praxis in our theatre classrooms, as we work toward authentic freedom, toward the "creation of a world in which it will be easier to love" (Freire 24).

Works Cited

Bakhtin, Mikhail. *The Dialogic Imagination.* Ed. Michael Holquist. Austin: U of Texas P, 1981.

Dolan, Jill. *The Feminist Spectator As Critic.* Ann Arbor: UMI Research Press, 1988.

Freire, Paulo. *Pedagogy of the Oppressed.* New York: Seabury Press, 1970.

———. *The Politics of Education: Culture, Power, and Liberation.* Trans. Donaldo Macedo. Granby, MA: Bergin & Garvey, 1985.

Freire, Paulo, and Ira Shor. *A Pedagogy for Liberation: Dialogues on Transforming Education.* Granby, MA: Bergin & Garvey, 1987.

Gusdorf, Georges. *Speaking (La Parole).* Trans. Paul T. Brockelman. Evanston: Northwestern UP, 1965.

hooks, bell. *Yearning: Race, Gender, and Cultural Politics.* Boston: South End Press, 1990.

Schechner, Richard. *Between Theater and Anthropology.* Philadelphia: U of Pennsylvania P, 1985.

Turner, Victor. *The Anthropology of Performance.* New York: Performing Arts Journal Publications, 1986.

———. *From Ritual to Theatre: The Human Seriousness of Play.* New York: Performing Arts Journal Publications, 1982.

Gay and Lesbian Studies and the Theatre Curriculum

Sam Abel

In recent years, courses have begun to appear in university curricula under the rubric of Gay and Lesbian Studies.[1] Gay and Lesbian Studies programs are in place in several schools, while many others have introduced individual courses dealing with gay and lesbian issues. Given the explosion of lesbian, gay, and bisexual issues on the national scene, and the rapid appearance of scholarly material about these issues, Gay and Lesbian Studies will soon take its place alongside existing cross-disciplinary programs in Women's, African-American, Native American, and other area studies. Theatre faculty will have great opportunities to participate in this growing field; more importantly, theatre has a heavy stake in Gay and Lesbian Studies, and major contributions to make equal to, if not greater than, the share it holds in other cross-disciplinary fields.

The purpose of this essay is to raise two questions: first, how does this new field of Gay and Lesbian Studies affect the curriculum and teaching methods of academic theatre; and second, what contributions can theatre educators make to courses dealing with sexual orientation, and what form should such contributions take? In short, what resources do Gay and Lesbian Studies provide for academic theatre; and how, in turn, can theatre educators contribute to Gay and Lesbian Studies? The observations presented here are based on experiences at Dartmouth College in developing courses that address gay, lesbian, and bisexual issues, in the theatre curriculum and in interdisciplinary courses. These discussions, then, reflect the situation of a small, private school, though many issues mentioned here will apply to any academic setting. I focus primarily on undergraduate education, though there are great opportunities for theatre studies to connect with Gay and Lesbian Studies on a graduate level as well.

Canon Fire, or Is There Such a Thing as a Lesbian and Gay Theatre?

The first (and potentially most divisive) question for gay and lesbian theatre studies is the validity of a genre of "Gay and Lesbian drama." Increasing numbers of plays in recent years have addressed issues of non-mainstream sexuality, but do these works constitute a genre? Do all plays that raise gay and lesbian issues belong in such a genre? Or are these concerns too loosely defined to warrant separate classification? Furthermore, if such a category is posited, the questions do not end there. Does gay male theatre belong in the same genre as lesbian theatre, or are they separate categories? Is there a distinct bisexual theatre? Does a play belong to this category if the writer is gay, but the subject matter is not, or if the subject matter is gay-related, but the playwright is straight? Where do the dividing lines end?

These questions are intriguing, but, in the end, moot. What matters is not the objective validity of a genre called "Gay and Lesbian Drama," but that the term is mentioned at all. As Thomas Postlewait argues in a series of recent articles in *Theatre Journal*, genre classification says more about the people who generate the categories than about the works being categorized. To posit a genre of gay or lesbian drama is, then, more than a mode of literary analysis; it is a political act. A lecture, or an entire course, on gay and lesbian drama tells students that issues of sexuality are important in society. The simple fact that plays labeled as "Gay and Lesbian Drama" are discussed at all asserts that there are sexual identities distinct from the mainstream population, and that such plays (and such identities) merit study.

What impact does the introduction of this genre have on the undergraduate drama classroom? If gay and lesbian drama follows the pattern of the drama of other marginalized populations, the first step is to recognize that many notable playwrights from the past were gay men, lesbians, or bisexuals. In the case of other marginalized populations, the process of recognition necessitates a literal act of recovery: finding works that rarely or never saw the stage or publication. Bringing the drama of marginalized populations to public attention means digging through archives, transcribing oral histories, and otherwise documenting that which has never been documented. But for gay writers (at least gay male writers) the process of recovery is less uncovering neglected works than it is revealing the author's sexual identity. Not being immediately identifiable as members of a sexual minority (unless choosing to be so identified), lesbians, bisexuals, and gay men have formed a continuous presence in the theatre, as in all of society. The process of recovery, then, is actually one of reassigning the identity of already familiar works, into a lesbian or gay male context.

Eve Kosofsky Sedgwick, in her landmark study *Epistemology of the Closet*, provides an incisive statement of this process:

> From the keepers of a dead canon we hear a rhetorical question—that is to say, a question posed with the arrogant intent of maintaining ignorance. Is there, as Saul Bellow put it, a Tolstoi of the Zulus? Has there been, ask the defenders of a monocultural curriculum, not intending to stay for an answer, has there ever yet been a Socrates of the Orient, an African-American Proust, a female Shakespeare? From the point of view of this relatively new and inchoate academic presence, then, the gay studies movement, what distinctive soundings are to be reached by posing the question our way—and staying for an answer? Let's see how it sounds:

Has there ever been a gay Socrates?
Has there even been a gay Shakespeare?
Has there ever been a gay Proust?

Does the Pope wear a dress? A short answer, though a very incomplete
one, might be that not only have there been a gay Socrates,
Shakespeare, and Proust but that their names are Socrates, Shakespeare,
Proust; and, beyond that, legion—dozens or hundreds of the most
centrally canonic figures in what the monoculturalists are pleased to
consider "our" culture, as indeed, always in different forms and senses,
in every other. (Sedgwick 51–52)

On the other hand, as Sedgwick adamantly argues, it is dangerous to accept
simple binary definitions of sexuality in identifying works by gay, lesbian, and
bisexual artists. There is little agreement about what, in fact, constitutes a gay
identity; this subject forms a major area of discussion in Gay and Lesbian
Studies. This debate goes beyond the "nature or nurture" argument about what
"causes" homosexuality; it is an issue of how society constructs sexuality, and
how individuals within society relate themselves to this construct. It is
problematic to assign a sexual identity if the person has not confirmed that
identity. For authors who have died without leaving this confirmation, and for
those who lived before the modern concept of homosexuality as an identity, the
problem is very difficult indeed.

In identifying a gay or lesbian drama, it is far too easy to say that a
particular individual is (or was) gay, and to construct a syllabus around that
identity alone: e.g., we will study the musicals of Noël Coward and Cole Porter,
but not those of Richard Rodgers. The author's sexual identity alone cannot
create a genre. If we study Coward and Porter, it is because their works embody
a gay consciousness, not because of their bed partners. On the other hand, "gay
consciousness" is a highly malleable category, and the farther we travel from
contemporary western society, the more difficult it is to define this sensibility.
What criteria do we use to determine whether a work or its author belongs in the
gay canon? What constitutes the standard for gayness in drama? How do we
construct a gay identity in the context of other cultures? These issues (which this
essay does not pretend to be able to resolve) must be raised in determining the
parameters of lesbian and gay drama, and will likely find a variety of solutions as
these debates evolve.

Another question in defining a gay canon is what to do with plays which
deal with gay and lesbian issues, but do so in a negative light, or which were well
meaning in their time, an attempt to create sympathetic feelings for the plight of
the "poor homosexual," but which today seem highly offensive: *The Children's
Hour, The Boys in the Band,* and so on. Vito Russo, in *The Celluloid Closet,*
traces the prejudicial depiction of gay men and lesbians in film; similar studies

have been written recently for the theatre, notably those by Kaier Curtain, John Clum, and Nicholas de Jongh. Just as a course on African-American theatre can profit from a study of minstrel shows and Jim Crow plays, the exploration of lesbian and gay identity on stage should include stereotyped portrayals, painful as these works might be. These works are part of the history of gay identity, and if nothing else, help to focus discussion on the issues of constructing sexuality on the stage.

While canon formation for the drama of gay men involves assigning identity more than textual recovery, for lesbian drama the issue, as with other marginalized groups, is the location, and generation, of plays at all. There is within lesbian and gay drama (hardly surprisingly) a wide disparity in the availability and visibility of dramatic works between men and women. The gayness of gay men is often hidden in their works, but lesbians as creators of theatre have been virtually invisible, at least until the most recent years. It is difficult enough to find canonical plays by women of any sexual orientation; to develop a canon of lesbian drama with any historical weight to it has seemed an almost impossible task.

The historical invisibility of lesbian drama, however, has fostered some positive developments. Because such works have been so thoroughly pushed to the margins of society, lesbian performance has been able to find a unique voice and form, with an innovative and creative energy that gay male drama has never achieved. Plays about gay men have, in the United States, largely been reflections of mainstream Broadway and Off-Broadway material, interesting because of their subject matter, but not for any new approach to dramatic structure or performer-audience relations. Thus, it is harder to argue that gay male drama is truly a separate genre. Lesbian performance, on the other hand, has flourished in underground venues, separate from mainstream theatre, with works that have since influenced other experimental performance. In some ways it is even misleading to call much of lesbian performance "drama," since its impulses are so far from the standard scripted work of traditional western theatre. Instructors may have difficulty finding these pieces, but they provide a remarkable resource, as an alternative to standard models of scripted performance.

If it is difficult to find works dealing with lesbian issues in general, then the task of finding plays by and about lesbians of color is utterly maddening. By a quirk of demographics, fully a third of the enrollment in the gay and lesbian theatre course which was offered at Dartmouth was made up of women of color. Finding plays of direct relevance to their lives posed the largest challenge of the course. One student made it her crusade to unearth everything she could find about theatre by and about lesbians of color, and made this topic the focus of her term paper. After extensive telephone calls and combing through the alternative press, she dug up a few relevant works, but her paper was largely a tale of frustration, and an impassioned plea for greater visibility.

This invisibility is slowly being remedied. There are a number of anthologies of lesbian plays appearing on the market, some of which include works by lesbians of color.[2] Smaller presses that publish these works are beginning to find a market, and some larger publishing concerns are even picking up a few titles. But we are still at a point where many people have trouble saying the word "lesbian," let alone documenting the progress of performance in the lesbian community. This work of making lesbian performance visible to a wider audience is one of the most important tasks of the teacher of gay and lesbian theatre courses.

Building Courses

How should this body of theatrical works by and about lesbians and gay men be incorporated into the theatre curriculum? Ideally, the material would appear in courses devoted exclusively to lesbian and/or gay male theatre. More than enough material on which to build such courses exists; one of the major problems with the Dartmouth gay and lesbian drama course was the overload of material in a ten-week term. Units in this class dealt with prejudicial representations of lesbians and gay men; plays about political issues, identity issues, and coming out, domestic dramas; gender roles and ambiguity; camp and drag; AIDS plays; performance art; street theatre; alternative performance; and issues of censorship. Each topic had at most one week, hardly enough time to go into depth. In many undergraduate institutions, however, an entire course devoted to these questions is an unlikely luxury. The next option, then, is to work these pieces into general courses in dramatic literature or theatre history.

As teachers add lesbian and gay concerns to general courses, it is vital to avoid the "Oh, god, not another minority to add to the checklist" syndrome. Beleaguered instructors, asked to cover all of dramatic literature and theatre history in a year, or even a semester, may sympathize with issues of multiculturalism and diversity, but feel overwhelmed by the amount of material they wish to cover. There are a number of approaches to this problem. Issues of non-mainstream sexuality arise frequently enough so that standard plays may be used to address this area. Instead of teaching *Doctor Faustus* to represent Marlowe, one might teach *Edward II*, or use Wedekind's *Pandora's Box* to illustrate German expressionism. Or, more to the point, instead of thinking of dramatic literature syllabi as checklists, either for a traditional canon or for a collection of canon revisions by marginalized groups, select plays based on their interest and merit. Plays belong in courses not because they are supposed to be important according to some external authority, but because they are artistically alive; raise vital social, political, or cultural questions; or influence the aesthetic or intellectual thinking of an artist or population. By such standards, issues of sexual difference are central to any survey of theatre today.

Beyond developing courses in lesbian and/or gay male drama and the including plays dealing with sexual difference in a broader course, finding a place for Gay and Lesbian Studies in the theatre curriculum becomes more complex. Is it possible, for example, to create a course in gay theatre history? Can there be a history of gay theatre prior to the development of the contemporary notion of gay identity? If a course in gay and lesbian theatre history is problematic, however, it is quite simple for a general theatre history course to draw on the resources of Gay and Lesbian Studies. The theatrical tradition of cross-dressing, for instance, provides some useful perspectives. Most theatre history, as typically taught to undergraduates, gives only the briefest nod to the fact that men played women's roles in fifth-century Athens and Elizabethan London, not to mention the long-standing traditions of transvestism in opera, music hall, and other less "serious" forms of performance. The study of this kind of gender-transgressive behavior is, however, at the heart of Gay and Lesbian Studies, and there is a great contribution to be made by its methodologies in finding ways to explain the practice of cross-dressing to theatre history students.

It is a comparatively easy matter to address the issue of Gay and Lesbian Studies in the "paper" courses, where there is some documentation of the presence of lesbian, gay, and bisexual people and issues in the material; but the question becomes more slippery when dealing with practical and performance-oriented courses. No genre of "gay and lesbian acting" or "gay and lesbian scene design" exists. Especially in an undergraduate curriculum, where an instructor must focus on conveying basic techniques and skills, it is hard to imagine how Gay and Lesbian Studies, with its frequent forays into high theory, can have an impact. Even so, gay and lesbian issues can play a role in the performance curriculum, though perhaps in less systematic ways than in literature courses.

The simplest connection between Gay and Lesbian Studies and a production program is in the performance of plays and scenes from gay and lesbian drama. All of the theoretical issues of the literature classroom may be explored on a more intense and immediate level in the rehearsal room and on stage. Scene work, scripted or improvisational, is an ideal tool to explore the complex social issues that surround the formation of sexual identity. A class can use a variety of exercises to explore how socially reinforced behavior patterns create sexual identities, and how an audience learns to read sexual identities. Portraying a gay identity provides a technical challenge for the actor of (whatever the student's own orientation) but, more importantly, offers the opportunity to explore identity formation and its physical portrayal in society. Lesbians and gay men have been characterized (usually negatively) by a wide variety of physical and vocal mannerisms. An exploration of these patterns through acting exercises can help students understand both the dynamics of reading the human body and the pervasive and problematic nature of all stereotypes.

Doing scene work on sexual identity in a closed classroom is relatively "safe"; such works can be more problematic when done for public performance. Few activities will make a general audience squirm more than watching two people of the same sex kissing passionately on stage. Note, for example, the furor (and occasional acts of violence) spurred by the production of Larry Kramer's *The Normal Heart* at Southwest Missouri State University in the fall of 1989. Such controversies, however, need not be avoided. This kind of public debate can demonstrate to students in a vivid and immediate way the vital importance of theatre to society. The theatre event can become a public learning experience, through public lectures, panel discussions, symposia, or post-performance discussions, as supplements to the performance itself.

Beyond acting classes and performances, Gay and Lesbian Studies has a less direct impact on other courses in the performance curriculum. The kind of work generally done in a scene or lighting design class has little room for in-depth connection to these issues. A designer will encounter plays about non-mainstream sexuality, or may draw on the visual vocabulary of a gay aesthetic. However, such knowledge is equivalent to the designer's need to know all genres of playwriting, and a wide range of visual vocabularies, and there is nothing which specifically privileges issues of sexuality above the many other factors that impact design work. By contrast, the technical skills taught in voice or dance classes, or in scene construction or technical production classes, rarely range beyond the tightly drawn worlds of these disciplines. Not every course in a theatre curriculum need connect directly to Gay and Lesbian Studies. Here, rather than introducing gay and lesbian issues, instructors can open themselves to these issues, and be willing and able to respond to them in class when they arise.

Costuming, on the other hand, is a production area where issues of sexual difference might be incorporated directly. Costume design deals with fundamental issues of identity formation, both from the point of view of the character (how does this person create an external image through the choice of clothing—what would this character wear?) and from the point of view of the audience (what will the viewer think about this character based on what she is wearing?). Gay and lesbian identity formation is heavily invested in clothing. Certain clothing styles are defined within the gay community as being gay or lesbian, femme or butch, while certain styles of dress are used by people outside the community (rightly or wrongly) to identify people as belonging to it. Gay men and lesbians, by force of social stigma, have developed elaborate symbol systems based upon dress. Leather, asymmetrical piercings (which ear—left or right—defines gayness?), colored back-pocket handkerchiefs—all become means by which clothing takes on discursive meaning. For a costume designer, these issues are important not only in the eventuality of designing a costume for a lesbian or gay character. They provide a vivid example of how the process of costume design works, how clothing is used to communicate.

Beyond Gay and Lesbian Studies in the theatre curriculum arises the issue of interdisciplinary work: how the study of gay and lesbian theatre contributes to other fields. With the work done by Judith Butler and Eve Sedgwick on the performative nature of sexuality, the various performing arts are "hot" territory as Gay and Lesbian Studies begins to define itself. There is a great opportunity to incorporate discussions of theatre into general introductory courses in Gay and Lesbian Studies, both from a textual and from a performance standpoint. Though such courses as yet have no standard form, many of the existing introductory level courses spend time covering issues of identity formation and societal portrayals sexual difference—subjects that are treated directly and extensively in dramatic texts, and which, as discussed previously, theatre performance techniques can serve to illuminate. Theatre studies can inform lectures and discussions of these issues; play scripts can be assigned as springboards to the issues involved; and units specifically on gay and lesbian theatre can be included.

Opportunities also abound for team-taught cross-disciplinary courses centering around gay and lesbian issues. A costumer might get together with a sociologist or anthropologist to teach a course on clothing, fashion and identity, with a unit on the gay and lesbian communities (not to mention the strong ties between gay men and the modern fashion industry). A recent course at Dartmouth paired film studies with comparative literature to explore prose and film versions of gay and lesbian fiction. The possibilities here are almost endless. As Gay and Lesbian Studies develops as an autonomous academic field, new ideas for such interaction will continuously arise, as scholars from different disciplines work together to understand the social, political, and aesthetic implications of sexual difference.

Struggles, Setbacks, and Advances

As with any other venture into issues of lesbian and gay concern, there is likely to be resistance to the introduction of Gay and Lesbian Studies into the theatre curriculum. College students can be extremely insecure about their own sexuality, and so reluctant to discuss such issues in public venues, where their vulnerabilities may come into question. Teaching is one of the professions most prone to public paranoia about non-mainstream sexuality, even at the college level, with lingering fears that gay teachers will "recruit" their students. Many faculty members are reluctant to associate with gay and lesbian issues, particularly junior faculty, who may feel that such associations jeopardize their chances for tenure. There is a strong likelihood that an instructor who teaches a course about lesbian or gay issues will be labeled as lesbian or gay, with the concomitant threat of prejudice, even if the person does not self-identify as such. Furthermore, the mere mention of sexuality raises a host of volatile responses that are not encountered by similar concerns around gender or racial inequality.

However, the fear of resistance to Gay and Lesbian Studies is often greater than the actuality. Prejudice is very real and often comes from unpredictable corners, but support can also be just as genuine and unexpected. (At Dartmouth, the Introduction to Gay and Lesbian Studies course passed easily through all faculty committees, though it has not yet, as of this writing, been funded).

Strategies can be used to answer resistance before it arises. Gay and Lesbian Studies courses need to be constructed carefully, with heavy documentation, so that faculty committees cannot question their academic rigor, or find excuses other than the subject matter for rejecting the course. Special topics courses may be easier to get approved than permanent curricular changes; strategically, it may be better to start with such classes, to establish their academic viability and student audience to reluctant administrators.

Private, non-denominational institutions will probably have less trouble introducing gay studies courses than schools that face the scrutiny of either religious or governmental administration. A state government that will not fund a gay student group is not likely to provide resources to introduce a curriculum in Gay and Lesbian Studies, nor are colleges associated with the Catholic Church or other bodies that specifically condemn gay relationships. No matter what the kind of institution, however, faculty attempting to develop courses in Gay and Lesbian Studies are, in the current political climate, likely to be challenged, and will be asked to address, with maddening frequency, a raft of issues: that these courses are immoral, that they promote homosexuality, or worse, "recruit" people to be gay or lesbian. In responding to these charges, it is vital to maintain as the central subject of discussion the academic validity of these courses.

Another, less obvious problem is the dangerous assumption, based heavily on stereotype, that a large percentage of theatre students (and faculty) are themselves gay or lesbian, and that therefore there is little need to address issues of homophobia in theatre departments. Even if the first point, that there are more openly lesbian and gay people in theatre, has a certain (if arguable) validity, the second assumption, that theatre people are further ahead in combatting homophobia, is certainly not the case. (Note that it took the Association for Theatre in Higher Education until 1991 to have a Lesbian and Gay Theatre division, far later than many academic organizations in other fields.) It is vital for theatre educators—for all educators—to be aware of sexual difference and to be sensitive to the problems students face in coming to terms with their sexuality, as well as to the abuse to which many of them are subjected. Our responsibilities as college teachers do not end when we leave the classroom. This responsibility is particularly acute in theatre, where we work closely outside the classroom with our students, who come to trust us and depend on us. Support for a student who faces problems of sexual identity can restore self-esteem to someone cut off from family and friends. This support, more than material conveyed in coursework, is the most important contribution Gay and Lesbian Studies can make to a university environment.

Theatre studies has found itself marginalized in academia, threatened by budget cuts, faculty reductions, and continued doubts about its validity as an academic field. Nevertheless, this marginalized position may also be turned into a strength. It is precisely theatre's paradoxical position in society, its existence simultaneously at the center of cultural production and on the margins of social acceptability, that allows theatre educators to engage in discussions of social marginalization. Theatre has always been a powerful voice for those with little access to the official channels of power. It is hardly surprising, then, that the lesbian, gay, and bisexual community has formed strong bonds with theatre, and has looked to theatre to express its feelings of social alienation. Now, as Gay and Lesbian Studies comes into greater visibility, theatre can reinforce this bond. In Gay and Lesbian Studies, theatre has a natural field in which to form ties to other academic disciplines—and simultaneously to reinforce the necessity of theatre in the world of higher education and in the world at large.

Notes

1. Throughout this essay, the academic study of issues of non-mainstream sexualities will be referred to as "Gay and Lesbian Studies," primarily because this term is the one most commonly used. There is a good deal of debate within the field regarding appropriate terminology, in particular regarding the inclusion of the term "bisexual" whenever "gay and lesbian" is used. Though I do not often use the term "bisexual" in this chapter, I intend for the discussion to include issues relevant to the bisexual community as well.

2. For example, *Chiaroscuro*, by Jackie Kay, is included in the anthology *Lesbian Plays*, ed. Jill Davis (London: Methuen, 1987). Two one-act plays, *Bert & Jessie* by Robin Barr Gorman and *What Do You See?* by Ana Maria Simo, are published in *Tough Acts to Follow: One Act Plays on the Gay/Lesbian Experience*, ed. Noreen C. Barnes and Nicholas Deutsch (San Francisco: Alamo Square, 1992). Some of the plays of Cherrie Moraga are in print, notably *Giving Up the Ghost* (Los Angeles: West End, 1986).

Works Cited

Butler, Judith. *Gender Trouble: Feminism and the Subversion of Identity*. New York: Routledge, 1990.

Clum, John M. *Acting Gay: Male Homosexuality in Modern Drama*. New York: Columbia UP, 1992.

Curtin, Kaier. *"We Can Always Call Them Bulgarians"*: The Emergence of Lesbians and Gay Men on the American Stage. Boston: Alyson, 1987.

de Jongh, Nicholas. *Not in Front of the Audience: Homosexuality on Stage*. London: Routledge, 1992.

Postlewait, Thomas. "The Criteria for Periodization in Theatre History." *Theatre Journal* 40 (1988): 299–318.

———. "Historiography and the Theatrical Event: A Primer with Twelve Cruxes." *Theatre Journal* 43 (1991): 157–78.

Russo, Vito. *The Celluloid Closet: Homosexuality in the Movies*. Rev. ed. New York: Harper, 1987.

Sedgwick, Eve Kosofsky. *Epistemology of the Closet*. Berkeley: University of California Press, 1990.

A Selected Bibliography of Gay and Lesbian Theatre

The following is a selected list of books and essays that specifically address issues relevant to Gay and Lesbian Studies in performance. The list of "Critical Works," which is only a sampling of relevant research, includes general critical and scholarly studies of lesbian and gay performance, or collections that include relevant essays; works discussing individual artists or plays have not been included. The list of "Play Anthologies" does not include collections of works by single authors. There are also numerous reviews and less scholarly pieces available on gay and lesbian plays, playwrights, and performers, and several dissertations on lesbian and gay theatre and performance. Many thanks to the students in my "Gay and Lesbian Drama in Performance" class in the winter quarter of 1992 at Dartmouth for their help in compiling this bibliography.

Critical Works

Brecht, Stefan. *Queer Theatre*. New York: Routledge, 1985.

Case, Sue-Ellen, ed. *Performing Feminisms: Feminist Critical Theory and Theatre*. Baltimore: The Johns Hopkins UP, 1990.

Case, Sue-Ellen, and Janelle Reinelt, eds. *The Performance of Power: Theatrical Discourse and Politics*. Iowa City: Iowa UP, 1991.

Clum, John M. *Acting Gay: Male Homosexuality in Modern Drama*. New York: Columbia UP, 1992.

Curtin, Kaier. *"We Can Always Call Them Bulgarians": The Emergence of Lesbians and Gay Men on the American Stage*. Boston: Alyson, 1987.

Davy, Kate. "Constructing the Spectator: Reception, Context, and Address in Lesbian Performance." *Performing Arts Journal* 10:2 (1986): 43–52.

de Jongh, Nicholas. *Not in Front of the Audience: Homosexuality on Stage*. London: Routledge, 1992.

Dolan, Jill. "Breaking the Code: Musing on Lesbian Sexuality and the Performer." *Modern Drama* 32 (1989): 146–58.

———. *The Feminist Spectator as Critic*. Ann Arbor: UMI, 1989.

Garber, Marjorie. *Vested Interests: Cross-Dressing and Cultural Anxiety.* New York: Harper, 1993.

Hart, Lynda, ed. *Making a Spectacle: Feminist Essays on Contemporary Women's Theatre.* Ann Arbor: U of Michigan P, 1989.

Helbing, Terry. "Gay Plays, Gay Theatre, Gay Performance." *The Drama Review* 25:1 (1981): 35–46.

Koestenbaum, Wayne. *The Queen's Throat: Opera, Homosexuality, and the Mystery of Desire.* New York: Poseidon, 1993.

Russo, Vito. *The Celluloid Closet: Homosexuality in the Movies.* Rev. ed. New York: Harper and Row, 1987

Senelick, Laurence, ed. *Gender in Performance: The Presentation of Difference in the Performing Arts.* Hanover, NH: New England UP, 1992.

Sisley, Emily. "Notes on a Lesbian Theatre." *The Drama Review* 25:1 (1981): 47–56.

Straub, Kristina. *Sexual Suspects: Eighteenth-Century Players and Sexual Ideology.* Princeton: Princeton UP, 1992.

Theatre Insight. Special Issue on Gay and Lesbian Theatre. (Spring 1991).

Wallace, Robert. "Gender, Sexuality and Theatre: To Become: The Ideological Function of a Gay Theatre." *Canadian Theatre Review* 59 (1989): 5–10.

(Mention should also be made of Donald M. Kaplan's intensely homophobic essay, "Homosexuality and American Theatre: A Psychoanalytic Comment" (*Tulane Drama Review* 9:3 (1965): 25–55), which links homosexuality as an illness with degenerate forces pervading Broadway.)

Play Anthologies

Barnes, Noreen C., and Nicholas Deutsch, eds. *Tough Acts to Follow: One-Act Plays on the Gay/Lesbian Experience.* San Francisco: Alamo Square, 1992.

Davis, Jill. *Lesbian Plays.* London: Methuen, 1987.

———. *Lesbian Plays: Two.* London: Methuen, 1989.

Helbing, Terry, ed. *Gay and Lesbian Plays Today*. Portsmouth, NH: Heinemann, 1993.

Hoffman, William M., ed. *Gay Plays: The First Collection*. New York: Avon, 1979.

Osborn, M. Elizabeth. *The Way We Live Now: American Plays & the AIDS Crisis*. New York: Theatre Communications Group, 1990.

Osment, Philip. *Gay Sweatshop: Four Plays and a Company*. London: Methuen, 1989.

Shewey, Don, ed. *Out Front: Contemporary Gay and Lesbian Plays*. New York: Grove, 1988.

Temerson, Catherine, and Françoise Kowolsky. *Gay Plays: An International Anthology*. New York: Ubu Repertory Theatre Publications, 1989.

Wallace, Robert, ed. *Making, Out: Plays by Gay Men*. Toronto: Coach House Press, 1992.

Wilcox, Michael. *Gay Plays*. London: Methuen, 1984.

———. *Gay Plays, Volume Two*. London: Methuen, 1985.

———. *Gay Plays, Volume Three*. London: Methuen, 1988.

———. *Gay Plays, Volume Four*. London: Methuen, 1990.

The Evolution of a Multicultural Theatre Course

Margaret Millen Swanson and Robin Murray

We have only to look at the flourishing Yiddish theatre in New York in the 1920s, the amateur productions of Chinese Opera on the West Coast at the turn of the century, or the Scandinavian variety shows that existed during the same period in the Midwest to realize the extent to which theatre can act as a lens through which a minority community can affirm its sacred myths and forge a sense of ethnic identity. Furthermore, we have only to look at the minstrel tradition, the stage Irishman, and the wild west show to realize the extent to which the theatre can create and perpetuate negative racial and ethnic stereotypes. Theatrical representations of race and ethnicity are an integral part of the American theatre.

University theatre programs have a unique opportunity to contribute to a multicultural university curriculum by creating new courses committed to the study of American racial and ethnic minorities. The Introduction to the Theatre course at our university had been a fairly traditional one which illustrated the theatrical process by using plays from the canon. In 1989 it was decided to modify this course on an experimental basis to incorporate plays by and about people of color. Plays by African-American, Asian-American, Latino, and Native American playwrights were included. Roughly half of those plays were written by women.

It is important to put this project in context: The authors of this article, Meg Swanson and Robin Murray, are members of the theatre faculty of a small public university located in the midwest. We are Caucasian, as are most of the students whom we teach. Our middle-class students come primarily from isolated rural communities and equally isolated suburban enclaves. Whatever their place of origin, they arrive on campus having experienced very little interaction with people of color. In recent years our university, like many others, has committed itself to an active recruitment program to bring students of color to campus. Their presence has led to some conflict. The university, also like many others, has encouraged faculty to develop courses that address cultural pluralism and embrace diversity. We decided, therefore, to conduct a modest experiment using our existing introductory theatre course as a laboratory to learn about student attitudes towards curricular diversity.

What follows is a brief description of the issues that emerged in the experimental setting, the ways in which what we learned affected the development of a permanent course, an assessment of how this permanent course was initially received by students, and a summary of our own feelings about teaching diversity using theatre as the focus. The information we employ in the article was culled from informal classroom discussion, short writing assignments, and written student evaluations of both the introductory course and a new course "Playwrights of Color." Since we are theatre practitioners and not social scientists, we are the first to admit that our methodology probably flawed; we are using our material anecdotally, and similar experiments conducted in different environments might well achieve different results.

The initial experiment took place in the Fall of 1989 in "Introduction to the Theatre," a course taught by Robin Murray. On our campus, "Introduction to the Theatre" is part of the core curriculum and attracts freshmen and sophomores from across the campus. Only a small percentage of students in the typical introductory class is likely to possess any background in theatre. Murray modified the class syllabus to include seven plays by playwrights of color. These seven plays represented approximately one-third of the plays to be studied during the semester-long course. Meg Swanson attended class meetings to observe student reactions and take notes on class discussions. Specifically, we wanted to know how students would respond when presented with material that challenged their assumptions about what was important to study. We also wanted to know what our predominantly middle-class, Caucasian students knew, or thought they knew, about people of color. We were surprised by some of what we discovered.

We discovered a vocal minority of students who were resistant, and even hostile, to the inclusion of culturally diverse material in the curriculum. In anonymous course evaluations one student told us he was "tired of this diversity stuff." Several students implied that the university's commitment to diversity was an educational fad that students were being forced to endure.

We also discovered that our students knew little about the specific history of racial and ethnic minorities in the United States. Many students did not know about the existence of a segregated military and were unaware of the race riots that occurred after World War I. They did not know about the Japanese internment camps or the Chinese Exclusion Act. Even more recent political figures like Cesar Chavez were unfamiliar to many of them.

Students in "Introduction to the Theatre" did not possess a vocabulary with which to discuss issues of race and ethnicity. They stumbled self-consciously over appropriate designations for various racial and ethnic groups. In a class discussion during which the term "cultural assimilation" was used frequently, several students heard "a simulation," and concluded that we were discussing something related to computers.

We also discovered that our students used white middle-class experience as the standard against which all other forms of experience should be measured. When this ethnocentrism was combined with stereotypic assumptions about social class among people of color, it became impossible for some students to read plays by playwrights of color with any degree of accuracy. The middle-class African-American family in Kathleen Collin's *The Brothers* was transformed by our students into an impoverished one. When informed that the characters were middle-class, one young woman concluded that they must, therefore, be white. Similarly, students read Eduardo Machado's *Broken Eggs* as a play about "the drug problem among the Hispanic underclass." Granted, drugs do enter into this play—one of the characters is addicted to valium and another makes social use of cocaine—but the play is clearly about family deterioration among the Cuban-American middle class. Our students, knowing little about the demographic distinctions among Latinos, found it difficult to attribute patterns of middle-class drug use to Cuban characters.

Students similarly assumed Black American English, such as that spoken by the characters in Cassandra Medley's *Ma Rose*, to be substandard. Black American English in *Ma Rose* is used as a sign of family solidarity. The protagonist, a young African-American woman who has achieved middle-class success at the price of alienation from her family, eases into Black American English as she becomes reconciled with them. Contrary to all of the signs present in the text, however, some of our students adhered to the belief that the language signified stupidity on the part of the speakers.

Finally, our students resisted political readings of these texts. When presented with David Henry Hwang's *M. Butterfly*, for example, students interpreted the issue of sexual "mistaken identity" in the text exclusively on psychological grounds. The notion that the gender confusion at the heart of the play is rooted in assumptions about "the other," which are *political,* went unnoticed by the student response and was resisted in class discussion.

Having finished our experiment, we wondered what we should conclude regarding our findings. Clearly some of the assumptions made by our students had racist implications. But their racism and ethnocentrism, it seemed to us, was the result of ignorance. Our students simply didn't know very much about people of color. Nothing in their experience or academic education had prepared them to frame history in anything but a Eurocentric perspective or to consider culture from other than a white middle-class point of view. Without understanding the cultural, historic, and social contexts which influenced the work of playwrights of color, it was impossible for them to appreciate the material aesthetically. If ignorance was one source of student racism, it seemed to us that anxiety was another. When students say they are "tired of all this diversity stuff," they may actually be saying that they are afraid of what they do not understand and feel threatened by a need to realign their value systems.

We tried to keep all these issues in mind as we developed a permanent course, "Playwrights of Color: Racial and Ethnic Diversity in the American Theatre." We decided we could not successfully teach the dramatic works of playwrights of color without addressing the issues of history, access to power, and cultural difference that frame them; without understanding the concept of marginalization, our students could not understand the plays; without coming to terms with their own stereotypic thinking, they could not grasp the playwright's intent; without understanding difference, they could not see the universal in the selected material. "Playwrights of Color," in short, became a course which was both about the theatre and about the society which the theatre reflects. Using theatre as the center, the course explores neglected history, introduces contemporary topics of social debate, and provides a vocabulary. The plays bring this material into focus, providing human emotions and compelling narratives through which to interpret specific facts. This approach requires that the course be viewed as an interdisciplinary as well as a multicultural one. Class content on any given day might well include material gleaned from historical sources, cultural studies, linguistic theory, or sociology.

At the center of the course are twenty-two plays written by American racial and ethnic minorities. Works by six African-American, six Asian-American, five Native-American, and five Latino playwrights were selected from the hundreds of possible texts. Nine of the selected plays were written by women. Our criteria for selection were whether we enjoyed the play, considered it to be good theatre, and looked forward to teaching it. Other criteria guided our choices as well— although history was an important part of the course, only contemporary plays were selected (arbitrarily deciding to define "contemporary play" as anything written after 1960). We limited our selection of plays to those which focus on the experience of racial or ethnic difference as the subject; and plays which we thought would be accessible to students. Further, having a choice between two wonderful plays by Native Canadian dramatist, Tomson Highway, we chose to incorporate *The Rez Sisters* rather than *Dry Lips Oughta Move to Kapusing*, believing that the obscenities in *Dry Lips* would so offend some of our students that they would be distracted from the important aspects of the play.

The class was divided into three major units: Stereotypes in the Nineteenth Century, Forging New Images and Telling New Stories, and Stereotypes in our Times. Paradoxically we begin a course about playwrights of color by addressing stereotypes created and perpetuated by nineteenth-century Caucasian playwrights; we examine the minstrel show, the inscrutable "oriental," and the wild west show as a means of understanding stereotypes. Those same stereotypes have taken on new dimensions, however, in the hands of playwrights of color; it is these revisions of the stereotypes which we want to introduce to students. The reading material for this unit includes Douglas Turner Ward's *A Day of Absence*, Luis Valdez' *Los Vendidos* and David Henry Hwang's *M. Butterfly*. All of these plays reference conventional stereotypes, turning them over to reveal what hides beneath them. We hope to introduce students to the way in which racial and ethnic stereotypes develop and how they circulate between the world and the stage. By including plays that challenge racial stereotypes while exploiting them, we hope to suggest that theatre can become a tool in destroying those very stereotypes it had been instrumental in creating.

The second unit is devoted to plays in which people of color forge new characters and voice their own experience. This unit was divided into three subsections: confronting prejudice and discrimination, issues related to cultural assimilation, and reclaiming cultural traditions. Included in the subsection on prejudice and discrimination are such plays as Alice Childress' *Wedding Band* which deals with lynching, Wakako Yamauchi's *12-1-A* which recounts day-to-day life in an internment camp, and William Lang's *Pow Wow* which explores Native American treaty rights. Here we teach some remedial history, in order to provide a context from which to view issues if race and ethnicity today. In the subsection on assimilation we include plays that address the difficulties and trade-offs involved in attempting to assimilate into dominant culture while maintaining an identity within one's community of origin. Included in this section of the course are Charles Fuller's *A Soldier's Play*, Kathleen Collin's *The Broghers*, and Eduardo Machado's *Broken Eggs*. Our purpose here is to suggest to middle-class students that the choice to become culturally assimilated is difficult and may be accompanied by loss. In the final subsection of this unit, we include plays in which people of color consciously employ traditional cultural forms within a theatrical context in order to renew them. Here we include David Henry Hwang's *The Dance and The Railroad* which utilizes elements of Chinese Opera, Diane Glancy's *Stick Horse* which explores some aspects of Native American spirituality, and George C. Wolfe's *Spunk* which utilizes African-American folk stories. Our intention is to enhance students' awareness of differing aesthetic conventions, and to increase their understanding of the various cultural traditions converging in the American theatre.

Having begun with nineteenth-century stereotypes, we conclude by addressing the role that the twentieth-century media play in forging new images or perpetuating old ones. This unit includes Phillip Kan Gotanda's *Yankee Dawg, You Die* which directly addresses the career frustrations of Asian-American performers. Adrienne Kennedy's *A Movie Star Has to Star in Black and White* uses film as a metaphor to address the issues of identity of an African-American woman. Carlos Morton's *Rancho Hollywood* creates a filmic overview of the history of Chicanos in the United States. We hope that by returning to the media in the last week of the course we provide some unity and remind students that the manipulation of imagery related to people of color continues. We further hope to persuade students that theatre and the related media must engage in a constant process of self-analysis if it is to do more than mindlessly reflect a culture back to itself.

Each of the plays considered is treated in a similar manner. We provide students with historical, social, or cultural material relevant to the play in order to create an appropriate social context in which to understand it. We also provide material relevant to the play as a theatrical or aesthetic work: genre, information on production style, production choices. Also included in the course is content related to the economics of the theatre industry and the role of mission theatres in producing works by playwrights of color. Finally knowing that students are curious about the lives and career paths of others, we include biographical information about famous and not so famous people of color involved in specific productions.

Our pedagogical techniques include extended use of the discussion format, concentrated small-group work, and short lectures. Since the class is team-taught we are able to model discussion behavior by entering into discussions with one another on issues related to the course. We also employ such discussion-starter techniques as asking students to hand in questions on a particular play which we then use as the basis of a discussion. Though we are sometimes surprised at the nature of the questions and the direction of the discussion, this approach permits us to learn a great deal about student attitudes and levels of awareness. Towards the end of the semester students are divided into groups, each of which is given responsibility for leading a discussion of one of the plays. We also incorporate large amounts of video material into the course. We do this in a self-conscious attempt to give people of color a position of authority in the classroom. We utilize whatever professionally made video material we can find, and have also created some of our own by videotaping on-campus presentations by scholars and playwrights of color. Grades are based on a combination of objective and essay tests, several brief paper assignments, and one group presentation.

"Playwrights of Color" was offered for the first time as an informal topics course which was not officially listed in the course catalogue and relied on the student grapevine to attract participants. Twelve students enrolled. Included among the twelve were one African-American, one Pacific Islander, and one Chicano. The remainder of the enrolled students were Caucasian. Given the demographics of our institution, this class was unusually diverse racially. The majority of the students in the class were women. Half of them had strong backgrounds in theatre; the other half possessed no theatre background.

The students in the class differed in one important way from the students we had previously observed in "Introduction to the Theatre": these students had enrolled in a class which they knew was to be about racial diversity and the theatre. The course content, after all, was baldly asserted in its title. These student were self-selected and were willingly participating in a class about diversity. This may explain why we did not encounter the level of resistance with which we had been confronted in the introductory class. The students enrolled in "Playwrights of Color" knew what they were there for. The "Intro" students may well have felt as if they had been tricked.

Having gotten into the habit of collecting information, we decided to continue to observe and monitor student reactions to the permanent course. We also devised a narrative questionnaire which we asked students to complete at the end of the semester. What we wanted to know was not so much what students had learned about theatre, but what they had learned about racial difference. We chose not to query them about racial attitudes or attitudinal changes which we understand are almost impossible to measure accurately. Instead we asked them about their comfort level in discussing race and what sorts of information about people of color they thought they had acquired during the semester. Among the questions we asked were: Did the course make you more comfortable talking about race? How was your understanding of racial difference expanded throughout the course? The questionnaire provided lots of blank space and we received some fairly lengthy responses. Some of the student comments were illuminating.

A majority of the respondents reported that they generally avoided discussing issues of race or racial difference in formal situations like a classroom, and were reluctant to engage in such discussions in social gatherings that included strangers. They were not reluctant, however, to discuss such issues among their friends. A typical response was "I can talk about anything with my friends." What this suggests to us is that talking about race is too risky to be undertaken unless students are fairly confident that the person to whom they are speaking will accept their comments non-judgmentally. Among the respondents who had acknowledged being uneasy talking about the issue, all agreed that taking the class had made such talk easier.

One of the things which had made it easier was the introduction of a vocabulary. Our students seem to have been lost among Hispanic/Latino, Black/African-American, Indian/Native American, Asian American/Oriental nomenclature, and had chosen to become mute rather than to reveal their naiveté regarding the appropriate language. It was a relief to students to understand why one term was preferred over another. It was also helpful to them to learn to differentiate between terms such as "discrimination," "prejudice," and "racism" which are frequently used synonymously.

Another thing which made it easier for the students to discuss racial issues was the possession of specific information. Several of the Caucasian students told us that most of what they had known about racial and ethnic minorities prior to taking the class had been information about their socio-economic position. By that we believe that what they meant was that they were aware of the existence of an urban underclass composed of large numbers of people of color. "Playwrights of Color," they told us, had provided them with specific, non-statistical information about people of color, particularly information about history and culture.

The students of color also told us that they had learned about their own culture through the class. The African-American student was interested to learn about the relationship between Black American English and West African languages. He later wrote a brief scene for a play which, while clearly a beginner's effort, featured some powerful dialect. The Pacific Islander who had been reared in the midwest by Caucasian parents, knew nothing about her culture of origin. While the course did not contain any plays by Pacific Islanders, she identified strongly with the various representations of Asian-American female characters whom she encountered during the course.

Students of color also confronted their own racial stereotypes and prejudices. The African-American student reported that he had always accepted the filmic representations of Native Americans as accurate. He became quite taken with Native American plays as he began to see through the stereotypes he had assumed to be true.

When asked how the course might be improved, most of the respondents talked about practical rather than theoretical concerns. They pleaded for more specific paper assignments, shorter readings, and more structure. Several students challenged our efforts to employ "innovative" pedagogy, pleading with us to lecture more often. We take such comments as examples of performance anxiety on the part of students and remain committed to the principles of active learning.

Two specific responses, however, stand out from the rest: One student saw the course as a bifurcated one. This particular student felt that we needed to decide whether the course was to be about the theatre or whether it was to be about racial and cultural diversity. To do both, the respondent implied, was impossible. What this comment suggests to us is that, while we imagined a class in which the social/political content merged seamlessly with the theatrical/aesthetic content, we did not fully achieve this objective. We attribute this, at least in part, to the fact that we were teaching the class for the first time and were doing research, and developing class material as we went along. When we next teach the class it should have a more integrated feel.

Another student offered the observation that the class was not sufficiently controversial and wondered why we had not selected plays with more confrontational content. This comment merits further consideration. There are some plays which we intentionally excluded from the course because we did not want to reinforce prevailing stereotypes. Miquel Pinero's *Short Eyes*, for example, is a fascinating play about prison culture. We excluded it thinking that many of our students already believe that young men of color spend most of their time in jail. Similarly Hanay Geiogamah's *Body Indian* presents a devastating look at the effects of alcoholism on Native Americans. We excluded it because we felt incapable to teaching it responsibly. It is certainly possible that we systematically excluded from the course those plays that made us uncomfortable as instructors and that might have led to volatile class discussions we felt unprepared to handle.

We see our own successes and failures somewhat differently from our students. On the trivial end, we know that some of our teaching strategies worked better in theory than in practice. The homemade videotapes, for example, were too unsophisticated to hold the attention of our media-conscious students. We also know that the students were less sophisticated about the theatre than we had expected them to be and that we needed to be as conscientious about providing students with a working theatrical vocabulary as we were in providing them with a vocabulary to talk about race and ethnicity. Though there is no way to measure the effectiveness of our teaching or to gauge how successfully we reached each individual student, we are confident about several basic things.

First, even though we are not ourselves from ethnic or racial minorities, we realize that we know more about the theatre of people of color than our students know. We also know more of the facts pertaining to the history and culture of people of color than our students—even the students of color—know. This is so because we have used our academic skills to teach ourselves about things we had not previously known. We know what linguists J. L. Dillard and Robert Hendrickson have to say about Black American English. We know about the Spanish language theatrical tradition in United States. None of our students, regardless of race or ethnicity, were familiar with this material. Moreover, even a student who was very familiar with the culture and traditions of his own racial or ethnic group is likely to be ignorant about other racial and ethnic groups. Even though, as Caucasian women, we cannot testify to the emotional and psychological experience of being a member of a visible minority, we nevertheless have much information to share with students. In addition, even though our knowledge and understanding is imperfect, we still have much we can teach.

Second, we realize that, though the information we possess gives us authority in the classroom, that authority is limited. It is limited because the experiences about which we are teaching are not our own. It extends only as far as the facts we are relating and the play being discussed. We have no special authority to interpret the psychology of characters of color or to make judgments about their behavior. Thus, we can present the class with the facts associated with Native American treaty rights and place the current debate about spearfishing and gaming rights within a historical context. We cannot insist that a student share our opinion about the current debate.

Finally, this class, like every class, was limited. It was limited because it was taught by theatre practitioners who were employing material from outside their home discipline. It was limited because it was taught by Caucasian women who could not speak authoritatively about the experience of being a member of a visible minority. It was limited because the majority of the students in the class were Caucasian. We feel confident in saying, however, the students who left our course knew more about people of color and the theatre than they had fifteen weeks earlier. They did not know it all and they did not know it perfectly. However, they knew more.

Our experience also persuades us that theatre programs have enormous contributions to make to a diverse university curriculum. If we can move beyond thinking of diversity as adding a single play by a playwright of color to an otherwise unchanged syllabus and use our creativity to explore the way in which the discipline of theatre intersects with others, who knows what innovative teaching and inspired learning might result?

What we cannot know is whether students who took "Playwrights of Color" emerged from it with open minds and increased tolerance of racial and ethnic difference. Our guess is that the results were mixed. In their chatty responses to the questionnaire, some students disclosed prejudicial attitudes even while struggling to sound enlightened. Other students openly acknowledged barriers, specifically religious barriers, which prevented them from understanding the issues or identifying with the characters in one play or another. If they emerged with a greater amount of information, a vocabulary with which to discuss racial and ethnic difference, and the confidence to use them, we consider our efforts to have been successful.

Works Cited

Childress, Alice. *Wedding Band*. New York: Samuel French, 1973.

Collins, Kathleen. *The Brothers. Nine Plays by Black Women*. Ed. Margaret Wilkerson. New York: NAL, 1986.

Fuller, Charles. *The Soldiers Play*. New York: Farrar, 1981.

Geiogamah, Hanay. *Body Indian. New Native American Plays: Three Plays*. Norman, OK: University of Oklahoma Press, 1980.

Glancy, Diane. *Stick Horse*. Ms.

Gotanda, Phillip Kan. *Yankee Dawg, You Die*. Ms.

Hwang, David Henry. "The Dance and The Railroad." *The Dance and The Railroad and Family Devotions*. New York: Dramatists Play Service, 1983.

———. *M. Butterfly*. New York: NAL, 1988.

Kennedy Adrienne. *A Movie Star Has to Star in Black and White. In One Act*. Minneapolis: U of Minnesota P, 1988.

Lang, William. *Pow Wow*. Ms.

Medley, Cassandra. *Ma Rose. Womenswork*. Ed. Julia Miles. New York: Applause, 1989.

Morton, Carlos. *Rancho Hollywood. Nuevos Pasos: Chicano and Puerto Rican Drama*. Ed. Nicolas Kanellos and Jorge Huerta. Houston: Arte Publico, 1989.

Machado, Eduardo. *Broken Eggs. On New Ground: Contemporary Hispanic-American Plays*. Ed. M. Elizabeth Osborn. New York: TCG, 1987.

Pinero, Miquel. *Short Eyes*. New York: Farrar, 1973.

Valdez, Luis. *Los Vendidos. Rereading America: Cultural Contexts for Critical Thinking and Writing*. Ed. Gary Colombo, Robert Cullen, and Bonnie Lisle. New York: St. Martin's. 1989.

Ward, David Turner. *A Day of Absence. New Black Playwrights*. Ed. William Couch. New York: Avon, 1970.

Wolfe, George C. *Spunk*. New York: TCG, 1991.

Yamauchi, Wakako. *12-1-A*. *The Politics of Life: Four Plays by Asian-American Women*. Philadelphia: Temple UP, 1993.

About the Contributors

Raynette Halvorsen Smith is an Associate Professor inthe School of Theatre and Dance at Kent State University where she served as School Director and Producing Director for the School's equity theatre company, Porthouse Theatre, for five years. Her work as a designer and scenic artist has taken her across the country to numerous theatres, including the Arena Stage (Washington, D.C.), the Music Theatre of Wichita, the St. Nicholas Theatre and CBS Television (Chicago,), and Porthouse Theatre Company (Ohio). Her articles on design and theatre pedagogy have appeared in *Themes in Drama, Journal of Dramatic Theory and Criticism, Theatre Design & Technology, Theatre Crafts, and Bühnentechnische Rundschau.*

Bruce A. McConachie is a theatre historian with over twenty years of teaching undergraduate and graduate students. As an educator he has held executive positions in the Association for Theatre in Higher Education and the American Society for Theatre Research. His books include *Interpreting the Theatrical Past,* co-edited with Tom Postlewait, and *Melodramatic Formations: American Theatre and Society, 1820–1870.* McConachie is Executive Editor of *Theatre Annual: A Journal of Performance Studies.*

Rhonda Blair is a Professor in the Division of Theatre at Southern Methodist University, Dallas, Texas. She is an actor, director, and writer whose most recent original solo pieces include *American Jesus,* and *I Used to Be One Hot Number: Ramonalogues about the body, desire, transcendence and the ugly truth about Snow White.* Her articles on performance, directing and theatre pedagogy have appeared in *Theatre Topics, Women and Performance: A Journal of Feminist Theory,* and *Upstaging Big Daddy: Directing Theatre as if Gender and Race Matter.* She is on the Editorial Board of *Theatre Topics* and a Contributing Editor to *Women & Performance.*

Sam Abel teaches couvrses in the Department of Theatre at the University of Vermont. He is the author of Opera in the Flesh: Sexuality in Operatic Performance.

Patricia Flanagan Behrendt is an Associate Professor, Graduate Faculty Fellow, and Director of the Introduction to Theatre program at the University of Nebraska-Lincoln; author of *Oscar Wilde: Eros and Aesthetics* (London: Macmillan, 1991) and a variety of interdisciplinary articles and conference papers on drama and theatre. She is currently completing a book manuscript on the Gothic tradition entitled *The Structure of Horror: The Aesthetic Codes of Gothic Drama from 1750 to the Present.*

Sarah Bryant-Bertail is Assistant Professor in the School of Drama at the University of Washington in Seattle, where she teaches theory and criticism and is chair of the PhD program. Her articles on epic theatre, contemporary French theatre, semiotics, and feminism have appeared in *Theatre Journal, The Journal of Dramatic Theory and Criticism, Assaph, Theatre Studies, Theatre Research International*, and *Journal of Kafka* Studies, and in anthologies *The Performance of Power, Strindberg's Dramaturgy, Brecht Yearbook, Semiotics 87*, and *Text and Performance*. She guest-edited the summer 1994 issue of *Theatre Research International* on performance analysis, and is completing two books, *Space and Time in the Epic Theatre* and *Women on the Road: The Picara in the Drama.*

Paul C. Castagno is the Director of the new Playwrights' Program and Head of the M.F.A. Playwriting/Dramaturgy Program at the University of Alabama. Costagno has published articles on the new playwriting in *New Theatre Quarterly, Theatre Topics*, and *Text and Presentation*. He recently published an essay on working with new playwrights in *Dramaturgy in American Theatre: A Sourcebook* (Hartcourt Brace 1999). In addition, Costagno served as editor for two volumes of *Theatre Symposium*, and published *The Early Commedia dell'Arte (1550–1621: The Mannerist Context* (Peter Lang 1994), reviewed as a "canonical work" by the *Journal of Dramatic Theory and Criticism*. A produced playwright, his most recent play, *Tyler's Trattoria*, has been selected as a finalist in several contests.

Stratos E. Constantinidis, Ph.D., is an Associate Professor in the Department of Theatre at the Ohio State University where he teaches primarily dramatic theory, criticism, literature, history, and research methods. His book, *Theatre under Deconstruction* (New York & London: Garland Publishing, 1993), was described as "a fascinating book, innovative in both its structure and its arguments" (*Theatre Journal* 1994:145). Dr. Constantinidis is the editor of *Classical Drama in Modern Performances* (Theatre Studies, 1989), *Modern Greek Drama* (Journal of Modern Greek Studies 1996), and *Greek Film* (Journal of Modern Greek Studies, 2000). He served as editor of *Greece in Modern Times: An Annotated Bibliography of Works Published in English in 22 Academic Disciplines* (Lanham: Scarecrow Press, 1999). His research papers have been published in various American, English, German, Greek, and Israeli refereed journals, including *Comparative Drama, Code/Codikas: Ars Semeiotica, New Theatre Quarterly, Journal of Dramatic Theory and Criticism, Poetics Today*, and *World Literature*.

Jerry Dickey is an Associate Professor and Director of Graduate Studies in Theatre Arts at the University of Arizona. He is the author *of Sophie Treadwell: A Research and Production Sourcebook* (Greenwood, 1997), and has published essays on Treadwell in *Theatre History Studies, Women in Theatre 4, Speaking the*

Other Self: American Women Writers (Univ. of Georgia Press, 1997) and the forthcoming *Cambridge Companion of American Women Writers* (Cambridge Univ. Press). Other essays and reviews have appeared in *Theatre Topics, Theatre Journal, Western American Literature, New Old-West: Centennial Essays* (Univ. of Idaho Press) and the forthcoming *Encyclopedia of American Literature.*

Marian E. Hampton is a Professor in the Department of Theatre at Illinois State University specializing in voice. She is a professional actor, singer, director, and voice coach who has performed and directed in San Francisco, New York, Chicago, and Alberta, Canada. She holds an MFA in Acting from Yale University School of Drama and a BFA from Illinois Wesleyan University. Her doctoral dissertation focused on teaching actors to sing. She is a member of Actors' Equity Association, Screen Actors Guild, the American Federation of Television and Radio Artists, has served as President of the Voice and Speech Trainers Association and was recently elected to serve on the Governing Council of the Association for Theatre in higher Education. She has published a number of articles, and her book, *The Vocal Vision*, a compendium of essays by voice professionals, was recently published by Applause Theatre Books in NewYork. Professor Hampton has taught at Allegheny College, the University of California at San Francisco, the University of Tennessee and the University of Texas.

Cindy Lutenbacher is Assistant Professor of English at Morehouse College, and Lecturer in Theatre and ESL at Georgia State University. She received her M.F.A. in fiction writing at Washington University, her doctorate in theatre at Northwestern University, and her MTESOL from Georgia State University. She co-authored and performed throughout the country with Tsehaye Geralyn Herbert in *Heart of the Matter*, their two-woman performance piece about racism. She is a member of the feminist satire troupe Southern Ladies Against Women (S.L.A.W.), and is currently at work on a piece about the choices of families in the margins.

Robin Murray is a Professor at the University of Wisconsin-River Falls and serves as Director of University Theatre. She teaches courses in theatre including Playwrights of Color, Costume Design, and Children's Theatre and Puppetry. In addition to designing costumes for University Theatre, she has also designed at St. Paul's Penumbra Theatre and the Wisconsin Shakespeare Festival. She co-authored a textbook with colleague Meg Swanson, *Playwrights of Color: Racial and Ethnic Diversity in the North American Theatre.*

JudyLee Oliva, formerly an Assistant Professor at the University of Tennessee and Northern Illinois University, is now a full-time playwright in the New York area. She holds an M.F.A. in Directing from the University of Oklahoma and a Ph.D. from Northwestern University, where her research and writing focused on script analysis and playwriting. She is the author of two books, *David Hare: Theatricalizing Politics,* and *New Theatre Vistas: Modern Movements in*

International Theatre, and has published over thirty articles and reviews in various theatre journals. At the University of Tennessee, she was honored with the Phi Beta Kappa Award for excellence in Liberal Arts and Humanities and was the first recipient of the Angie Warren Perkins Award for excellence in scholarship and teaching in the theatre. Her first play, *See Jane Run* was the winner of the prestigious Agnes Nixon Playwriting Award. Other award winning plays include: *The Fire and the Rose, Pasture,* and *Mark of the Feather.* Dr. Oliva has spent the last seven years working on a musical, *Te Ata,* based on the real life story of a Chickasaw Indian woman who performed a one-person show for over seventy years. *Te Ata* received an Off-Broadway staged reading and is currently in development. Other plays that are being considered for regional productions include: *On the Showroom Floor* and *Angel's Light.* A descendant of the Chickasaw tribe from Oklahoma, JudyLee serves on the Advisory Board for the Native American Women Playwrights Archive (NAWPA), is a member of the Native Writers Circle of the Americas, and is an Adjunct Advisor at the New Actors Workshop in New York City. In addition to her playwriting, she is currently working on a film project; "Five at Dawn" produced by Bateman Productions, California.

Robert N. Schmidt is an Associate Professor and Associate Chair with the University of Texas at Austin. He has designed scenery at major theatres nationally and internationally. His drawings and models have been exhibited in New York, Chicago, Hong Kong, Austin, Houston, Seattle, and Prague. In addition, Prof. Schmidt has served on the Board of Directors of the University/Resident Theatre Association, as Scenic Design Commissioner for the United State Institute for Theatre Technology, and as a member of the editorial board for *Theatre Design and Technology.*

Robert Skloot is Professor of Theatre and Drama and Jewish Studies at the University of Wisconsin-Madison. He is a stage director and author of works on drama, the Holocaust, pedagogy and diversity, including *The Theatre of the Holocaust* (ed. vol. 1, 1982; vol. 2, 1999) and *The Darkness We Carry: The Drama of the Holocaust* (1988). He serves as Associate Vice Chancellor for Academic Affairs with a particular focus on teaching and learning issues.

Anna Deavere Smith is an internationally renowned actress, writer, and teacher, on the faculty of Stanford University. Her work includes the critically acclaimed *Twilight: Los Angeles 1992* and *Fires in the Mirror* for which she won an Obie Award. She continues to do "On the Road" performance pieces which examine issues of race, gender, and community through workshops and performances and traveled with '96 presidential candidates. Smith is a MacArthur Foundation Award recipient. Her current piece, *House Arrest*, is about the US presidency.

Margaret Millen Swanson is a Professor of Theatre at the University of Wisconsin-River Falls, where she teaches courses in theatre history and directs plays. With her colleague Robin Murray, she has co-authored a textbook, *Playwrights of Color: Racial and Ethnic Diversity in the North American Theatre.*

Patricia VandenBerg, Ph.D., is the former Director of Theatre at Calvin College in Grand Rapids, Michigan. She is currently Assistant Vice Chancellor for Communications and Marketing at the University of Massachusetts Amherst. She teaches in the Professional MBA program at the University of Massachusetts and is on the faculty of the Smith Management Program, a program offered at Smith College for executive women. Using theater and classical rhetoric training, she consults in the areas of leadership and communication to a wide variety of business and academic organizations. Published in both scholarly and popular journals, Dr. VandenBerg has authored numerous articles on communication, management, theater, and gender issues. Her articles on theater pedagogy and design have appeared in *Theatre* Topics, *Theatre Design and Technology*, and *Bühnentechnische Rundshau.*

Gary Jay Williams is a Professor and the Associate Chair of the Department of Drama at the Catholic University of America in Washington, D.C., where he has taught theatre history and theory for twenty-five years. His is the editor of *Theatre Survey* and author of *Our Moonlight Revels: A Midsummer Night's Dream in the Theatre*, winner of Theatre Library Association's 1998 George Freedley Award. He is the co-author of an annotated bibliography of *A Midsummer Night's Dream* and author of a stage history of Shakespeare's *Timon of Athens*. He has published over forty articles and reviews in such journals as *Shakespeare Quarterly, Theatre Survey, Theatre Journal, Theatre Research International, Theatre Annual*, and *Theater*. He has recently held fellowships from the Folger Shakespeare Library and the Harvard Theatre Collection for work on Shakespeare on the American stage in the twentieth century.

J. Robert Wills is Professor of Theatre and Dean of the College of Fine Arts at Arizona State University. He previously served as Provost and Dean of Graduate Studies at Pacific Lutheran University, and as Dean of the College of Fine Arts at the University of Kentucky and at the University of Texas at Austin. In each of these places, he also served as Professor of Theatre. A graduate of the College of Wooster (B.A.), the University of Illinois (M.A.), and Case Western Reserve University (Ph.D.), he holds a Certificate in Arts Administration from Harvard University. The author of three books and more than sixty articles, he is also an active director in theatre, having directed more than 90 plays. He has made over a hundred professional presentations, has served as president of the University and College Theatre Association, and has been active as a consultant in the arts to such divergent groups as the National Endowment for the Arts, the U.S. Department of Education, and the Republic of Taiwan.

Stacy Wolf is an Assistant Professor in the Department of English at George Washington University. She has published on theatre audiences in *New Theatre Quarterly*, the *Journal of Dramatic Theory and Criticism*, and *Theatre Research International*.